The Cave Divin Manua

![CDG logo]

Copyright © Cave Diving Group.2008

Publishing editors: A M Ward, C P Hayward.

ISBN number 978-0-901031-04-4

Reprint December 2015

Front cover: AMW, Back cover: SG.

Printed by TPM (UK) Limited

i

Safety Statements

Cave diving is a potentially hazardous activity. The underwater cave environment is very unforgiving, injuries are rare and when something goes wrong divers will either survive or die. Any mistakes in the planning or execution of a cave dive can easily result in death. Anybody considering taking up the sport should first ensure that they have enough time to learn fully and maintain the skills that increase the chance of survival. Even when a fully skilled diver correctly plans and executes a cave dive well, death can still result.

Scope

This manual covers the activities of the UK Cave Diving Group. Cave diving in the UK is almost always undertaken by solo/independent divers using a side mount configuration. The skills required to cave dive come from a mixed base of theory and anybody wishing to master them will have to learn from a wide variety of sources. This manual is aimed at providing the information specific to UK cave diving.

i. Aims

- *To meet the constitutional requirement for the CDG to publish techniques.*
- *To lay out the body of theory used to support side mount cave diving in UK conditions for the benefit of the membership of the UK Cave Diving Group and the wider cave diving community.*
- *To support the CDG training standard both in content and approach and aid mentors and trainees with the training process.*
- *To introduce trainees to the activities of the CDG, both in the UK and abroad.*

ii. Limitations

- *Whilst this manual covers the background theory of UK cave diving, it is not on its own, a guide to how to do it. It must not be used on its own to train for cave diving. There can be no substitute for undertaking a full apprenticeship through the CDG mentoring system under the guidance of experienced active cave divers.*
- *In some areas the CDG training standard only calls for an understanding of the subject matter. This manual can be used to gain this and as such, does not provide sufficient detail in these areas to support a full training program; it only provides an introduction to these subjects. References to further reading are provided where appropriate.*
- *Trainees joining the CDG will come in with either a caving or diving background (although both is preferable). This manual does not attempt to provide basic information in either area, but focuses on cave diving. As part of the training process it falls to the trainee to obtain training and experience, to a standard laid down by the CDG in the areas of dry caving, open water diving and first aid, prior to and in parallel with cave diver training.*

This manual is dedicated to the members of the Cave Diving Group past and present.

Editors' Notes

The Cave Diving Group was founded in 1946 and has a history of which CDG members are justifiably proud. This manual is the distillation of that history. The CDG has highly experienced cave divers within its ranks; it also draws on the experience of its past members. This manual contains some of that experience. The manual also reflects the dry caving roots that the CDG springs from and from where it continues to draw most of its membership. In many ways cave divers within the CDG can be seen as technical cavers. A good dry caving back ground can not be underestimated for the aspirant CDG member.

Cave diving is a pursuit that is continually evolving (although it is hoped this manual will stay current for a few years). Each new site or project may require adaptation of the techniques within this manual. Some of these adaptations may even find wider favour within the CDG. New equipment will also bring about change in techniques and the application of them. In this way the CDG moves forward. The CDG is not a prescriptive organisation and looks to foster technical progress in its membership. In this way the CDG builds the path to a continuing future by remaining progressive.

To produce this manual submitted text has been edited. In some cases material was taken from the previous CDG Manual published in 1990. The text as it appears is the work of multiple authors although it has been edited into a consistent format.

This manual is not designed to teach cave diving but to be used in conjunction with the CDG's mentoring system. Cave diving is a potentially dangerous pursuit and should only be conducted after rigorous preparation and training. The benefits of a good dry caving background can not be underestimated.

The CDG (editors and contributors) can not be held responsible for the application of the contents of this manual or any errors within.

Andrew Ward, Colin Hayward

Special thanks to

Clive Westlake, John Cordingley, Rick Stanton, John Volanthen

Contributing Authors

Some of the text in this manual has been taken from the previous manual. It has been updated and reformatted for publication in this manual. That work and the contribution of new text has been carried out by:

Dave Brock, John Cordingley, Colin Hayward, Duncan Price, Rupert Skorupka, Rick Stanton, Mike Thomas, John Volanthen, Andrew Ward, Clive Westlake.

Photographs

The copyright for all pictures included in this manual remains with the authors. The pictures are reproduced herein with the kind permission of the authors who are identified on each picture by their initials. All sketches and drawings are copyright of the Cave Diving Group except those that are initialled.

JNC (John Cordingley), MWC (Marcus Crabbe), PD (Phil Davis), SG (Steffen Gross), CPH (Colin Hayward), FM (Fred Maxant), TS (Toby Speight), FV (Frank Vasseur), SW (Steve Walker), AMW (Andrew Ward), SPW (Sue Ward), CDW (Clive Westlake) RF (Rob Franklin).

Thanks for Information and Assisting

Dave Bater, Thomas Baum, Terry Birtles, Richard Dearden, Peter Devlin, J Hayward, M Hayward, Chris Howes, Gary Jones, Maxime de Gianpietro, Mike Jeanmaire, Andrew Roca, Dave Ryall, Bryan Schofield, Sue Ward, Rachel White.

Introduction 1

Chapter 6 Specialist skills and equipment 95

Chapter 7 Awareness of mixed gases............................... 113

Introduction

35 years ago I dipped beneath the surface of the first lake in Wookey Hole as a novice cave diver. With several months worth of Friday evening training at Bristol University pool under my belt I felt quietly confident. However by today's standards the techniques I adopted and the equipment I used left considerable room for improvement.

After a few rudimentary instructions on line signals from my trainer, Oliver Lloyd, I slipped under the roof of the upstream sump. Eager to explore I was soon over 30m in and experiencing the rapid learning curve that is an essential part of cave diving. Forward progress was becoming a struggle as the friction from my base fed line increased and the sense of exhilaration of my first dive was quickly being overtaken by the onset of hypothermia. "The pepper pot" caving wetsuit and "Marigold" washing up gloves I was wearing were clearly not up to the job. I gave my signal to return and shivering uncontrollably I followed the gentle pulling as I was wound in. My progress out through swirling clouds of mud was abruptly halted by a head-on impact with a roof projection. A trickle of water entered my mask and simultaneously my only lighting, a single miner's lamp, flickered. I carried on with more care and less haste making a mental note to carry additional lighting next time.

Throughout the dive I had fought a losing battle with the single side mount I was wearing which had been determined to slide under my stomach. Back at base with warmth returning to my body it occurred to me that I would be much happier with two sets and that a piece of line across my back tied to each bottle band would keep them in place.

Cave diving is all about solving problems as they present themselves and trying to predict them in advance. Rather then being put off by the rigours of my first wetting I was quickly developing an appetite for more.

Earlier this year I was invited to inspect a friend's dive store. As one of our leading exponents of deep, long duration diving his stash was an Aladdin's cave of kit, unimaginable when I first started: Huge cylinders; a KISS rebreather; a side mounted rebreather; a variety of dry suits; scooters; a device for mixing gases; perfectly designed harnesses; dazzling, duplicated and reliable lights; and dive computers. The list went on and I roughly estimated a total value in excess of £10,000: well beyond the budget of a 1970's student and indicative of years of dedication and commitment.

The pages of this manual are a testament to the huge practical advances made by our group in exploring the flooded underworld. Its pages are an instruction in caution but cave diving will always be a blend of caution mixed with daring. The former we can put to print but the latter is for the individual to understand and control.

Geoff Yeadon
CDG President

Chapter 1 The Cave Diving Group

Early rebreather diving, in the 1950s.

New members to the CDG will find that it has a unique character and method of working, which is due to the structure and history of the Group, the oldest amateur diving organisation in the world. People from a caving background will find that it differs from a caving club in its more structured approach to training and qualification. Those who are more accustomed to the recreational diving environment will find the group requires more from them during training, over a longer period than they are used to giving.

The following chapter is aimed at helping the trainee understand the way the CDG operates and trains. It is hoped that armed with this understanding trainees will be able to make the most of the opportunity offered by the CDG and become active qualified divers in the CDG.

A) History

i.   Beginnings

Cave diving in the United Kingdom did not originate or develop in isolation from caving. Cavers learnt to dive; cave divers did not become cavers. It was regarded simply as another technique to further cave exploration. Just as a ladder or rope is used to overcome a vertical drop, so diving equipment was used to overcome a flooded passage. Being underground and underwater doubled the skills to be mastered by the pioneers, so with the additional problem of equipment that was in its infancy, the dangers confronting the first cave divers were incalculable. Submerged cave passages, then pointedly known as "traps" rather than as "sumps", would not be places in which to lose one's nerve or have equipment failure. No manuals were available to educate the uninitiated and no organised cave rescue teams existed at the time should anything go wrong. Those participating were on their own.

The early history of cave diving reveals the independent outlook needed by those involved. By modern standards their progress was slow but sure. In the 1930s and 1940s it took many years merely to explore and pass the sump between Chambers 3 and 9 in Wookey Hole, now a regular training dive. The equipment was in its infancy and the fears and mental obstacles that existed were far different from what they are today. Any step forward in those days measured up to any advance achieved today. In France, the Fontaine de Vaucluse was reconnoitred by a diver on an air line to –23m in 1878, in 1893 a Swiss diver with equipment made a 15m penetration in a cave, and in 1894 a diver with equipment valiantly tried to assist in the rescue of a trapped caver also in Switzerland. Norbert Casteret made his now celebrated free-dive through a sump in Montespan in 1922. But the moment cave diving was really conceived came when cavers carried a respirator underground and succeeded in breathing underwater to explore a virgin sump.

Those principally concerned were Graham Balcombe and Jack Sheppard, the cave was Swildon's Hole on Mendip, and their objective was to push the sump that had held up exploration of the streamway since its discovery in 1921. The dive took place on 17th February 1934, and the lightweight respirator was home-made from parts of a bicycle. At the time, the Swildon's Sump was one of the deepest points reached in any British cave and the "Bicycle Respirator" had to be carefully portered for several hundred metres along a potholed streamway that includes two wet pitches. Whilst they did not pass the sump for another two years, they had sown the seeds of cave diving that day.

Although it was not known for sure until January 1967, the Swildon's stream feeds the subterranean River Axe that rises from under Mendip at Wookey Hole Caves. These well-known caves were lit and opened to the public by the owner, Gerard Hodgkinson in the 1920s. In 1932, they attracted over 38,000 visitors, paying one shilling each. Three chambers with lakes could be seen and the water entering the show cave was noted for its clarity. By releasing the 1852 dam at the resurgence, it was possible to lower the lakes and open an airspace between the Third and Fourth Chambers. The way on upstream was unknown, although earlier water tracing had shown that stream sinks at Eastwater Cavern and from the Priddy Minery (now St Cuthbert's Swallet) were sources of the Axe. Both swallets are in similar geological locations to Swildon's Hole. After the Swildon's dive in 1934, Balcombe approached the long established diving company Seibe Gorman for assistance. This firm was in the forefront of designing and building respirators for use in mines with bad air, in flooded tunnels and at sea for submariners in particular. Sir Robert Henry Davis, who started work for Seibe Gorman in 1882 and had been its managing director since 1904, responded favourably. Jack Sheppard visited him and, grateful for any equipment to further cave diving, accepted Sir Robert's generous offer of standard helmets and diving dress fed by air lines from hand pumps. Sir Robert also agreed to provide an experienced diver to train those wanting to learn, and the pools at Priddy Mineries were chosen as "base camp".

The sheer bulk of all the helmet diving gear forced the pioneers to focus attention on the roomy and easily accessible Wookey Hole Caves throughout 1935. It was an accident that resulted in a success story. The excitement and rewards of that summer are best gleaned from The Log of the Wookey Hole Expedition, 1935, by The Divers. This now classic book of cave diving history was written and produced largely by Graham Balcombe during the following months. From a diving base in the Third Chamber his team progressed beyond the already known Fourth Chamber and entered new Fifth, Sixth and Seventh Chambers. Being restrained by base-fed air lines and weighted for bottom walking, they were restricted and unable to travel more than 61m. But the way on was tantalisingly wide open; cave diving had a promising future.

Wookey Hole Caves are thus regarded as the birthplace of cave diving. In the years following the Second World War, the River Axe became the cradle of the Cave Diving Group. The 1935 expedition and the nature of Wookey Hole's commodious sumps set the standards for years to come - safe-water training, kit testing, meticulous log keeping, good lighting, line laying, navigating, surveying, and the accurate recording of every dive became rules. Porters (or sherpas), dressers, photographers and a controller were needed. Bottom walking ruled, for the need to swim, let alone the opportunity, had simply not arisen.

Another aspect of the early days at Wookey Hole that considerably influenced later cave diving was the need to fit in with the owner's requirements since the cave was, after all, a major tourist attraction. In fair return, the cave owner expected full media coverage of any discoveries. Some cave divers learned to perfect the art of publicity themselves and it is fundamental to the larger expeditions of today. But the preferred outlook that still appeals to many cave explorers is the unsung pushing of a streamway in the independent manner shown by Balcombe and Sheppard down Swildon's Hole.

The prize for the first ever cave dive that led to further exploration of a streamway fell to Jack Sheppard on 4th October 1936. Having learned the hard way that it was necessary underwater to have a pressurised supply of gas, he made a lightweight drysuit with a hood and breathed from air pumped to it through a long hosepipe. Using this, he passed Sump One and found another 274m of Swildon's. Shortly afterwards, on 22nd November 1936, Graham Balcombe made the next crucial step. He connected a hand-held Oxygen cylinder to the old "Bicycle Respirator", opening the valve when he wanted to breathe and turning it off to exhale. Without any waterproofs, he thus dived about 12m through Sump Two to surface in the Bell Chambers. Apart from a lifeline, he was on his own—the first self-contained cave diver. Again, the option of swimming had not even been considered. It would have been inappropriate given the lighting available and the size of Swildon's sumps let alone the unfamiliarity of such a venture. The potential for cave diving was proven. Only the threat and arrival of the Second World War held up further exploration.

During the early 1940s, on a posting to Yorkshire, Balcombe found time to experiment with an oxygen rebreather respirator which he had built. He probed the rising at Keld Held several times, climbed down a ladder underwater at the bottom of Alum Pot, and pushed the sumps in Goyden Pot. As a solo diver, all his pre-war training and experiences on Mendip were strictly followed; this included bottom walking and carefully recording every moment, whether good or bad. The early 1940s were a period of gestation that led directly to the formation of the Cave Diving Group.

At the end of the war during Easter 1946, Graham Balcombe and Jack Sheppard held court at the Ffynnon Ddu resurgence in South Wales and, although failing to discover the great cave of OFD that lay waiting upstream, they succeeded in converting several cavers to the cause. Most came from the Bristol area, and so Wookey Hole Caves' became the main focus of attention for the rest of the decade. Peak Cavern played a similar role in Derbyshire. Thus, the CDG was co-ordinated on a regional basis with Somerset, Welsh and Derbyshire sections. "HQ" was at Balcombe's home in London.

ii.   The tentative approach to horizontal swimming

The availability of surplus War Department diving gear was a boon in the austerity years. Ex-WD equipment shaped all aspects of caving until the 1960s. National Service had a big impact upon cavers and cave diving in particular. Transport was difficult and time-consuming. The support of Sir Robert Davies and Gerard Hodgkinson, who had reached the rank of Wing Commander during the war, underwrote the strong links fostered between the CDG and Royal Navy. The 'Wing Co' encouraged the divers and provided them with a substantial wooden hut in the Wookey Hole car park which became known as Crooks' Rest. It soon filled with diving gear.

By 1949, the CDG had explored the subterranean Axe to the majestic Ninth Chamber and pushed beyond to the submerged Eleventh. Here the river wells up a steep slope at a point well below the depth limit of 9.1m for oxygen rebreathers. It marked the introduction of mixed gas rebreathers alongside oxygen rebreathers at Wookey Hole but Graham Balcombe's influence remained strong through his authoritative chapter on cave diving in British Caving edited by Cecil Cullingford (1953).

Swimming with fins in the manner of wartime frogmen and French divers was first considered in 1949. It was likely to be faster and stir up less mud. The steep descent in the Eleventh Chamber of Wookey Hole would probably be best attempted in this way. A highly experienced naval diver, Gordon Ingram-Marriott, was invited to demonstrate the technique. After visits to Wookey Hole and Peak Cavern in March, the dive to Eleven was arranged on the evening of 9th April. All the leading divers of the CDG were there. Somehow, on the return journey from the Tenth Chamber ahead of Robert E Davis, Marriott went missing in poor visibility. His body was subsequently found by Donald Coase just upstream of the Sixth Chamber. Desperate attempts to resuscitate him on the nearby diving platform in Six failed. He had run out of Oxygen and inexplicably lost his reserve cylinder. Wookey Hole Caves had claimed the first cave diving tragedy. It was a traumatic event for the CDG and Graham Balcombe in particular.

The inquest concluded that a faulty test pressure gauge must have been responsible, but the divers were not so sure. Their uncertainty reinforced the old rule that aspiring cave divers should be cavers first and that the trusted routines, which included bottom walking, were intrinsically safer. A lull in pushing dives followed into the early 1950s.

When Bob Davies became lost beyond the Eleventh Chamber whilst finning with an aqualung on 10th December 1955, and returned to tell of a remarkable escape from a Thirteenth Chamber that he had luckily chanced upon, the dice seemed loaded against swimming and breathing air in cave diving. For the rest of the 1950s, the divers, led by John Buxton and Oliver Wells, perfected the use of P-Party Oxygen/Nitrogen mixture re-breathers to increase depth potential. They preferred bottom walking and the longer duration of the re-breathers compensated for the necessarily slower but traditionally surer navigation on foot. Good progress was made to record depths of 21m in Wookey Hole Caves; the Swildon's streamway was broken into beyond Sump Three and Sumps Four and Five were passed. The latter involved several mammoth expeditions, still some of the largest and most complex diving operations ever undertaken in Britain.

iii.   Slimming down and independence

The large-scale approach to diving began to slim down in the early 1960s as a direct result of tackling the constricted Sump Six in Swildon's Hole and Sump Two in Stoke Lane Slocker. Diving was also coming into its own in every caving region as cavers found more sumps. Changes in the availability and pricing of diving equipment occurred as the commercial markets expanded. A new and freer phase in our social history helped. Cave divers slimmed down their gear and immediately met with success in passing tight sumps. In underwater squeezes the question of walking or swimming simply did not arise. Divers became virtually self-supporting and capable of pushing farther ahead. Steve Wynne-Roberts and Fred Davies, made ingenious modifications were made to the smallest oxygen rebreathers available; whilst Mike Boon opted to use air and tiny "tadpole" cylinders. On 7th July 1961, Mike succeeded in passing Sump Six in Swildons, the first of many successes using air sets. The following year, on 9th June, he forced his way through the very tight Sump Seven by removing his kit and feeding it ahead by hand. It was a daring (some would say utterly mad) technique that had been carefully rehearsed in a swimming pool. During this period there were few thoughts about pushing the 21m-deep sump in Wookey Hole whilst short and shallow ones were "going" elsewhere on most weekends.

It was a great shock and setback when E. J. Waddon died whilst practising with a newly modified Oxygen re-breather in the Priddy Minerys pool on Saturday 3rd November 1962. Jack had encouraged and helped train the younger divers of the day and, in their eyes, he embodied the traditions of the CDG. Naval experts blamed the equipment at the inquest but, yet again, other factors seemed just as likely to those who used the very same set before and after the incident. Once more, uncertainty clouded CDG affairs. There were critical moments when its regional framework might have collapsed but for a strengthening of the constitution, training procedures and tests under Michael Thompson's leadership and Dan Hasell's commonsense presidency. Cave divers in the regions rallied to the overhauled CDG.

Whilst all this was going on, three students from Bristol University set about training themselves during the autumn of 1964 and by Christmas formed the self-styled Independent Cave Diving Group. Mike Wooding, Dave Savage and Dave Drew adopted Mike Boon's approach: they bought a couple of Scubair regulators and cylinders and got on with it. Cylinders were slung from waist belts, weights were kept to a minimum, only wetsuits were worn, a single NiFe lamp on an ordinary helmet sufficed and they carried fins for swimming the longer sumps. It was a logical reduction of the old view that ordinary cavers with the bare minimum of diving equipment could get results. Solo caving and diving was the ultimate development of course.

By the 20th March 1965, the ICDG trio had pushed the Swildon's streamway to Sump Twelve. The final choke beyond Sump Seven in Stoke Lane Slocker was reached on the 22nd May and passed to 100 feet of passage on the 30th October. Neither has been passed since - a remarkable legacy and vindication of their work. Later in March they joined the Cave Diving Group. Dr Oliver C Lloyd (OCL) also submitted himself for tests with them. He was 54 years of age and became the oldest active cave diver to qualify. OCL had taken on the task of running the CDG the previous Easter after Alan Clegg drowned because of tangled lines in the Master Cave Sump of Lancaster Hole.

The next twenty years of the CDG until the mid-1980s were dominated by OCL in many ways. He ran Friday night training sessions for the Somerset Section and all-comers in the Students' Union swimming baths at Bristol University. The Severn Bridge and M4 to South Wales ensured close links with the Welsh Section. He organised and held most of the equipment at his home in Westbury-On-Trym. Editing the CDG Newsletter and other publications was one of his great pleasures for it kept him in touch with everyone, and in control. His distinctive editorials and comments were very influential far afield, and he was a good correspondent for active divers around the world. The modern phase of cave diving bears his stamp, a phase which has seen rapid advances in equipment and techniques with record long and deep dives in every caving region of Britain and in other countries. The pages that follow contain much that is traced back to OCL.

Oliver Lloyd died after going to Priddy on Mendip on the weekend of 18th-19th May 1985 to show the film that he made in Swildon's Hole in 1960 about sump rescue for the Mendip Rescue Organisation. So, sadly he missed the fiftieth anniversary celebrations of cave diving and reunion of cave divers who represented the full 50 years, held in the Third Chamber of Wookey Hole Caves on 4th October. The recollections of those involved in pioneering and pushing sumps under Mendip have been compiled into a commemorative volume. This will provide a much fuller history than is briefly summarised here.

British side mount, late 1980s.

iv.   Rapid change

To bring this brief history of the CDG up to date, the present era has seen rapid change. Deeper, more remote, and more inaccessible caves and sumps, together with increased and more complex technology, have forced divers to change at a very rapid rate. Traditional breathing gas in tanks is being replaced by modern re-breathers in some cases, hand-held or ride-on diver propulsion vehicles are increasingly common, especially for large sumps abroad, gases containing Helium are commonplace, and underwater digging techniques are constantly being developed and honed. However the problem of devising a dive plan that will safely meet the challenge posed by a site still requires an in depth understanding of the equipment and techniques used in the cave environment. Cave divers are, if nothing else, inventive and resourceful. If a problem needs solving, they will usually find a way. In the first report of the CDG (1946), Jack Sheppard wrote:

"A dive, or job of underwater exploration, is abandoned when the total of all difficulties and danger becomes equal to the diver's determination to complete the job. To push any job to its limit it is therefore necessary to eliminate every possible weakness or imperfection in the apparatus used, so there remains nothing to overcome except the natural hazards of the cave..."

B) Structure

i. Central Committee, Sections and officers

The membership of the CDG is divided between sections, each of which is linked to a major caving area in the UK. When someone joins the CDG they do so by joining a section. There are four sections, each named after the geographical region they represent, Somerset, Northern, Derbyshire and Welsh. Each section has a duty under the constitution to maintain and publish a sump index for the local area and to elect officers as required by the constitution. The constitution requires the election of a secretary and treasurer, but most sections also elect other officers to meet the requirements of the section membership. This will typically be a training officer, an equipment officer and one or more examiners.

The Group's AGM is hosted in rotation by each section. At this meeting a central committee is elected, other than the regional secretaries who are elected at regional AGMs. The Central Committee meets throughout the year to run the affairs of the CDG. Amendments to the constitution and other documents are proposed, discussed and voted on at the AGM. It is these documents that form the framework for the sections to operate within; they are not however a complete set of instructions and each section will operate in a slightly different way, mainly varying in the degree of organisation and formality of structure. The central Committee Consists of the following, President(s), a Chairperson, a Secretary, a Treasurer, a Foreign Officer, a Technical Officer, an Editor, a Distribution Manager, a Librarian, a Web Site Manager and the secretary of each regional section plus any member nominated by the central committee.

A copy of the Group documentation can be found in Appendix i) of this manual; the copy is correct at the time of writing but the contents are subject to change. For an updated copy see the Cave Diving Group website at http//:www.cavedivinggroup.org.uk

ii. Membership and qualification structure

Membership of the CDG is divided between diving and non-diving status, with most members having diving membership. Within diving membership there are two levels: qualified and trainee. The different types of membership have been created so that the group can meet the needs of its members with respect to services and fair distribution of costs, particularly insurance.

Anyone can apply to join as a non-diving member, but people applying for diving membership must join as trainees. Applications to join a section of the CDG are submitted in writing and must be proposed and seconded by qualified divers. The application is then subject to a vote at the next section meeting where it is expected that the applicant will attend.

Qualified Diver status is granted by simple majority vote of a section's Qualified Divers, at a section meeting, once a trainee diver has meet the necessary criteria as laid down in the constitution/rules. Qualified Divers have additional voting rights; they are the only members allowed to vote on matters of qualification.

iii. Updating and amending of the Constitution and Rules

Any member of CDG may propose an amendment to the Constitution or Rules unless it relates to a matter of qualification. Only Qualified Divers may vote on matters of qualification. Any such amendment must be proposed and seconded at the Group AGM or an EGM and be presented to the group in accordance with the Constitution. The membership at the meeting then discusses, amends and finally votes on the proposal. It is however commoner for this process to be started or guided by the Central Committee, who will ask an individual or group to put together a proposal in a specific area for the following year's meeting.

C) Suitable candidates for cave diving

A suitable candidate is fit, intelligent, aware and self-reliant as well as being an active caver. A basic general technical ability is useful as is a basic understanding of diving physiology. The candidate appreciates the history and traditions of the Cave Diving Group and the fast-changing face of the activity and is prepared to put as much back into the Group as they gain from it.

i. Minimum CDG requirements

The current Cave Diving Group requirements are that a trainee should be over 18 years old, physically fit, and be a reasonable swimmer who is comfortable in the water. Most commonly they will be experienced UK cavers; a basic knowledge of open water diving can be an advantage. Any candidate who does not meet these requirements will be expected to put considerable amount of effort into correcting the shortfall.

These requirements set a minimum standard. The applicant who does not satisfy high standards of competence in caving and diving is likely to be rejected, not only for their own safety but for the safety of others who dive with them.

ii. Individual attitude

Cave diving calls for complete self-reliance and independence of judgement but this does not imply ignoring the experience of others as embodied in codes of practice. Nevertheless, each cave diver is always responsible for their own safety. The trainee would do well to examine the whole question of danger in relation to caving and cave diving and should consider carefully the following ways of reducing the risks of this hazardous activity.

Motivation: Examine the motives for cave diving. Is the aim to dive in UK conditions or limited to trips abroad? Will the primary reason to dive be exploration/digging, a means of getting to more dry passage or tourist dives? Is the individual pursuing another dive qualification card?

Temperament: What are the relative proportions of boldness/caution and how easily does the candidate panic? Is the trainee susceptible to outside pressures - will dives be undertaken in inadvisable circumstances?

Thorough approach: Cave diving requires much time, thought and preparation. A diver must be in good physical condition for the caving and diving activities planned. The diver must ensure that equipment is suitably prepared. This is easy to state and easy to agree to but very hard to adhere to in practice. Nevertheless it must be adhered to. If a diver's equipment is unsuitable for a dive, the dive must be postponed until it is suitable. The diver will also make good use of experience, both learned and gained from others through the scattered but considerable volume of literature on diving and especially cave diving. Time must be spent interpreting the merits of different techniques in various circumstances. For the active UK cave diver the sport becomes a passion.

Site suitability: Match dive sites to ability, limiting the number of dives to projects where the chances of achieving the goal outweigh the risks involved. Sumps engender enthusiasm that is often misplaced, so a careful assessment of the chances of a successful dive should be made. This is a hard doctrine for an enthusiastic recruit to accept; nevertheless it is a doctrine of experience.

By their nature, cave divers tend to be determined and stubborn individuals and, like it or not, some exhibit a certain degree of machismo. The onus is on the diver to make the decision to dive. Divers must be prepared to turn back if the situation is not right. It is far better to swallow pride and turn back, rather than take unnecessary risks. All divers have off days and there will always be another opportunity; the cave will still be there next week.

D) Training within the CDG

i. How training is organised

The CDG uses a mentor system for training. A trainee will initially be introduced to the basics of cave diving by a qualified diving member, usually the person who proposed or seconded them. Once the basics have been learned, the trainee will then dive with other (maybe more experienced) divers to gain a wider range of experience. The training period lasts for a minimum of twenty varied dives. In the CDG one dive is counted as a trip to a point and returning regardless of how many sumps are passed during the dive. Trainees do the twenty dives at a variety of sites during their training period (trainees typically do more dives than this when multiple dives at the same site are considered). Each dive is written in a log by the trainee. This log should be available for inspection at any section meeting by the qualified members and acts as a useful guide to the training process as well as forming part of the application for qualified status. Trainees will also have to record and submit a dry caving log when applying for qualified status.

ii.   Who trains within the CDG

Within the CDG any qualified diving member can act as a mentor. The training officer (if the section has one) may mentor people directly on a practical level or may organise training events to provide some background theory; the role is defined by the person who carries it out.

The Cave Diving Group does not franchise out its cave diver training. Training provided by outside agencies does not provide a "fast track" route through the training process.

iii.   What trainees can expect from the CDG

The CDG will introduce trainees to cave diving in a progressive manner; the process takes upwards of a year. Over this period the members of the Section that the trainee has joined will provide the trainee with the opportunity to learn a wide range of cave diving skills. This will highlight shortcomings in a trainee's theoretical knowledge and practical skills and suggest ways to remedy them. Training given will probably be limited to cave diving skills and will be almost exclusively based around side mount diving. Some trainees who have a strong caving background and no experience in open water diving may find someone within the Section of the CDG they join who is prepared to mentor them through the basic use of scuba equipment. Trainees will not be charged for any part of the training for cave diver qualification and will be required to pay only the annual Group subscription.

iv.   What the CDG expects from trainees

The CDG expects a proactive approach to training from trainees. The CDG does not charge for training and members involved in mentoring trainees give up their free time to do so. As a result of this trainees are not spoon feed on a structured "how to do it" course; they must be prepared to seek out the knowledge they need from the membership and to change their views on their personal training requirements based on advice given. Trainees must also organise their own background reading to improve theoretical knowledge, based on advice and published reading lists.

Traditionally the CDG has drawn membership only from the caving community. Now divers from an open water background may join as trainees. However they are expected to put considerable effort into gaining dry caving experience by joining a caving club and doing a lot of caving in a variety of caves. Trainees from a caving background are expected to seek out training that meets the CDG open water diving requirements from other agencies or from within the CDG.

All trainees are required to maintain a logbook of all caving activity, both dry and diving during the training period. This is used to assess the progress of the trainee and act as proof of experience when qualified status is requested.

v.   The importance of dry caving

Cave diving in many UK sumps can be seen as caving with scuba gear. There is limited free swimming and progress is frequently made by moves that would be more recognisable to a dry caver than an open water diver. It is possible to do free swimming sumps in the UK, but the suitable sites are limited to a handful and the weather conditions further limit availability. Most trainees will encounter these sites at a very early stage of their training before moving on to more typical UK sumps. The conditions also dictate that dry caving skills and knowledge of dry caving form a useful part of a diver's skills. An experienced caver will have an understanding that can be useful in interpreting the shape of a passage from touch when visibility is reduced to zero, as it frequently is in UK sumps. In addition experienced cavers develop a good memory for finding the (reverse) route out of a cave. This can also be very useful as the diver deprived of vision will still have a mental picture of their whereabouts in the sump; this goes a long way to reducing the stress on the diver.

The other more obvious importance of dry caving is that most sumps are located beyond dry passage. The number of resurgences is very limited. To increase the number of accessible sites, the trainee must venture underground with dive gear; this forms part of the training requirement. Without good dry caving skills the trainee will find it very difficult to get even the simplest diving equipment to a sump and still be in good enough condition, both physically and mentally to complete a useful dive.

Boulder floored bedding typical of UK sumps.

vi.　　Core skills

During the learning process the trainee will cover a wide range of subjects related to cave diving, caving and open water diving. As has already been stated, this manual only covers in depth the areas that are special to cave diving in UK conditions. The areas listed below represent the most important knowledge and skills that must form the core of a cave divers training, but on their own they are not enough; all areas must be understood by the trainee. With this core of knowledge and skills a diver can greatly reduce the risks of a dive.

Study fatalities: Analyse what goes wrong and why, learn from situations that have resulted in deaths, and learn procedures to survive such situations. (See, Appendix ii: Accident analysis.)

Learn to plan a dive: How to gain and use knowledge of a dive site, gas margin calculations, decompression considerations, special equipment needs, understanding of how a poor dive plan increases the risk in the water.

Learn to modify equipment configuration: Design a configuration that can support a plan, be usable in the site and meets the safety principles for gas supply, lighting and line control drills.

Practiced dive skills: Master the drills that support survival.

Learn to turn a dive: Be able to judge the condition of a dive and know when it is prudent to turn and come back another day.

vii.　　Progression of training and election to qualified diver status

A trainee will come into the CDG with either a strong background in caving or diving or both. Where one area of skills is low the trainee will be expected to work on improving their experience to increase ability. How quickly this happens will be largely dependent on the level of motivation displayed by the trainee. Trainees without a strong caving background will start doing dry caving trips to help them build a body of experience. To meet the requirements laid down in the assessment schedule all of these trips should be recorded in the trainee's log book. Trainees without diving experience are expected to gain a basic knowledge of open water diving techniques either from within the group or from outside agencies. At this time the trainee will also be expected to study background theory both independently and with a mentor. The method used for this will vary between mentors.

Once the mentor is satisfied that the trainee fully understands the risks, difficulties and dangers of cave diving, along with how to cope with some of them, an understanding of equipment configuration will be developed to a point where basic cave diving can start. Diving in a cave rig (developed by the trainee under guidance from the mentor) will then be started either in an open water site or in a very simple cave (or mine) situation. These early dives will be supervised. Once the trainee has demonstrated to the mentor an adequate level of competence, the trainee will be directed towards other sites; these will be of progressively increasing difficulty for the trainee.

At all times the trainee should be diving in line with the CDG's Safety Code which states that:

1. A trainee should be accompanied by a qualified diver unless he has had considerable cave diving experience before joining the group.

2. A trainee diver on his first cave dives should either be accompanied by an experienced diver, or should have a fully kitted, experienced diver at base.

(See, Appendix i: CDG Documentation, for the full Safety Code.)

Once a trainee has successfully completed some initial dives, it is appropriate for the trainee to start diving with other divers and to start practising solo diving. The trainee should discuss this progression thoroughly with a suitable mentor before taking this significant step forward. Solo diving is one area where UK cave diving differs considerably from open water diving. There are significant hazards associated with buddy diving in the confined spaces of UK sumps. The CDG advocates an ethos of solo diving as an appropriate method of managing the risks associated with UK cave diving. In order to pass the CDG Qualified Diver Test the trainee must be familiar and comfortable with the theory and practice of both solo diving and team solo diving. The trainee diver must seek help from more experienced diving mentors in order to find effective ways of practising solo diving whilst maintaining a suitable level of safety. It is important that both the mentor and the trainee have a good understanding of the trainee's development needs and current skill level when balancing the risks associated with a particular solo diving exercise against the risks of not practising the essential skill.

At all times during the training process the trainee should ask questions of and seek guidance from any Qualified Diver. This is seen as the best way to gather experience within the CDG, as the trainee can gain from the collective experience of many divers. During the training period the Section will review the progress of each of its trainees, offering guidance on how best to progress with training and giving each trainee the opportunity to meet with the Section's Qualified Divers with a view to furthering training.

Once the trainee and mentor are in agreement that the trainee is ready to take the qualification tests an examiner will be asked to administer the theory test and carry out the practical test in accordance with the rules. The examiner will report the result to the Section meeting where the qualified diving members will review the trainee's results, dry caving logbook and cave diving logbook. A vote is then held and in the event of the trainee being accepted, qualified membership is granted.

E) Legal aspects of cave diving

When things go badly wrong during a cave dive the authorities hold an investigation using legal methods and scrutinise all aspects of the dive including the diver's training. This means that anything the CDG does can be subject to inspection by lawyers. Most CDG members go cave diving for pleasure. The diving is recreational with as little bureaucracy and trouble as possible. The CDG is a voluntary organisation and offers services to its members. The more services the CDG offers, the more the members get from membership but there is also more potential for trouble for the members.

Cave diving is always an evolving sport. A real issue is that some of the changes are viewed as increasing the potential for trouble from a legal standpoint and so are resisted. This section looks at some of the issues and terminology surrounding this problem from a lay person's perspective. The purpose is to allow members to engage in the running of the Group with a level of confidence that although the Rules cannot be indefensibly vague, they do not need to be untenably prescriptive.

Although this section deals with legal issues it has not been written or verified by anybody with legal training and as such cannot be taken to be a legal opinion; it merely serves as an introduction to the topic to help members understand the legal framework they are operating within.

i.   Duty of care

The first key concept is Duty of Care, which can be looked at in three ways:

- *Our legal responsibilities.*
- *Our insurance small print.*
- *What we feel to be ethically correct.*

The Legal Dictionary defines Duty of Care as "a requirement that a person act toward others and the public with watchfulness, attention, caution and prudence that a reasonable person in the circumstances would". As a lay person it is an accepted position that a CDG member does not need to get hung up on the legal technicalities. The Group and its members just need to act in a way that seems reasonable to reasonable people. If something is fully considered by the Group and said to be acceptable then it is.

So what specifically are the CDG's standards of Duty of Care? Although they are not explicit, the standards can be inferred from our published material. The starting point is to examine the objectives of the Group:

- *To explore submerged caves and cave passages.*
- *To lay down codes of practice for that purpose.*
- *To review and publicise new diving techniques.*

This sets the scope of what the Group sees as its duties. Clearly members have a duty to go diving, lay down codes of practice and review techniques. The detail of the CDG Codes shows the boundaries. For instance the CDG has a duty "to ensure that Trainee Divers have reasonable access to suitable training". It also has a duty to "establishing mentoring relationships both as mentors and mentees with other members of the Group". Again, the code shows the direction of the duty but is not prescriptive of the degree. The best way to understand the CDG's Duty of Care is to read through the constitution and rules.

Not all Duties of Care are written down. Some rely on common sense. The acid test on what constitutes a Duty of Care is when a case is placed before the courts. Case law involving breaches of Duty of Care during diving in the UK is minimal.

A precedent comes from the case of Milner versus Rowbottom in 2000 where two amateur open water divers were diving together and one of them lost his life. The judge, Sean Overend, ruled that a Duty of Care existed between the divers hence it seems likely that the CDG has a Duty of Care to its members. The prosecution argued that a commercial diver would have been able to save his buddy and that the surviving diver had not done enough. Judge Sean Overend ruled that commercial divers were under a more stringent Duty of Care and it was not reasonable to apply these levels of standards to an amateur organisation. The surviving buddy was exonerated. It would seem that although the CDG has a Duty of Care there are limits and those limits will not be as onerous as for a professional organisation.

Another source of concern to CDG members is the legal role of the Health & Safety Executive (HSE). The HSE provides practical guidance for what is expected from professional organisations including Duties of Care and have jurisdiction to enforce safe working practices. The Cave Diving Group does not have a single paid employee hence does not fall within the remit of the HSE. This is a view shared by other voluntary diving organisations. For example, section 3.3.3 of the BSAC Branch Officers' Handbook (January 2004) states "Instructors within a members club teaching recreational diving skills to other club members do not (currently) come under the Diving at Work Regulations 1997." Although the CDG does not have a legal obligation to follow guidance from the HSE, such guidance does represent an excellent source of material and the CDG should consider their recommendations where it is within the Group's capability. For instance, the HSE advise that a key aspect to ensuring safety is to perform a risk assessment and the HSE publish a leaflet on this topic called "5 Steps To Risk Assessment". Where possible CDG members should follow this simple advice. Many other voluntary organisations do, including diving clubs.

The insurance industry's approach to Duty of Care varies from insurer to insurer. Without setting any direct legal requirement, the Association of British Insurers (www.abi.org.uk) has published a leaflet to help voluntary organisations, like the CDG, to manage risk. The leaflet is called "Living With Risk,

Risk Management and Insurance Advice for the Voluntary and Community Sector". Their advice focuses on five areas:

- *Assess the potential risks you face.*
- *Take action to minimise risks.*
- *Appoint someone to be responsible for safety.*
- *Assess risk regularly.*
- *Seek help and advice.*

So the legal and insurance advice provides a starting point when considering the Duty of Care for one another, but moral and ethical obligations that should go further. The Group must also set realistic requirements for itself.

ii. Tort of negligence

Of course things go wrong and that is why there are accidents. Not all incidents where things go wrong are accidents. Sometimes incidents are caused by people who should have known better and these incidents are considered to be acts of negligence or in extreme case they are criminal acts. As an organisation the CDG has responsibilities to its members and as members we all have accountability for the actions of the Group through joint and group liability. To protect the membership and allow it to continue to discharge the Duties of Care in peace of mind, the Group has chosen to take out insurance against Public Liability claims.

Claims of negligence are made under the Tort of Negligence, which comprises three elements:

- *The existence of a duty of care.*
- *A breach of the duty of care.*
- *Damage caused by the breach of a duty of care.*

As stated above a duty of care does exist but it is limited. The Group can use procedures to help set limits for the duty of care.

For both ethical and legal reasons the Group must not tolerate breaches of our Duty of Care. It is therefore important that members stay within the letter of the Rules and that the Rules never impose an impossible obligation upon the membership. It is important that the Rules are regularly reviewed to ensure that there is a justified and reasonable compromise made between being indefensibly vague and being untenably prescriptive. It is also important that the Rules are communicated effectively to the membership.

The rise of a litigious culture and the no-win, no-fee lawyer is an area of concern for organisations like the CDG. Currently government is considering legislation aimed directly at voluntary organisations like the CDG. This legislation will introduce regulation into the no-win, no-fee industry and hopefully go some way towards curbing spurious claims. Such legislation will also introduce a requirement on a court considering a negligence claim to have regard to whether the Duty of Care requirements would prevent a desirable activity or discourage persons from undertaking functions in connection with a desirable activity. Cave diving is considered a desirable activity and the court should take account of the limitations on the Duties of Care that can be provided whilst participating in cave diving.

The damage caused refers to the subsequent loss; the outcome of a failed cave dive includes the possibility of death. Clearly death would be considered to be substantial damage. A proven case of negligence would probably result in compensation and for this the CDG has Public Liability Insurance.

iii. Release and waiver

The CDG requires all members to sign a release and waiver stating that in the event of an accident the member will hold the CDG blameless. This has value as it undermines the ability of someone to bring a spurious claim for negligence. It does not affect the rights of a member to claim for genuine negligence or damage from a criminal action because rights cannot be waived by signing a release.

Chapter 2 Dive planning

Photographic dive in a spacious bedding.

Although cave diving uses some of the equipment, techniques and theory of open water diving, it also relies on additions to all of them. The risks faced by a diver in a cave environment are very different from open water which results in a very different dive planning process. The cave environment is very unforgiving. Simple mistakes and misjudgements can place a diver in a highly stressful situation with no easy escape route. Open water training is totally inadequate to prepare a diver for cave diving both on the practical side and the theoretical base. To be able to cave dive in UK conditions a full understanding of the special difficulties they present should be developed at the earliest stage of cave diver training.

A) Risk factors

i. Risk identification

Risk identification can be used to reduce the hazards of cave diving. Before entering a sump a diver should be aware of the hazards that will be faced and how to reduce them. All aspects of a diver's equipment and procedures must be assessed to ensure that they are adequate to minimise the risks that may be encountered. If a diver identifies a hazard that has not previously been considered, some way must be found to cope with it before the dive can be attempted.

If during a dive a hazard is spotted that has not been considered, the dive will have to be abandoned if there is no procedure for coping with the new hazard. In the conditions found in sumps, divers should have a solution to a problem available before the problem occurs.

The hazards that a diver can face fall into three categories:

- *Inherent.*
- *Specific.*
- *Real time.*

Inherent: All trainees have to study the CDG Risk Assessment to be accepted into the Group. By doing this they will develop an understanding of the general risks involved in UK cave diving. The Risk Assessment (see Appendix 1: CDG Documentation) has been published by the Group to cover the risks that may be encountered in any UK sump. It is not a complete risk assessment. It does not cover all the possible risks in any sump.

Specific: A more specific analysis covers the risks anticipated for a particular dive. During the planning process the diver should attempt to predict the hazards that will be encountered owing to the nature of the sump or the tasks to be carried out on the dive. This may lead the diver to reduce the hazards involved by organising the tasks to be carried out into a sequence and spread the diving over several trips. An individual diver does a specific hazard analysis for each dive; it is not published by the CDG. The assessment can be done as a paperwork or mental exercise. For trainees the exercise can be reviewed by a more experienced diver. For the less experienced cave diver the paperwork method is more useful as it will develop the diver's ability to foresee and plan to cope with the hazards. Experienced divers will have developed an approach to the specific hazards that they are likely to encounter. These will include procedures, equipment and an order of priorities for the reduction of risk.

Real time: Once a dive has been commenced the process of noting hazards does not stop. A cave diver must maintain an awareness of the sump environment so that any change of the conditions is observed. If any change in conditions introduces hazards that compromise the diver's hazard analysis, the dive should be abandoned. The same is true when a diver encounters a task that was not foreseen in the dive plan. If the new task is something the diver cannot safely cope with, the dive should be abandoned.

Each hazard assessment process will be carried out in a different way. The inherent risks of cave diving must be fully understood and mitigated by the diver's training. The specific hazard analysis should be carried out by every diver as part of the dive planning process. It may be in paperwork form or a mental exercise depending on the diver's level of experience and the perceived complexity or severity of the dive. The real time hazard awareness is a mental exercise that involves the diver knowing the anticipated hazards and noting new ones that were not considered for the dive plan, procedures or equipment.

ii. Accident analysis

Several attempts have been made to analyse cave diving accidents in the UK. Some of these have included data from all rescues that involve divers. The result of this type of study is to show that the most common type of rescue incident involving divers was to aid non-divers or inexperienced divers trapped beyond sumps or flood waters. This is not representative of the risks involved in cave diving. The current approach to accident analysis is two fold. Fatalities that happen to cave divers of all levels of experience are studied and incident recording is used to identify the causes of non-fatal incidence.

Investigating fatalities is part of the legal procedure that occurs under UK law and coroner's recommendations may result. Divers who have been involved in non-fatal incidents can report them for distribution to other divers using the Groups on-line reporting system. Using this method a much larger pool of information can be gathered. This may give a better picture of the frequency and severity of incidents that occur during UK cave diving. The information provided will potentially be of better quality as it will be reported by the diver rather than being the result of a third party investigation.

The most recent accident analysis carried out by the CDG is in Appendix 2 of this manual. It uses incidents that have occurred since the previous analysis and compares the results of the two studies. The results show that divers with lower levels of training and experience are far more likely to have an incident. Well trained and/or experienced divers are far better equipped to survive a cave dive. From this it can be seen that Trainee Divers should make every effort to learn the basic skills of cave diving outside the cave environment. Once learned, these skills should be practised on their own and together until the diver is competent and comfortable with them. Any dive in a cave or mine puts the diver in a situation where a controlled ascent to air is not possible. A cave diver cannot abandon a dive and exit to air without overcoming the hazards and stresses of the cave environment. Open water training cannot reproduce the same types of stress as a cave dive. A diver will experience cave dive related stress only on a cave dive and for some any amount of training will not reduce this. This does not negate the importance of training. A well trained diver will be better prepared for problems that may happen and an untrained diver may be unable to cope with a problem that occurs on an initial cave dive.

Diver setting off into typical UK sump conditions.

iii.   Stress

How a cave diver responds to and copes with stress is very important. Stress affects individuals in different ways. Cave divers rely on equipment and techniques to complete any dive successfully. They also rely on their ability to cope with stress. All cave divers should be aware of their own personal limit for coping with stress. This limit can be extended by training, practice and experience. If the limit is exceeded the diver is likely to become stressed and may not be able to cope with the problems that would otherwise be routine.

For a diver, stress can be divided into two distinct categories; direct stress and indirect stress. Direct stress is related to something that is immediate to the environment. Indirect stress is related to background stress on the diver from matters that are not related to the dive.

The main causes of direct stress are:

- *Equipment failure.*
- *Poor visibility.*
- *Other divers.*
- *Line loss.*
- *Time pressure.*
- *Distance.*
- *Depth.*
- *Physical stress.*
- *Peer pressure.*

Factors that can create indirect stress can include:

- *The diver being stuck in traffic.*
- *Rushing to make up lost time.*
- *Problems at work.*
- *Problems at home.*

Any of these causes of stress will become more significant as a diver approaches their personal limit. This may not be immediately obvious to the diver but some signs of stress will be apparent. These may include:

- *Increased gas consumption.*
- *Faster movement.*
- *Loss of technique.*
- *Inability to execute routine diving drills.*
- *Reduction of environmental awareness.*
- *Fixation on one element of the dive.*

When a diver's level of stress is rising to an uncomfortable level the solution is to stop, secure the line, read the contents gauges and assess the dive. If the diver feels sufficiently in control, the dive can continue (as long as the turn point has not been reached) or alternatively a controlled exit can be made. Simply abandoning a dive will frequently reduce stress levels but the diver should be mindful that in the rush to return to base errors can occur. If the diver does not spot the early signs of stress, the effect can significantly increase the risk to the diver.

The effects of stress may include:

- *Problems become magnified.*
- *Drills become more difficult to execute.*
- *Problem solving abilities become reduced.*
- *Following the line and not looking at the sump.*

With reliable equipment and a good grounding in cave diving theory it is easy for inexperienced cave divers to go beyond their personal limit. Although good training and practice will reduce the levels of stress on divers the best way to reduce the effects of stress is by gaining experience. Experienced cave divers will have a greater awareness of their own limit and will have more confidence to deal with situations within that limit. Trainee divers should gain experience within their limit in simple sites before attempting more challenging sumps. Thorough dive planning and good equipment preparation can both help to reduce stress. The most important element when dealing with stress is to be able to recognise it. If a diver can do that, then appropriate action can be taken before the situation becomes hazardous.

iv. Decompression factors specific to cave diving

Diving in open water allows a diver to choose a dive profile as part of the dive planning process with the advantage that profiles that conform to decompression theory can be used. The profile of a cave dive is fixed by the course of the cave passage that is being followed. A cave diver can influence a profile by varying travel speeds throughout the sump but the depths cannot be changed. The result of this is that the majority of UK cave dives do not conform to the algorithms used in dive computers or to construct dive tables. Cave dives are not square profile or multi-level dives with decreasing depths. Cave dives are considered to be saw tooth profile dives, meaning that the depths vary both up and down throughout the dive. Most dive tables are based on theory and tests for square profile dives. As such, UK cave dives can be considered to be outside the algorithms used to construct the dive tables. The no stop and decompression stop limits from the tables may not be correct for a cave dive, even if the diver plans the dive as a square profile based on the maximum depth of the sump. The tables will assume a constant rate of on-gassing that may not occur during the shallower parts of a saw tooth profile dive. The tables will also assume a rate of off-gassing that will not take into account any reduction in off-gassing efficiency caused by increased bubble formation. When a diver ascends, off-gassing occurs from the tissues into the blood. At any time the human body will have bubbles in the blood stream but these are small enough that they cause no harm and can bypass the lungs. These bubbles are called micro bubbles. During tissue off-gassing micro bubbles act as a starting point for bubbles formed by the excess gas. As the diver continues to ascend the bubbles expand until they cannot bypass the lungs and instead become trapped. Each bubble trapped in the lungs reduces the available area for off-gassing and therefore reduces the rate of off-gassing. A saw tooth profile may have multiple ascents, each of which may contribute to a reduced rate of off-gassing.

Fortunately most UK cave dives are not very deep or long and so most dives will not approach decompression. However this does not mean that the increased risk caused by the saw tooth profile can be disregarded. Micro bubble theory indicates that repeated changes of depth can increase the risk of a decompression sickness. UK cave divers can reduce the risk of a decompression sickness by not diving close to the limits of the (square profile) dive tables, adding safety stops when doing so and carefully controlling the rate of ascent used for every ascent of a dive not just the final one. This cannot be considered as a complete solution to the problem.

B) Information about sumps

Dive planning for an undived sump in the UK will be limited by the distance that a diver can cover when laying line and unless the sump turns out to be deep it can be carried out with basic equipment and small cylinders. For dives in sumps where one of the objectives is to dive along an existing line, details about the profile and general passage condition will aid the dive planning process. Information about a sump may already include gas quantities and types as well as the appropriate level of thermal protection for the diver.

i. Obtaining information

When dives are known to have taken place at a particular cave site by members of the CDG, the first resort should be the various Sump Indices produced by the Group. Earlier Indices tended to use an historical approach, but the more recent ones have been more site-descriptive, with references to the relevant CDG Newsletter for precise details of previous dives. Indices include surveys of major sumps and underwater caves. This obviously is good only to the date of publication of the appropriate Index and should be supplemented by information from later Newsletters.

Newsletters are published every three months or so by the Group, and contain details of all exploration dives submitted to the Editor, as well as information about existing dive sites that is considered to be worth recording (condition of lines, changes in sediment patterns, dry exploration beyond, etc.). These newsletters, together with the Indices, constitute the most easily accessible and thorough record of underwater caving in the UK. Annotated ten-year cumulative indices to newsletters help identify previous published accounts of dives at particular sites.

Other information, especially about early dives, may be gleaned from area guide books or caving club journals where more detailed accounts of particular explorations are found. Caving magazines contain accounts of exploration at major sites. The best information of course is from the diver who last dived at the site.

Information about diving sites outside the UK can be gained either by contacting the local cave diving organisation, or by subscribing to foreign cave diving magazines. The CDG Foreign Officer can help with preliminary contacts, and holds some foreign magazines in archive. In some countries, groups or individuals are reluctant to publish exploration records and personal contact may be the best approach.

ii.   Recording information

Obviously, for information to be available for succeeding generations of cave divers, it is vital that each original dive is recorded with the Group. Divers may also wish to send in notes on dives that may otherwise be relevant to members of the Group. The Group prides itself on the ongoing practice of its members, unless the dive site is sensitive or secret for some reason, to reveal their exploits for the benefit of others, both current and future, and for posterity.

Most cave divers keep some sort of personal logbook and submit details to the Group Newsletter when they feel it relevant. This manual does not and will not stipulate how such information should be noted down. Standard log sheets have been designed in the past but realistically these are seldom used by divers who will design their own log format. Suffice it to say that the style and content of the record has to defer to common sense. It is a record of what was planned and what was actually achieved. So, notes should be made as to the sump conditions encountered, original explorations made, condition of lines and belays, depth of sump, length of sump, equipment used (including size of cylinders) and its suitability, sediment patterns, flow conditions, visibility (outward and return), and any other information deemed interesting. The account should be detailed but concise. Mention of helpers on long and arduous carries is polite, and will probably help get them down for a return bout.

A survey is preferred where any original exploration is made and this should be drawn in black ink as clearly as possible. This need not be detailed at first, and a rough sketch is better than nothing. When the occasion allows, a more precise survey should be undertaken and published in the Newsletter.

Where secrecy is preferred, perhaps because of access difficulties, conservation management or other reasons, the Editor operates a Secret File. This is not available for publication within or outside the Group unless the diver concerned gives permission, but is useful to have on record for several reasons, a major one being an accident to the exploring diver when otherwise there would be no record of where the diver might be.

Where dives are made under circumstances that would be covered by the Health & Safety Executive regulations (for paid work including filming, journalism, scientific research, training, etc) more detailed information may be required from each dive.

C)   Preparation

A diver should have a plan for every dive. How formal the dive plan will be varies depending on the type of dive and the individual doing the dive. For a complex dive using mixed gas a more formal approach will be needed than for a dive to pass a short and simple sump breathing air.

For most UK sumps the plan will be an informal mental exercise. The information needed to plan the dive will be common knowledge, or be easily ascertained from the cave description or survey.

This information will cover:

- *Cave access.*
- *Equipment movement through dry cave.*
- *Maximum depth and length of the sump.*
- *Cylinder size needed.*
- *Type of diving suit to be worn.*
- *Line and navigation details.*

For a more complex dive in a UK sump the basic steps for creating a plan will be the same but carried out in a more formal way.

These will include some, but not all of the following:

Declare aim: All UK cave dives should have an aim whether it is a working dive or a tourist trip. The risks created by the sump environment are only worth taking if there is a clear objective including the limitations of the dive.

Collect information: A considerable body of information exists about UK sumps (See Sections Ch2.B.i & ii, Ch5.B.vi) and this should be consulted before a plan is drawn up. For a complex dive the diver will have to collect as much information as possible. For a simple dive the diver may wish to collect the same amount of information. The minimum information should include:

- *Access requirements.*
- *Location of the sump.*
- *Length of the sump.*
- *Maximum depth.*
- *Nature of the passage.*
- *Temperature.*
- *Static or active sump.*
- *Anticipated visibility.*
- *Susceptibility to a flood pulse.*
- *Number and position of any air bells.*
- *Condition of the line.*
- *Orientation of the sump.*
- *Number and type of line junctions.*

Assess profile: Based on the information collected the diver will be able to start to plan the specifics of the dive using the profile. This can take the form of a survey, a dive computer download or a hypothetical square profile based on the length and maximum depth of a sump. The duration of the dive should then be planned using either the information of the nature of the sump passage, the computer download or an assumed rate of movement. From these two exercises the diver will have an idea of the duration of the dive and the depths that will be reached. This will be true only of a known sump. When undertaking an exploratory dive, a diver should plan for a maximum distance (or less) dictated by the amount of line being taken on the dive and a guess at the probable maximum depth and conditions in the sump.

Identify special risks: From the information gathered about the sump it will be possible to identify risks that may be specific to the dive. These may or may not appear in the CDG Risk Assessment. Typical risks may be related to the line. If the sump is infrequently visited the line may be in a poor condition and be in need of replacement/repair. Exploration divers frequently leave a line reel at the limit of exploration. If the fabric of the reel has degraded over the intervening time the line on the reel may spill creating a significant hazard. If a project is being undertaken at such a site, sorting the line out first can reduce the risks. Other risks may relate to digging activities or some other specialist skill.

Identify special equipment: For a dive through a sump to gain access to the dry passage beyond the diver's standard equipment will be used. Any equipment needed beyond the sump will have to be carried through the sump in suitable containers. When the aim of the dive is to carry out some specific task, special equipment may be needed. This may take the form of something that the diver has used before such as a survey slate or something chosen for the specific task. This may include digging tools or materials or some other equipment. When something unusual is to be taken into a sump it should be assessed in the same way as all of the regular diving equipment to maintain an effective equipment configuration.

Plan dive run time and gas requirements: From the profile information gathered about the sump it will be possible to estimate the likely dive time and maximum depth. Using these two factors and the diver's rate of gas consumption it will be possible to estimate the required gas quantities for the dive. The dive time will be an estimate based on information from other divers, or the diver's own judgement of the normal rate of travel in the type of sump passage. When a project is being planned the gas requirement will be based on the experience gained on each dive and will take into account different work loads.

Select cylinders and cylinder configuration to support the gas requirements: (section Ch2.D.v)

Visit the cave: Although this step may not always be necessary for all dives (especially for the caver with good knowledge of the cave) it can prove useful to visit a cave the diver knows less well. The visit will give the diver to opportunity to assess the cave for possible equipment movement problems.

Plan movement of equipment: Whether or not the cave is well known to the diver, a plan to suit the caving party will need to be devised. The diver will have to consider the number of supporters and their ability levels as well as the tackle needed in the cave. The plan may call for multiple trips to carry in caving tackle (leaving the cave rigged) and stage lead.

Plan rescue call out procedure: Finally when all the other planning is done and the planned date and duration of the trip is known, some form of call out procedure will be needed. This will take the form of the normal cave call out procedure, but with extra attention paid to the planned route underwater. It is especially important that in the event of a call out the cave rescue team knows that diving may be involved. Any information from the dive plan may be useful to divers on the call out. Details of the plan should be left with the person responsible for making the call out. If the dive plan changes on the day, a note should be left at dive base explaining the new plan.

D) Gas management

Gas management is a basic skill for all cave divers. For UK cave divers the gas management techniques are based on the use of two or more independent breathing sets. The Rule of Thirds underpins the techniques used but its limitations mean that proper gas management is the result of understanding the principles rather than simply following the rules.

The Rule of Thirds states that a diver must use no more than one third of the available gas on the inward journey leaving one third for the journey out and one third for emergencies. This forms the basic principle of gas management but does not properly and fully describe the process. Correct gas management obeys the principle of thirds; it also ensures that the distribution of gas in the cylinders allows sufficient gas for the outward journey should one breathing set fail at any point during the dive. Other factors that influence gas management mean that the simple application of the thirds rule can leave a diver without enough gas in the event of a breathing set failure. Conversely a strict implementation of the thirds rule without understanding the basic principle can result in a dive plan that fails to maximise the potential offered by the available gas.

The aim of gas management is to calculate the turn point of a dive (measure by cylinder pressure), so that a diver still has enough gas to exit from the furthest point in the event of one breathing set failing.

Depending on the type of dive the turn point will be worked out in one of two ways:

The simple method: For most dives the turn point is reached after one third of the available gas has been used. This simple method of gas planning is commonly used by divers whose aim is to gain personal experience or knowledge of a site. The same method is also used on exploratory dives where the diver will have no way of predicting accurately the profile or duration of the dive and must therefore turn the dive when the safe limit of available gas is reached.

The modified thirds method: Is used for a dive to a known limit such as the other end of a sump or a dig site where the bailout gas needed to return to dive base from that point can be calculated first. The gas needed for the inward journey, the outward journey plus any gas needed for other tasks is then added together to determine the total gas for the dive. For this type of dive the turn point may exceed one third of the available gas, but will still allow enough gas for the diver to exit in the event of one breathing set failing.

i.   Practical considerations

For any dive the gas requirements can be divided into clear phases. For a simple dive this will include the inward phase, the outward phase and the reserve gas. On a more complex dive additional phases such as a working phase and a decompression phase may also be included. The distribution of gas in the cylinders also dictates the level of complexity involved. For two cylinders of equal size and pressure the calculations can be based on pressures. For more than two cylinders or cylinders of different sizes or pressures the calculations have to be based on the gas volume held in each cylinder measured in litres.

Once a turn point has been calculated it has to be useable in UK sump conditions. Pressure gauges typically read to the nearest 10 bar. Using numbers between these steps means that the diver has to guess the reading. To reduce the risk of an incorrect reading all figures for thirds calculation should be calculated to a whole 10 bar number. To do this the total cylinder contents is always taken as the next lowest 10 bar when calculating the third. The third itself is also taken as the next lowest 10 bar increment. When the turn point is calculated by subtracting the third from the total cylinder contents (not the nearest increment number used for thirds calculation) the result is increased to the next biggest 10 bar increment. In this way each move to the nearest 10 bar will reduce the amount of gas available for the inward journey. Moving to the opposite 10 bar increment will increase the amount of gas available for the inward journey and may result in the diver not having enough gas in the event of a breathing set failure. The cylinder pressure used for calculations will be the measured pressure of gas in the cylinder, not the maximum working pressure. Since the cylinder pressure may vary with each fill, the available gas may vary for each dive.

A further consideration is the working pressure required by a demand valve first stage. Valves cannot deliver gas at below ambient pressure. A diver at 30 m cannot breath the last 3 bar (gauge) from a cylinder. To ensure that all the gas used for calculating thirds is available to the diver at any point in the dive 10 bar should be subtracted from the total cylinder pressure before any other calculations start.

Once in a sump the cylinders and the gas in them will usually cool owing to the water temperature being lower than the air temperature. This will reduce the pressure gauge reading. Whilst it is possible to include this effect in the thirds calculation it is unnecessary to do so. In UK conditions the effect is limited to about 10 bar and reduces the amount of gas breathed before the turn point is reached thereby increasing the margin of safety. If a dive is planned at a UK site when the water temperature is higher than the air temperature the effect can again be discounted as the difference will be minimal.

Rounding examples:-

A cylinder pressure is measured before a dive and shows a reading of about 207 bar.

For calculating thirds 207 bar is rounded down to 200 bar.
From that 10 bar is subtracted for the valve giving 190 bar.
One third of 190 is 63.33 bar which is rounded to 60 bar.
The turn point will be 207 bar – 60 bar = 147 bar rounded up to 150 bar.
The turn point is 150 bar.

Slightly less than 60 bar will be used on the way in and the diver will have slightly less than 150 bar available for the exit (the valve cannot be guaranteed to access the full 150 bar at all depths).

Throughout the calculation the direction of rounding always acts to increase the margin of safety. In the above example the figures are not very favourable for getting the most out of the available gas, but they may be suitably cautious for an inexperienced diver.

With different cylinder pressures the level of caution changes:-

A cylinder pressure is measured before a dive and shows a reading of about 220 bar.

For calculating thirds 220 bar does not require rounding.
From that 10 bar is subtracted for the valve giving 210 bar.
One third of 210 is 70 bar, a number that does not require rounding.
The turn point will be 220 bar – 70 bar = 150 bar which does not need rounding.
The turn point is 150 bar.

The full 70 bar will be used on the way in (ignoring the cooling effect) and the diver will turn with almost 150 bar available to the valve. Two thirds of the gas is available for the outward journey and the diver has maximised the available gas for the inward journey but the cylinder has very little spare gas to provide additional safety. If a diver wanted to be more cautious the third could be reduced form 70 bar to 60 bar resulting in a turn point of 160 bar.

Once the turn pressure has been calculated for a dive it is good practice to write them on a slate to provide a backup to the diver's memory.

ii.   Gas calculations

With cylinders of the same size and pressure a diver can calculate thirds as a mental exercise, but for cylinders of different sizes and/or pressures written calculations will probably be needed.
These calculations will include:

- *Cylinder capacity*
- *Respiratory minute volume (RMV)*
- *Gas needed*

When paper calculations are used not all of the formula will be needed for every dive plan. The first formula is the most frequently used. The second formula is used to establish a rate of gas consumption which will only be used to calculate gas needed in the third formula. This will typically be used only for the modified third method in cases when the gas needed has to be estimated by calculation.

Cylinder capacity: For all but the simplest gas planning the free gas capacity of the cylinders should be used. From this the diver can plan gas usage for cylinders with different working pressures and calculate the dive time that can be supported. For cylinders with a working pressure of 232 bar or less the ideal gas laws can be used and the free gas capacity can be calculated using:

FGC   =   Free Gas Capacity ....in litres
CP   =   Cylinder Pressure...in bar
CS   =   Cylinder Size (measured by water volume) .....in litres

In the formula:

$$FGC = CP \times CS$$

E.g.   For a 7 litre cylinder at 220 bar the free gas capacity is:-

$$CS \times CP = FGC$$
$$7 \times 220 = 1540 \text{ litres}$$

For cylinders with a working pressure of greater than 232 bar the compression of gas is less as pressure increases. Initially the reduction is very small but as the pressure rises the effect becomes more noticeable. To calculate the free gas capacity for cylinders above 232 bar the Van der Waals equation can be used.

Respiratory Minute Volume (RMV): All divers will have an average rate of breathing in the water that can be converted to a surface equivalent. This rate can be used to calculate gas consumption at any known depth. The rate will vary depending on the level of activity, stress, task loading, water temperature, experience, fitness and other considerations. RMV is expressed in litres per minute and is calculated from diving experience. A diver can calculate a rate by swimming at a constant depth for a measured period of time and calculating the amount of gas used based on cylinder pressure readings. From the depth, time and volume of gas used, the consumption rate can be calculated using:

RMV   =   Respiratory Minute Volume..............................in litres per minute
GU   =   Gas Used..in litres
T   =   Time ....in minutes
D   =   Depth..in metres

In the formula:

$$RMV = (GU / T) / ((D / 10) + 1)$$

Knowing the cylinder volume plus the starting and finishing pressures the Used Gas Capacity can be calculated using:

GU	=	Gas Used	in litres
SP	=	Start Pressure	in bar
CS	=	Cylinder Size	in litres
FP	=	Finish Pressure	in bar

In the formula:

$$GU = CS \times (SP - FP)$$

E.g. A diver breathes a 12 litre cylinder down from 180 bar to 90 bar whilst swimming at a constant depth of 10 m for a period of 30 minutes. The divers RMV is calculated as follows:

$$GU = CS \times (SP - FP)$$
$$GU = 12 \times (180 - 90)$$
$$GU = 1080 \text{ litres}$$

$$RMV = (GU / T) / ((D / 10) + 1)$$
$$RMV = (1080 / 30) / ((10 / 10) + 1)$$
$$RMV = 18 \text{ litres/minute}$$

Typical figures for minimum RMV gas consumption rates fall around 15 to 20 litres per minute for a relaxed diver. This is an average figure which can fall in good conditions or rise sharply when hazards are encountered. For this reason using an unrealistically low gas consumption rate when calculating gas requirements can result in a diver not having enough gas during a bailout. It is advisable to use a higher gas consumption rate for calculating gas requirements to allow for more gas when stress increases the breathing rate. In a stressful situation a diver's RMV can exceed 30 litres a minute. Allowance should be made for this in a gas plan.

Gas needed: To calculate the quantity of breathing gas needed and thereby choose appropriate cylinders a diver will have to combine several factors. The length of the sump and the type of passage will determine how long a dive will take. The depth will increase the gas consumption rate resulting in the need to calculate the rate of consumption related to the profile. The gas consumption rate will vary with workload if additional tasks are planned. The normal rate of travel for a side mount diver will typically be between 5 metres per minute and 20 metres per minute, sometimes slower in more challenging passage. If a full dive profile is available from a published dive log or can be estimated from a survey the depths during the dive can be used to calculate the quantity of gas needed. When no detailed profile or survey information is available the maximum depth and sump length can be used to calculate a square profile. The gas needed for a dive can be calculated using:

GN	=	Gas Needed	in litres
IJT	=	Inward Journey Time	in minutes
RMV	=	Respiratory Minute Volume	in litres per minute
D	=	Depth	in metres

In the equation:

$$GN = 3 \times (IJT \times RMV \times ((D / 10) + 1))$$

This Gas Needed will be measured in litres and can be used to select cylinders based on their capacity, also calculated in litres. The result of the calculation will be an estimated amount of gas needed for the inward journey and the bailout gas.

E.g. Working from a survey a diver estimates that a dive will take 40 minutes in total (in and out) with a depth of around 12 m for most of the way. The diver uses a RMV of 20 l/minute for calculations even though it is normally about 15 l/minute.

The dive time of 40 minutes is first divided by two so that it represents only one direction and therefore one third of the gas:

40 / 2 = 20 minutes

GN = 3 X (IJT x RMV x ((D / 10) + 1))
GN = 3 X (20 x 20 x ((12 / 10) + 1))
GN = 2640 litres total gas, including one third in one third out and one third bailout.

Knowing the quantity of free gas needed for the dive the diver can then choose the appropriate cylinders.

iii.   Cylinder configurations

Several cylinder configurations are possible with side mount diving. Each configuration has different applications but all must provide a safe quantity of gas for the planned dive and the planned bailout.
This subsection will consider the following models:

- *Two even cylinder model.*
- *Two uneven cylinder model.*
- *Stage cylinders.*
- *Single cylinder.*

Two even cylinder model: The simplest model for gas planning is when two cylinders of the same size and measured pressure are used for a dive that does not include a working phase. The limit of inward gas consumption can be calculated using only the cylinder pressure. As both cylinders are the same size the same amount of gas will be used from both if the pressure used from both is the same.

Two uneven cylinders model: Divers will sometimes dive with uneven size cylinders as part of a dive plan or because of limited cylinder availability. Cylinders are considered to be different sizes when the free gas capacity of the two is significantly different. This may be owing to different cylinder volumes or different cylinder pressures or both (note that the actual cylinder pressure is used here not the maximum working pressure). When planning a dive that will use an equal amount of gas from each cylinder, the turn point should be calculated for the smaller of the two. This amount of gas measured in litres is then converted into a cylinder pressure for the larger cylinder. The turn point will then be one third of the smaller cylinder and the same amount of gas from the larger cylinder, which will be less than one third of the larger cylinder. Diving beyond the turn point on the larger cylinder may result in a shortage of gas if the larger cylinder fails and the diver has to rely on the smaller cylinder for the journey out.

If the diver is planning to minimise carrying cylinders through dry passage at a regular project site, uneven cylinders can be used so that only one will need replacing after each dive. If the smaller of the two cylinders contains enough gas to pass the sump in one direction, it can be considered as bailout if none of its contents are used on the inward journey. To make both the inward journey and the outward journey the diver breathes from the same cylinder (the larger one) which contains enough gas to complete both. If at any point during the dive the main breathing set fails, the diver switches to the other set and exits. It should be noted that valve testing both pre dive and during the dive will deplete the contents of the bailout cylinder (see Section Ch.4.F). Provision should be made to decant gas from the primary cylinder to the bailout cylinder when needed. Alternatively the bailout cylinder will have to be removed from the cave periodically for topping up. For dives that include a working phase (digging, surveying etc) a diver may choose to use uneven cylinders to provide additional gas for the work. The turn point is calculated using the modified thirds method.

Stages: Stage cylinders are a useful method of extending the range of a dive, but correct balancing between the sizes of the two main side mount cylinders and the stage cylinder/s used is important. When planning a dive involving a stage cylinder it is normal practice to still provide sufficient redundancy to allow for only one breathing set failure. When more than one stage cylinder is used the diver will have to decide if more redundancy is appropriate. For dives that use a stage cylinder of the same capacity or smaller than the main cylinders, the stage cylinder can be breathed down to half way if the thirds rule is followed for the other two cylinders. In the event of one of the side mount breathing sets failing (after the stage cylinder has been dropped) the diver will be able to return to the stage cylinder on the working breathing set. The stage cylinder being half full will still have enough gas for the diver to exit. If only the stage cylinder fails the diver will be able to exit using the remaining gas in the side mount cylinders. Each will be one third full and therefore have more gas between them than has been lost from the stage. For dives planned with a stage cylinder that is larger than the side mount cylinders the size of the stage is limited by the amount of bailout gas in the side mount cylinders. The quantity of gas breathed from the stage on the inward journey must not exceed the amount available from the two side mount cylinders at the point where the stage is recovered on exit. If the side mount cylinders cannot provide the required amount of gas there are several ways to change the gas plan to provide enough gas in the event of one breathing set failing:

- *Take two stages and use the thirds rule to calculate gas margins, effectively dividing the dive between two sets of cylinders.*
- *Calculate the side mount gas quantities to save enough gas to allow a return to base; useing less than one third from each cylinder on the inward journey after the stage has been dropped off.*
- *Take a fully redundant breathing set that can be staged in the sump and will only be used to bridge the gap between the limit of the side mount cylinders and the exit if the main stage fails.*
- *Calculate the inward limit of usable gas for the stage cylinder based on the capacity of the side mount cylinders.*

Single cylinder: In some cases sumps are short and open enough to be free dived or dived on a single breathing set. A breathing set with a small cylinder can be taken for emergency use when free-diving a sump. Alternatively a single set can be used for short sumps as long as the valve is designed to free flow on failure. In the event of a failure the diver will have to turn the dive towards the nearest airspace on the free flowing valve. This method should only be considered for use if the diver is confident of passing most of the sump without breathing. This is not a method that should be used when a diver has no previous experience of diving at a site. It is advisable to use two breathing sets wherever possible.

iv.   Calculating a turn point

To work out a turn point a diver must calculate the minimum cylinder pressures that will provide enough gas for an exit in the event of one breathing set failing at any point in the dive.

a.   Simple thirds model

To calculate the turn point based only on the available gas the pressure in each cylinder must be measured, rounded and used to calculate how much gas is held in each. From this the third point can be calculated and checked to see that it meets the requirement of bailout if any one breathing set fails.

For cylinders of equal size and working pressure it is possible to base thirds calculation on the pressures only.

E.g.   A diver plans to use a pair of 232 bar 7 litre cylinders on a dive. When measured their pressures are 225 bar and 200 bar.

225 bar rounds down to 220 and subtracting 10 bar for the valve gives 210 bar
200 bar needs no rounding and subtracting 10 bar for the valve gives 190 bar

210 divided by 3 gives 70 bar (no rounding)
190 divided by 3 gives 63.33 which rounds to 60 bar

225 subtract 70 gives 155 rounds up to 160 bar turn point
200 subtract 60 gives 140 turn point (no rounding)

Check.
The gas used on the inward journey will be 130 bar (60 bar + 70 bar)
130 bar is smaller than the amount remaining in either cylinder at the turn point.

Turning at the pressures of 160 bar and 140 bar on the 225 bar cylinder and the 200 bar cylinder respectively will meet the requirement of thirds rule to have enough gas available it the furthest point in the event of one breathing set failing.

If cylinders of unequal size or dissimilar pressures are used (if equal size cylinders fail the Check part of the calculations above) then the gas capacity of each cylinder must be calculated and used as the basis of the thirds calculation. For this the rounding process is applied before the gas capacity in litres is calculated.

E.g.   A diver has a 7 litre cylinder with a measured pressure of 225 bar and a 6 litre cylinder with a measured pressure of 190 bar.

225 rounding and subtracting 10 gives 210 bar
190 rounding and subtracting 10 gives 180 bar

Cylinder capacity is calculated using the equation FGC = CP X CS

For the 7 litre cylinder
        210 x 7 = 1470 litres
For the 6 litre cylinder
        180 x 6 = 1080 litres
Dividing each by three gives 490 litres and 360 litres respectively.
Check:
490 litres + 360 litres = 850 litres used on the way in.
At the turn point the diver will have 980 litres available in the 7 litre cylinder (1470 – 490)
At the turn point the diver will have 720 litres available in the 6 litre cylinder (1080 – 360)
As a result if the 7 litre breathing set fails the diver will be left with insufficient gas to make an exit. The gas plan fails the test of thirds rule.

To correct this error the amount of gas calculated as one third of the smaller cylinder (measured by free gas capacity) is used as the third of both cylinders. Doing so reduces the gas used from the larger cylinder and therefore the total gas used in the inward journey which is now calculated by doubling the gas used from the smaller cylinder. The turn point is then calculated for the larger cylinder using the volume of gas used from it rather than one third of its contents.

Gas used for the inward journey becomes 720 litres (360 litres + 360 litres)
Check:
The six litre cylinder holds 720 litres at the turn point and therefore can provide enough gas for an exit in the event that the 7 litre breathing set fails at the turn point.

The next step is to convert gas in litres into a pressure reading for each cylinder. This is done using the same formula as before but in a different format:

CP X CS = FGC
CP = FGC / CS

For the 6 litre cylinder the pressure that represents the third is:

CP = 360 / 6
CP = 60 bar

And for the 7 litre cylinder

CP = 360 / 7
CP = 51.42 bar which is rounded to 50 bar

From these two figures the turn point for each cylinder can be calculated:

For the 7 litre cylinder
225 – 50 = 175 rounded to 180 bar

And for the 6 litre cylinder
190 – 60 = 130 bar

The turning point for the 7 litre cylinder is 180 bar and for the 6 litre cylinder it is 130 bar. This meets the requirements of thirds but it is clear that this cylinder configuration does not give the diver optimal use of quantity of breathing gas available.

If the cylinder capacities are very different the diver may benefit from using the available gas in a different way. With unequal cylinder sizes it is sometimes best to use only one cylinder during the dive, keeping the second in reserve as the bailout.

E.g.   A diver has a 6 litre cylinder measured at 195 bar and a 3 litre cylinder measured at 205 bar.
Using the method above the size of the third would be very limited by the 3 litre cylinder and would result in the diver turning after only using 360 litres of gas. By treating the 3 litre cylinder as bailout only the 6 litre cylinder can be breathed down to half way if the 3 litre holds enough gas to get the diver out from the turn point.
To calculate and check the turn point only using the smaller cylinder for bailout the free gas capacity of each cylinder is calculated first:-

For the 3 litre cylinder:-
205 rounded and subtract 10 gives 190 bar
190 x 3 = 570 litres
And for the 6 litre cylinder:-
195 rounded and subtract 10 gives 180 bar
180 x 6 = 1080 litres

The turn point will be the larger cylinder divided by two:-
1080 / 2 = 540 litres

At the turn point the diver will have used 540 litres from the larger cylinder and will have 540 litres available for the journey out. The bailout cylinder contains 570 litres and so the rule of thirds is met in this case. If the gas used from the larger cylinder was greater than the amount available from the bailout cylinder, the rule of thirds would not be met and the turn point would have to be recalculated using the capacity of the bailout cylinder.
From the turn point in litres the turn point in bar can be calculated:-

540 / 6 = 90 bar

195 – 90 = 105 bar rounded to 110 bar

The turn point for the dive will be 110 bar on the larger cylinder and no gas used from the smaller cylinder.

SIMPLE THIRDS

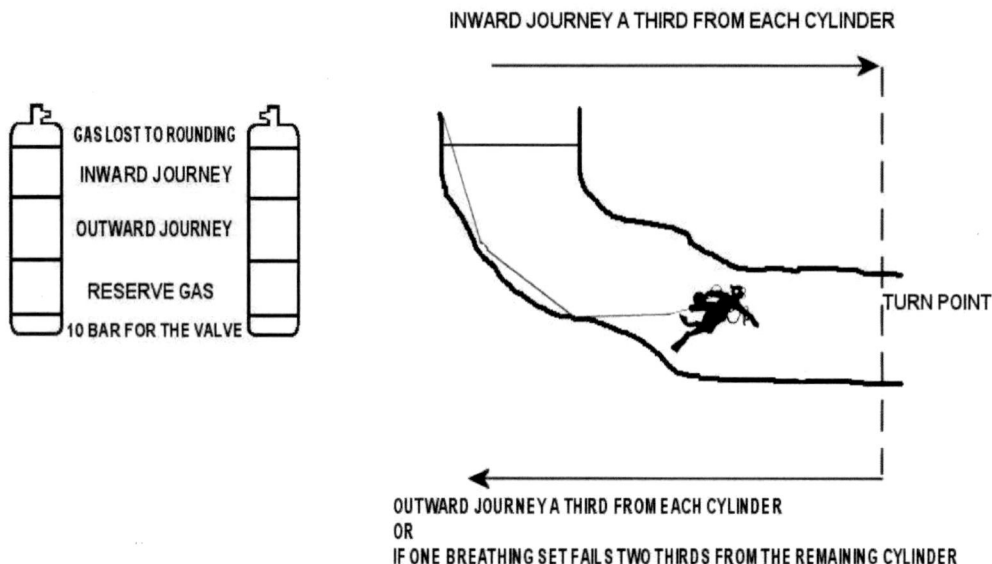

INWARD JOURNEY A THIRD FROM EACH CYLINDER

GAS LOST TO ROUNDING

INWARD JOURNEY

OUTWARD JOURNEY

RESERVE GAS

10 BAR FOR THE VALVE

TURN POINT

OUTWARD JOURNEY A THIRD FROM EACH CYLINDER
OR
IF ONE BREATHING SET FAILS TWO THIRDS FROM THE REMAINING CYLINDER

b. Modified thirds model

The modified thirds model allows the diver to plan for more complex dives than the simple thirds model. It still follows the same principle that the diver must always have enough gas in reserve to exit in the event of one breathing set failing, but differs because it makes better use of the available gas. Using the modified thirds method the gas required in each cylinder for an exit (in the event of one breathing set failing) is calculated first and then the other gas requirements for the dive are added to that. The diver must still turn the dive once (or before) the turn pressures are reached, but the turn point can be more than one third of the available gas.

For the modified thirds method dives can be divided into different phases for gas management. The phases are:

- *Bailout.*
- *Inward travelling phase.*
- *Working phase.*
- *Decompression (if applicable).*

Bailout: the amount of gas needed for an exit in the event of one breathing set failure. The actual figure can be known from experience of the site or estimated by calculation and corrected on the dive.

Inward travelling phase: the amount of gas needed to reach a point where a planned task is to be carried out. As above this can be based on experience or estimated by calculation.

Working phase: the amount of gas available to the diver once the inward travel gas and the bailout gas have been subtracted from the cylinder contents. The working phase of a dive will start when a diver has reached a desired point in a sump. The diver can work to the limit of the available gas, but should not violate the turn point for bailout gas. If the working phase of the dive takes the diver further into the sump, the turn point will have to planned (or adjusted underwater) to ensure that the diver will not run short of breathing gas when trying to exit should one breathing set fail.

Decompression: although decompression is rare in UK cave diving, when it is required the gas plan must provide enough gas for a full decompression in the event of one breathing set failing. If a diver is involved in a project that requires decompression when air is used as the breathing gas, alternative breathing gases should be considered (see Ch.7). Starting from the dive profile, the required decompression stops can be calculated and converted to a gas quantity in litres that will be breathed. This quantity is then subtracted from both cylinders before other calculations are carried out using the quantity of gas remaining in the cylinders. Alternatively a separate cylinder can be staged to provide the decompression gas as long as the two main side mount cylinders hold enough gas in reserve in the event of the stage failing to work. If they do not then more than one decompression stage should be used to provide for the shortfall.

To make a dive plan a diver will have to calculate the gas needed for each phase whilst ensuring the safe level of bailout gas if one breathing set fails.

For the inward and outward phases this calculation will take the same form as used for calculating gas needed for the simple model. To this is added the gas needed for the working phase of the dive. This is known either from experience at the site or is estimated by calculation using the divers RMV with the depth and duration of the working phase. For digging work the diver should anticipate a higher RMV than would be used for a normal swim.

E.g.   A diver plans an underwater dig knowing from a previous visit to the site that it takes 420 litres of gas to get there. The diver wants to use two uneven cylinders so that only the larger cylinder will have to be carried in and out of the cave for each dive. The cylinders available are a 232 bar 3 litre and a 232 bar 7 litre.

Each cylinder can hold:
CP X CS = FGC
232 x 3 = rounded and subtract 10 gives 220 X 3 = 660 litres
232 x 7 = rounded and subtract 10 gives 220 X 7 = 1540 litres

The 3 litre cylinder can be used as bailout because 660 litres is more than the 420 litres required for exit in the event of the other breathing set failing. The amount of gas in the cylinder will be depleted slightly on each dive by valve pressurisation and testing. To calculate the minimum cylinder pressure that will allow it to be used for bailout the same equation is used:

CP X CS = FGC
FGC / CS = CP
420 / 3 = 140 bar plus 10 for the valve gives 150 bar.

Once the 3 litre cylinder pressure drops to 150 bar (owing to valve testing) the cylinder must be topped up either in the cave by decanting or by compressor outside of the cave. In practice the best method would be to decant from the larger cylinder as often as possible to maintain the highest possible pressure in the bailout cylinder.

To calculate the turn point for the larger cylinder the diver will use the same equation as above:

FGC = CP X CS
FGC / CS = CP
420 / 7 = 60 bar plus 10 bar for the valve gives a turn point of 70 bar.

The diver must stop working at the dig when (or before) the 7 litre cylinder reaches 70 bar pressure. Turning before the 70 bar point is reached will have the advantage that some pressure will be left in the cylinder after the dive. This will protect the cylinder and a diver who has been working and may use more gas on the way out because of diving through reduced visibility created by digging.

The amount of gas available for the working phase of the dive will vary with different fill pressures, but the turn point will not. Working phase gas can be calculated as the measured gas in the cylinder minus the turn point and the inward travel gas. Knowing how much gas is available for the working phase, the diver can estimate the duration of the working phase using the RMV figure. From the duration and depth of the dive the decompression requirements can be predicted. If decompression may be required, the outward journey gas will have to be recalculated to include it in both cylinders. This will raise the turn point pressure and reduce the digging time available.

E.g. The working phase of the above dive will be at 7 metres and the diver has a measured cylinder pressure of just over 190 bar in the 7 litre cylinder. For the working phase of the dive the diver uses a RMV of 25 litres per minute (which the diver has deliberately chosen as a higher value).

From the above calculation the diver must turn at 70 bar, so the available gas for the inward journey and the working phase of the dive will be:

Just over 190 rounded down to 190 − 70 = 120 bar

In this case there is no need to subtract 10 bar for the valve as this has already been included in the exit calculation of 70 bar.

The diver also knows from the above calculations that 60 bar of gas will be used from the 7 litre cylinder on the inward journey. From that the gas available for the working phase can be calculated and then the anticipated duration of the working phase can also be worked out using the RMV.

120 bar − 60 bar = 60 bar available for the working phase.
Using:
$RMV = (GU / T) / ((D / 10) + 1)$
As:
$T = GU / (RMV X ((D / 10) + 1))$
In this case GU is the gas available for the working phase, or:
60 bar X 7 litre = 420 litres
So:
420 / (25 X ((7 / 10) +1)) = 9 minutes 52 seconds

This number is an estimate based on several guesses. If the diver has over estimated the RMV for the working phase of the dive, then it may last longer than this calculation shows. Alternatively if the diver has underestimated the RMV, the working phase will be shorter. In both cases the diver must turn the dive when or before the turn pressure is reached.

The diver knows from previous experience that the journey time one way is 14 minutes, so the total dive time will be two journeys of 14 minutes plus the working phase of 9 minutes:

14 + 14 + 9 = 37 minutes at a depth of 7 metres.

From a set of dive tables the diver can see that the planned duration of the dive does not exceed the no stop time for its depth. The diver does not have to plan for decompression for this dive. At this depth the available no stop time is 300 minutes and the diver is clearly not going to get close to this limit. If the calculations showed that the diver's plan did approach the no stop time for the depth, the diver would have to monitor the elapsed time of the dive as well as the cylinder pressure. The dive would be turned when either of the two limits is reached. This ensures that the diver could abort the dive before spending long enough underwater to require decompression stops which were not planned.

MODIFIED THIRDS

INWARD JOURNEY GAS FROM THE LARGER CYLINDER

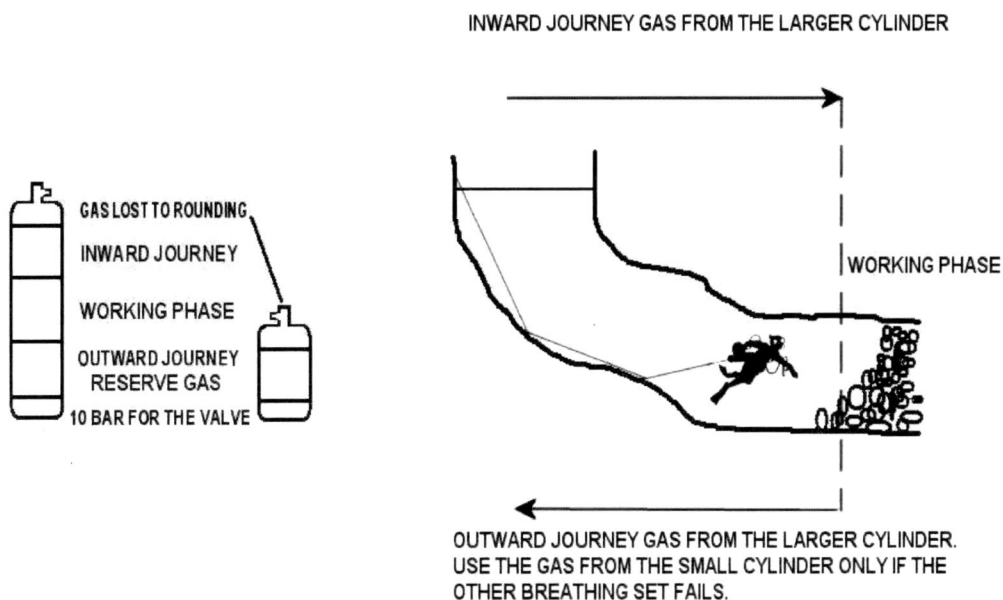

GAS LOST TO ROUNDING

INWARD JOURNEY

WORKING PHASE

OUTWARD JOURNEY
RESERVE GAS

10 BAR FOR THE VALVE

WORKING PHASE

OUTWARD JOURNEY GAS FROM THE LARGER CYLINDER.
USE THE GAS FROM THE SMALL CYLINDER ONLY IF THE
OTHER BREATHING SET FAILS.

v.   Cylinder selection

From the gas needed figures cylinders can be selected (based on their free gas capacity) to carry the gas for the planned dive and to provide bailout. Inexperienced divers are advised to use larger cylinders than the dive plan requires where possible.

E.g.   A diver wants to use two cylinders of the same size and pressure to carry out a dive that has been calculated to need 2640 litres of gas. The cylinders available are pairs of 5 litre, 7litre and 12 litre; the 5's have a maximum working pressure of 207 bar and the 7's and 12's have a maximum working pressures of 232 bar.

For each cylinder the diver has calculated the free gas capacity as:-

5 x 207 = 1035 litres or 2070 litres for the pair
7 x 232 = 1624 litres or 3248 litres for the pair
12 x 232 = 2784 litres or 5568 litres for the pair

With the dive plan requiring 2640 litres of gas the 5's will not hold enough gas and the 7's will hold more than required. The diver chooses the 7's and then calculates the minimum cylinder pressure that will be need for the dive:-

Total gas for the dive is 2640 litres and it will be split between two cylinders giving 2640 / 2 =1320 litres per cylinder. Each cylinder is 7 litres, so the pressure required is:-

1320 / 7 = 188.57 bar (From FGC = SC x CP above)

A cylinder with more than 188.57 bar should contain enough gas to carry out the dive. But owing to the rounding needed to make the turn point easily readable and the requirement for 10 bar to ensure the valve will work throughout the dive, the minimum cylinder pressure will be higher than this. For a practical gas plan the third will have to be 70 bar (188.57 divided by 3 gives 62.86 which is rounded up to 70 bar) or more. Thus the minimum cylinder pressure becomes:-

10 bar + (3 x 70 bar) = 220 bar

This is close to the maximum capacity of the cylinders and the diver will need a good fill to be able to provide enough gas for the plan. If during the dive the diver finds that the amount of gas needed has been underestimated, then the dive must be turned when thirds is reached and before the planned end point of the dive. After the dive the diver can compare the calculated estimated gas needed figures with the amount used. For future dives at the site the figure for the actual amount of gas used on the dive should be used for calculations instead of the estimated figures.

vi.   Accounting for a decompression phase

To calculate the quantity of gas required for a decompression stop a diver can use the RMV figure calculated above or base the figure on the diver's experience of decompression. Once the quantity of gas needed to support the decompression phase of the dive has been established, it should be subtracted from the available gas before the turn point is calculated.

E.g.   A diver who has an RMV of 15 litres/minute has estimated that a dive may require a stop of 10 minutes at 3 metres depth.

From the equation:-
RMV = (GU / T) / ((D / 10) + 1)
Reworked as:-
GU = T X (RMV X ((D / 10) + 1))
GU = 10 x (15 x ((3 / 10) + 1))
GU = 195 litres rounded to 200 litres.

For a simple thirds model this would mean subtracting the 200 litres of decompression gas from each cylinder before calculating the turn point.

E.g.   If the diver is using two 10 litre with nearly 230 bar measured pressure, the turn point will be:-

200 litres / 10 litres = 20 bar of gas for decompression in each cylinder. (If one breathing set fails, the remaining operational set will have enough gas for a full decompression)

nearly 230 bar rounded and subtract 10 bar gives 210 bar.
From this the 20 bar for decompression is subtracted:
210 bar – 20 bar = 190 bar
Thirds is then calculated from 190 bar in the normal way:
190 / 3 = 63.3 rounded to 60 bar

nearly 230 bar – 60 bar = 170 bar can be used without rounding as the diver will use less than 60 bar on the way in owing to using the reading of nearly 230 bar for the calculation. (If the diver had a cylinder pressure reading of 228 bar instead of nearly 230 bar, the turn point would still be 170 bar. 228 – 60 = 168 rounded to 170 bar).
The turn point for each cylinder is 170 bar.

Check:
total gas used on the way in is 120 bar (60 bar + 60 bar)
and to bailout the diver will need 140 bar from 120 bar + 20 bar for decompression in each cylinder.

As the turn point is 170 bar for each cylinder, the gas plan is well within thirds.

For the modified thirds model the diver would again subtract the decompression gas from the cylinders before calculating the available gas for the other phases of the dive. Alternatively the diver may wish to include a separate decompression cylinder.

E.g.   To supply the decompression gas for a dive a diver chooses to use a 2 litre cylinder.

From the equation:
CP X CS = FGC
Reworked as:
FGC / CS = CP
200 litres / 2 litre = 100 bar
100 bar plus 10 bar for the valve gives a minimum pressure of 110 bar for the decompression cylinder.

For the dive plan the diver will now have to provide sufficient gas held in one or more of the other cylinders to be used on the dive to allow for the failure of the decompression breathing set. This can be done by ensuring that the amount of gas remaining in the two side mount cylinders at the end of the dive is more than the decompression gas if all three breathing sets work.

E.g.   From the example above the diver has two 10 litre cylinders with just under 230 bar in each. As the decompression phase is to be supported by a third cylinder (the 2 litre already mentioned) the diver does not have to subtract the gas needed for decompression prior to calculating the turn point:

nearly 230 bar gives a turn point of 160 bar in each cylinder (the third is 70 bar)
the diver will breathe each cylinder down to 90 bar on the way out.
If the 2 litre decompression breathing set fails, the diver still has enough gas for the decompression, held in the combination of the two working breathing sets.

90 bar X 10 litre = 900 litres of gas in each cylinder or 1800 litres in total
1800 – 200 = 1600 litres of gas spare after the decompression.

vii.   The weaknesses of thirds rule

The application of thirds rule can only calculate reserves needed to allow a diver to exit a sump after suffering a breathing set failure in one of its various forms. There are other problems that a diver may encounter during a dive, such as lost line, line entanglement etc. Without prior knowledge of the exact nature of each incident it is impossible to calculate how much time (and therefore gas) will be needed whilst the problem is solved. It is hoped that the extra gas available from the application of the thirds rule will give the diver sufficient time to solve a problem when it occurs. This may not always be the case.

Thirds rule also assumes that a diver's gas consumption rate remains constant throughout the dive. Several factors can cause a diver's breathing rate to increase:

- *Stress.*
- *Swimming into a current.*
- *Carrying extra equipment.*
- *Poor visibility.*
- *Moving too quickly.*
- *Poor buoyancy control.*
- *Multiple attempts to pass an obstacle.*

Given that failure of one breathing set at the limit of the dive will leave the diver with only just enough gas to get out, an increased rate of gas consumption can leave a diver short of gas. If this situation is exacerbated by a further problem, the diver will be under significant time pressure. If a diver knows that some of these factors will affect the journey out, the gas plan should be adjusted to compensate. If a diver is planning a dive in a sump with a strong current, the gas margins should take account of this. If the diver is travelling against the current on the way in the normal thirds rule should be followed. This will give the diver more gas to cope with problems that may be created by being swept along by the current on the way out. If the diver is travelling with the current on the way in, more gas will be needed for the journey out and bailout. For an exploratory dive in these conditions it is normal to dive to a reduced margin such as quarters or sixths. For a dive of known profile the divers RMV should be adjusted down for the inward journey and adjusted up for the outward journey and bailout gas. The amount of adjustment will depend on the strength of the current in the sump. If the diver has no data for this, then a shorter dive to gauge the conditions and gather information should be made. When this is done the diver should dive to quarters or sixths and calculate the two gas consumption rates (inward and outward) after the dive. This information can then be used to plan dives in that sump when it has similar flow rates.

Thirds rule works on a fixed amount of gas irrespective of the cylinder size or the depth of the dive. The amount of time available to cope with any problem will be small if a diver is using smaller cylinders or is diving deep. For a diver on a long shallow dive using larger cylinders the third of gas that is held in reserve for bailout and coping with problems will last for quite a long time. For some dives this could be 30 minutes or more. When a diver is using smaller cylinders on a shorter dive, the third held in reserve may only last for 10 minutes. Thus both dives give the same apparent margin of safety, but the small cylinder dive provides a much shorter amount of time to cope with problems. For deep dives the problem will be the same as the advantage of the larger cylinders is negated by the increased gas consumption rate at depth.

It should be noted that diving to the limit of gas supply calculated to thirds is high risk. It is prudent allow extra gas in all breathing sets for the outward journey. This is particularly important when using unbalanced first stages that can free flow at lower cylinder pressures.

E)   Theory

i.   Solo diving

There are many hazards associated with cave diving. Some but not all, of the hazards of cave diving have been identified by the CDG in the Risk Assessment. The CDG views solo diving techniques as safer than buddy diving techniques for diving in UK sump conditions. The buddy system was introduced in open water diving to minimise the risks associated with open water diving hazards, but when applied to the UK sump diving situation, buddy diving introduces additional risks:

- *One diver can become physically jammed in a passage, possibly trapping the diver's buddy.*
- *If one diver gets tangled in the line and has to cut it, the diver's buddy will be left with no continuous line out unless the diver is able to repair the line.*
- *A second diver past a line junction may disturb the first diver's out tag at the junction.*
- *Two divers moving through the constricted passages typical of UK sumps will potentially cause a greater reduction in visibility.*
- *Buddy diving techniques are often based on one diver providing the alternative breathing supply to the second diver rather than each diver having two independent breathing sets. In UK sumps air sharing of this type would be difficult even with the long hose system.*
- *In UK sump conditions, communication can be confusing and varies from being difficult to being impossible because of poor visibility.*
- *The buddy system can result in a diver being distracted by the buddy and not concentrating on the safety of a dive.*

As a result of these risks CDG training is based on solo diving for UK sumps. A fully independent diver who has redundant breathing supplies and is responsible for all aspects of the dive will not be put at additional risk by the factors listed above. Thus all CDG divers should always consider themselves to be solo divers even when diving as part of a group. Due consideration must be given to redundancy of equipment. If an item of equipment is essential for survival, the diver should have two or more. In the event of essential equipment failure the diver will swap to the backup, abandon the dive and return to base. If an item of equipment is important, but not essential the diver should take only one as this will reduce task loading. In the event of non essential equipment failure the diver can choose to abandon the dive and return to base or continue without completing the task dependent on the failed item of equipment.

Proper training for solo diving is important as there will be no other divers to offer help. Any solo diver must be well practised in the core skills that will allow the diver to survive in the sump environment.

ii.   Team diving

Diving with multiple divers in a sump does have a role to play in UK cave diving. There are certain tasks, such as underwater construction, that benefit from more than one diver being present at the same time. Additionally, there is a social dimension to recreational cave diving that results from diving in a group. This is particularly likely if a caving project is conducted beyond a sump where mutual support may be critical to the success of a task. The overriding philosophy of the CDG remains that divers entering a UK sump bear the full responsibility and accountability for their own actions. As such there is a deeply ingrained belief that a philosophy of solo diving is an essential requirement for safe sump diving within the UK. Multiple divers are effectively a team of solo divers, where each individual diver must be considered by all of the divers as a potential source of hazard. This form of diving is more accurately thought of as team solo diving.

Buddy diving is very different from team solo diving. When buddy diving a pair of divers is considered to be a unit and thus share responsibility and accountability for their actions. Buddy diving has been developed and modified for many different environments including some cave environments. It would, however, be a grave and possibly fatal error to use an unmodified buddy diving system in the majority of UK sumps. Similarly it would be incorrect for a diver familiar with team solo diving to consider themselves fully conversant with buddy diving or to consider that solo diving is appropriate for all forms of diving.

Diving in a group creates additional hazards for each diver. A diver who is being followed can feel pressured to hurry through hazardous obstacles when they are better passed slowly and carefully. There may also be a tendency to overlook equipment problems so as not to spoil the dive for others. The nature of the sump must be considered when diving in a group. For short constricted sumps, it is best to maintain enough separation to allow each diver time to pass the sump before the next diver starts. Elapsed time and absence of movement of the line is an indication of when it is safe to proceed. When diving multiple sumps, the advantages of redundancy can be fully utilised. Air space between sumps can be used to render assistance or repair equipment. For longer sumps, it is often safe for divers to travel in pairs, one diver a safe distance behind the other. Often, owing to the lighting effect from the diver in front, it is possible to see more of the passage in this way. Should a problem occur both divers might be able to proceed to a larger area and take advantage of the redundancy which pair diving can offer. For very large clear sumps, it is often normal for pairs or groups of divers to swim together down the line. In this case it is very important that each diver monitors the line for breaks and potential junctions. Each diver is responsible for their own route finding and safety. A diver should never rely on someone else for route finding on the way out. Each diver should mark line junctions as would be done on a solo dive. When exiting junction markers left by other divers should not be disturbed.

Diving with others is most effective when individual aims and roles are pre-planned and best when the divers have developed a considerable rapport based on years of diving and caving together. They must be familiar with the use of signals and slates and should agree beforehand on any marks and techniques to be used at junctions or difficult sections. Otherwise, especially on original exploration dives, it is probably safer to dive alone.

iii.   Types of sump

The conditions that a diver will experience in the UK will be largely dependent on the flow characteristics of the sump. Some procedures used by the diver when planning and executing a dive will have to be adjusted to compensate for the conditions. The condition of the sump will change with weather, both in the short and long term. Some sumps will need sustained dry weather before they offer the best diving conditions. Other sumps can benefit from seasonal changes in flow rates to give acceptable diving conditions.

Sumps can be classified into one of two types, but may belong to either dependent on the weather.

The types are:

- *Static.*
- *Active.*

Static: sumps have little or no flow. They can be feed from percolation water or from an intermittent stream. Percolation sumps have a characteristic blue hue to their clear water that is lost once the water is disturbed. As the water has been filtered whilst draining through the cracks in the limestone, these sumps will have little suspended vegetation. Stream-fed static sumps can have suspended vegetation and their colour will be dependent on the soil type in the stream's catchment area. Static sumps will clear if left undisturbed as the suspended particles and silt will settle to the floor or may cling to the walls and ceiling. This can be disturbed by a flood pulse or by diving activity. General caving activity will not affect static sumps unless the water is disturbed in some way. Once a flood pulse or dive has happened in a static sump the disturbance caused will take some time to clear. A diver will have the opportunity of good visibility on the inward dive in a static sump, but will frequently suffer very poor visibility on the outward journey. Every effort should be made to avoid disturbing silt deposits and the line should be checked and any line junctions clearly tagged. Flood pulses can move silt banks in sumps. In static sumps the space available to the diver can depend on the positioning of the silt banks after the last pulse. As there is little or no continuous flow in a static sump this may leave a sump blocked until the next flood pulse. Most static sumps will be perched above the level of the resurgence and be the result of water being trapped in a 'U-tube' between sections of dry passage. When prolonged dry weather is experienced active sumps can become static when flow ceases. If this allows suspended particles to settle visibility may improve: the best time to dive some normally active sumps is when they are static.

Active: sumps have a high enough flow through them to prevent suspended particles from settling. The amount of vegetation in the water can vary with seasonal changes. The colour of the water will be dependent on the soil type in the stream's catchment area. The intensity of the colour staining will be related to the flow rate. In some caving areas the staining can be enough to reduce the visibility significantly. A good local knowledge of the way visibility in a sump reacts to rainfall will be needed to select the best conditions to dive. Active sumps will usually have poorer levels of visibility on the inward journey than static sumps owing to the staining affect and the suspended particles. On the outward journey the flow may help to clear deposits disturbed by the diver on the inward journey. The flow rate can also be helpful to divers involved in project work in a sump as anything they disturb will be washed away from their static position. When planning dives in active sumps, divers should be aware of the effect the flow rate will have on gas consumption and take this into account when calculating bailout gas. In some flow conditions the force of the water will be high enough to prevent a diver from moving when swimming against the current. The condition of active sumps can be affected by general caving activity. Cavers moving through the stream further up the cave will disturb deposits which will be washed into the sump. For some active sumps the best diving conditions will be on a Friday, just before the weekend's dry caving activity.

iv.   **Visibility in sumps**

Unfortunately, good visibility in UK sumps cannot normally be expected. Where good visibility exists, however, it is important to maintain it as much as possible for a number of reasons.
These are:

- *To make the dive safer.*
- *To allow as full a visual examination of the passage as possible.*
- *To make route finding easier.*
- *To maintain visual communication between divers.*
- *To preserve the cave environment.*

Layered affect in an active sump.

Various factors affect the visibility in underwater caves. The type of sump and how it reacts to the local weather conditions has a significant effect. How the water feeds into the sump is also important. Occasionally, flowing stream water may overlie static water (or vice versa), creating a layered effect similar to cloud inversion, where either the upper or lower layer is considerably clearer than the other. This may be due to temperature or density differences, but the phenomenon has not been fully studied.

Suspended materials, caused by either active surface run-off or human disturbance of cave or surface sediments, offer the greatest problems. Choosing the most opportune moment to dive and using correct technique are the best ways to maximise visibility. Once disturbed heavy particles will settle fairly quickly, but fine, light particles may remain in suspension in water for hours, or even days. Any limitation of visibility on a cave dive increases the risk, and any reduction of visibility during a dive simply reduces the odds even further.

The position of a diver's light can create different levels of backscatter from suspended partials. Lights held further from the eyes (e.g. hand-held) are more effective in reducing backscatter.

v.   Diving at altitude

A small number of UK cave dives and a large number of cave dives outside of the UK can be classed as altitude dives. The difference in atmospheric pressure at altitude may be very small compared with the pressure changes experienced by a diver's body during a dive, but the effect on decompression can be significant. Decompression tables are designed to allow the diver out of the water only when the level of gas dissolved in the body's tissues has reduced to a level above the atmospheric pressure that the tissues can hold without bubble formation. At sea level dive tables achieve this with the last stop being at 3 m or deeper if mixed gas techniques are being used. At altitude the lower atmospheric pressure reduces the amount of gas that the body's tissues can hold without bubbles forming. To reduce the gas loading to a safe level for the altitude the diver will have to follow a decompression schedule designed for the atmospheric pressure at the altitude of the dive site. Therefore more decompression will be needed and no-stop times for all depths are reduced. To reduce the amount of dissolved gas in a divers tissues the decompression profile will typically involve reduced accent rates and require stops that start deeper and finish shallower.

Divers contemplating diving at altitude should ensure that their depth measuring equipment is appropriate and that they have the correct decompression tables. Depth gauges measure pressure and represent it as a depth. It is therefore important to calibrate any depth measuring device to the atmospheric pressure at dive base. Some depth gauges and dive computers will need to be user set for altitude compensation, where some computers and digital dive timers will automatically set themselves. In the case of computers, selecting the altitude mode will modify the algorithm used to calculate decompression. For decompression tables it is important to ensure that the tables being used are correct for the altitude of the dive. Decompression tables for altitude diving are classified by their altitude, which will be designated as a height above sea level.

Altitude diving is an area of decompression theory that adds another complexity to a body of theory that is incomplete. Proper training is important to fully understand the subject. Modern electronic dive computers and gauges are complex and a diver must be fully competent in their operation in line with the manufacturers' instructions. Diving at altitude will frequently involve travelling to and from the dive site through a range of altitudes. During these changes of altitude (and therefore pressure) the body's tissues will be on and off gassing. Moving from a dive site to a higher altitude will result in off gassing; if a diver has just completed a dive this can increase the chance of decompression sickness. For a diver intending to carry out complex dives at altitude a twelve hour period of acclimatisation before the dive will allow the body's tissues to have the correct gas loading for the tables being used.

Diving at altitude also affects partial pressure calculations for divers using accelerated decompression based on high Oxygen mixes. Proper training and the correct tables and/or software are important when planning such dives.

vi.   Turning a dive

One of the most important parts of any dive plan is the turn point of a dive. This may be dictated by gas margins, the completion of a task, sump conditions or apprehension. A diver must be monitoring cylinder contents gauges frequently enough to know when the gas turn point is being approached. For some dives the diver will have to carry out tasks prior to turning such as securing a line reel, belaying the end of the line or tidying up tools. Time must be allowed for these tasks so that the diver can complete them without using any of the bailout gas. If a diver is on an exploratory dive the rule of thirds must be followed. The diver's planned turn point must be observed. If drawn forward into unexplored passage a diver would use some of the bailout gas and extend the distance that the bailout gas has to cover. In the event of breathing set failure the other already partly depleted breathing set will have to sustain the diver over a greater distance to the exit. When working on a project in a sump divers should develop a routine for the work that includes frequent contents gauge reading. This will reduce the chance of a diver becoming engrossed in the task and missing the turn pressure.

Divers should also be prepared to abandon a dive if conditions deteriorate to a point where the difficulty of the dive exceeds the divers' ability or makes a planned task unacceptably hazardous. Knowing when this point has been reached is a skill that divers develop with experience. Divers with limited experience should be cautious and be prepared to abandon a dive before the level of difficulty approaches the limit of their ability. A small problem that occurs on a cave dive can quickly develop into something more serious if other small problems or poor conditions are encountered. An inexperienced diver will be able to learn from a dive that was abandoned before the planned turn point owing to a small problem. Experienced divers will abandon a dive at any point if that is their decision. If this happens when the diver is one of a group, the decision will not be questioned. In this instance the other divers will react in accordance with the pre-dive plan and either carry on with their own dives or turn at the same time. It is not considered good etiquette to question another diver's decision to abandon a dive. A decision to carry on with a dive that should have been turned can be questioned.

Chapter 3 Equipment and configuration

Sharp roof pendants can dictate the route over a smooth floor.

To become a proficient cave diver in UK conditions trainees must build on their knowledge of caving and diving to develop the techniques used in sumps. Since cave diving is entirely dependent on equipment, a great deal of time and effort must be put into developing a solid understanding of the equipment and how it is used. This chapter does not attempt to explain the basic operation of scuba equipment (which is dealt with in basic scuba training) but instead focuses on the specific equipment requirements of cave diving. The reader is assumed to already have a basic understanding of scuba equipment. Likewise the equipment configuration details in this chapter are specific to side mount cave diving.

A) Equipment

Equipment for cave diving is taken from three main sources: open water diving, dry caving and home building. The equipment must work well together to keep the diver safe in the demanding passages of UK sumps. Thorough testing of new kit must be undertaken before its use in a sump to ensure it works as required. It should integrate well with the rest of the diver's equipment. Many different kit configurations are used by CDG divers; individuals having found a way that works for them. Despite this there are some configuration guidelines that the group has adopted:

- *Two independent breathing sets.*
- *Three or more lights.*
- *Knife or other cutting device.*

The specific equipment used on a dive will vary for different sumps. Factors such as temperature, depth and duration will have a very significant effect on the type of suit worn as well as other items. Belay devices will be chosen to match the nature of the sump; even if no line laying is planned, a small number of belays will still be taken for repair work if needed. Special elements of the dive plan will dictate additional equipment.

The equipment commonly used is described below:

i. Wetsuits

These are known to all cavers, but unfortunately the standard caving wetsuit will not keep a diver warm in all but the shortest sumps. For use on longer dives, a semi-dry two piece suit with attached hood made from a thicker, diving grade neoprene material, typically 5 or 7 mm, is needed. The standard configuration is long john and jacket, but for caving beyond sumps some divers use a full suit with a separate vest (with attached hood) which provides additional thermal protection and can be removed and easily carried after the dive.

This sort of suit offers the advantages of low drag, robustness, mechanical simplicity and predictable buoyancy characteristics. The disadvantages are limited protection from cold, limited depth range and lack of buoyancy compensation.

Typically this sort of suit has limited application below around 15m depth and 45 minutes duration, as they become less efficient as water temperature drops. For short, shallow sumps with caving beyond, they are ideal.

ii. Dry suit and underclothing

The alternative to the wetsuit is the dry suit and underclothing. This combination is used when the depth, duration or temperature of a dive exceeds the comfort limits of a wetsuit. Dry suits are available in two basic types: neoprene and membrane. The former are traditionally used in UK sumps but the latter are becoming more popular as manufacturers produce more robust models. Irrespective of the type chosen there are some basic considerations that apply to both types when purchasing a dry suit; neoprene seals (latex seals are to flimsy and cold), medium weight zip (light weight aren't robust enough and heavy weight limit flexibility), zip cover (to prevent damage from grit and abrasion) and a cut that allows a better range of movement than might be found in an open water dry suit. Other features of a dry suit are the position and type of dump value. Both cuff and auto (shoulder) dumps are used in caving, front or rear zip (front zips suits are designed to be diver operated, the rear zip design relies on someone else for operation) and hard or soft boots (soft boots allow the diver to wear caving boots over the dry suit). The inflator valve, which for open water diving is normally placed in the centre of the chest, must be offset to the side or up towards the neck (but avoiding the route of any harness straps) so that it doesn't snag when the diver is in constricted passage. The dump valve also needs to be positioned to avoid harness straps and other equipment whilst not compromising its operation.

There are two commonly used materials for dry suit construction:

Neoprene: Dry suits are made using expanded neoprene (the same material as wetsuits) or a compressed neoprene; both offer good warmth and don't lose all their buoyancy characteristics in the event of flooding. They are bulky for carrying through a cave and can restrict movement if they have a tight cut. Under suits can be worn to increase thermal protection.

Membrane: Dry suits are made from a range of materials (some similar to caving oversuits). They have no inherent buoyancy characteristics and offer no significant thermal protection; for these reasons the type of underclothing worn is very important. The normal caver's under suit is not capable of maintaining warmth or buoyancy in the event of a suit flood and the diver will have to look for a suitable open water diver's under suit to combat these problems. Alternatively a wetsuit could be worn under the dry suit to achieve the same result. Membrane dry suits can be packed much smaller than neoprene suits especially if they have soft boots and are therefore ideal for carrying through caves. The diver can use caving boots over the top and thus have footwear to cave in beyond the sump once the dry suit has been removed.

In some cases divers have added an independent air cell to a suit with its own inflation and dump valve to provide redundant buoyancy. This is a custom feature and not all suit suppliers will provide it.

iii.   Gloves, hoods and wet socks

Gloves will need to offer adequate protection for the depth, duration and the temperature of the dive. Gloves can be bought with a range of surface treatments; the harder protective layers can make the glove less flexible and colder but will offer good protection when digging.

Wet socks, when worn with a wetsuit or semi-dry must be of diving grade (normal caving wet socks will not be warm enough in most sumps). They may not be available from all diving shops in a soft soled design. The hard soled designs are unsuitable because they prevent caving footwear from being worn and do not offer enough support or grip to do the job themselves.

Hoods are usually supplied with dry suits or they can be bought separately for use with wetsuits or semi-dry suits which don't have an attached hood.

With all these items long overlaps where they meet the suit help to reduce heat loss.

iv.   Fins

Fins are used in most but not all sumps. They provide propulsion and must therefore attach firmly as well as comfortably to the diver's footwear. Modern fins come with a wide range of (foot) pocket sizes and a huge variety of shapes and designs with an equally wide range of price tags. Only pocket fins are suitable, shoe fins (sometimes called pool fins) aren't suitable. When buying fins it is a good idea to take the footwear to be worn into the shop as this is the only effective way of checking the fit before the purchase. This usually means the diver's dry suit or caving boots as worn when diving with a semi dry/wetsuit. The only general rule on fin choice is that shorter fins offer better control but less thrust and longer fins offer more thrust but less control. Some designs go against this rule and it is best to borrow several types of fin from other divers to try them out before making a purchase. When choosing fins bright colours should be considered an advantage. They allow other divers to see and avoid the fins in the water and recovery can be easier in the event of loss.

The most likely point of failure on a fin is the strap. If the original strap is left on, a spare strap should be carried as a matter of routine. There are aftermarket metal spring straps available that make taking the fin on and off easier. They are also less likely to break. Some CDG members have experimented with replacing the strap with thick bungee cord.

v.   Mask

The modern dive mask is available in a wide range of designs but since the main criterion on choosing one is an airtight comfortable fit, each diver's choice is usually limited. A diver may find that it takes time to find the right mask. After fit, the other criteria for selecting a mask are the field of vision and packing size. There are several masks that offer a wider field of vision to the diver, but this type of mask is often bigger and more difficult to pack for transport through a cave. The alternative is the low profile mask which is small, packs well but has a much smaller field of vision. A compromise has to be struck between the two, or more than one mask can be bought, one being big for easy access sites and the other smaller for the more difficult trips.

As with fins, mask straps can break, so a spare strap should be carried as routine. On longer dives a spare mask should also be carried.

For divers with poor eyesight some masks can be fitted with corrective lenses.

vi.   Cylinders

For UK cave diving, steel cylinders with a working pressure of 200 bar, 232 bar or 300 bar are common with most divers having a choice of capacities ranging from 3 litre to 15 litre. For the trainee diver a pair of smaller cylinders will prove sufficient; sizes of 3 litre, 5 litre or 7 litre will all work well. The smallest size, (3 litre) are the best for carrying through dry cave but will only allow the shortest dive. If only able to buy one set of cylinders then the idea size would be 5 litre or 7 litre. If a diver wants smaller cylinders then 3 litre scuba cylinders of 232 bar or preferably 300 bar if these can be filled properly, can be used.

Cylinder valves are usually whatever comes with the cylinder but if there is a choice the diver should try and get the most robust thick walled valves. Some cheap valves have very thin walls and will not survive a carry though a cave without becoming deformed (see Ch.9.B.ii). DIN fitting types are essential for cave diving. An A-clamp is not as mechanically strong as a DIN fitting. There is also the potential for the diver to turn the wrong knob, thus separating the valve first stage from the cylinder tap.

vii.   Demand valve

Demand valves are designed to be sold into the recreational diving market, not the UK cave diving market. This means that despite the fact that they all pass the same European standard for air delivery with low breathing resistance at depth, very few are suited for carrying through caves and diving in UK sumps. When choosing a demand valve the best source of information will be the trainee's mentors and other qualified divers. As demand valves are expensive, safety critical equipment, trainees should inspect several kit configurations, gain advice and use several different valve types before buying their own. Some valve types may look ideal when viewed in a shop but are not used because experience has shown them to be unsuitable.

The following factors are important for cave diving:

The first stage: must be capable of taking the knocks when carried through a cave, have the hose outlets in the correct place for hose routing and be capable of performing in cold water. The only common standard among UK cave divers is the choice of DIN fitting to connect the first stage to the cylinder. All first stages will have either one or two high pressure ports for the SPG plus one or more (typically four) low pressure ports that will be at interstage pressure.

The second stage: The choice of second stage is more difficult than the choice of first stage. The position of the exhaust valve, purge button and the hose routeing, or "handedness" must be taken into account. All second stages work in the normal swimming position, i.e. face down, or with the body upright or horizontal. The cave diver may get into a head up or sideways position for extended periods. A cave diver needs a second stage that will work effectively in all these positions. Some second stages may not. Whichever second stage is chosen the mouthpiece must be comfortable; if the one supplied with the valve isn't, there are aftermarket models available. One of the functions of the exhaust valve is to drain any fluid that has collected in the second stage. If it is operating correctly no water should enter the valve. However, fluid can enter from a poorly fitting mouthpiece, as saliva from the diver's mouth, or from a minor malfunction on the valve (a hole in or poorly fitting main or exhaust diaphragm are the most common examples.) During normal diving this fluid may not be a problem, but if allowed to build up it can become at the least an annoyance. For the second stage to drain the fluid away, the exhaust valve needs to be lower than the mouth. This allows water to drain to the lower part of the breathing chamber where it is blown out on the next breath out. Most second stages have the exhaust port located at the bottom front of the main air chamber. If the valve is used upside down (i.e. the diver is head down or upside down) this draining cannot occur until there is sufficient fluid in the valve for some of it to be blown out of the exhaust. Before this becomes effective the diver will be aware of the build up as some of the fluid will enter the mouth on each breath. This orientation problem depends on the type of valve. Those with exhausts at the side probably perform better as they work just as well when the diver is upside down, because there is no upside down for them.

Cave divers in the UK almost always use side-mounted cylinders and this requires the second stages to come to the mouth from each side. Most valves are "handed" i.e. they only have the air inlet on one side, with the exhaust valve below. If two left-hand valves are used, your air hose will have to be twisted through 180° to reach the mouth. This should be avoided. There are two solutions to this problem. You can use only demand valves that are not handed and can therefore be inserted from either the left or right side (i.e. side-exhaust valves such as the Poseidon Cyklon). The alternative is to have one valve of each side. Many manufacturers will supply both right and left valves and different models of valve may be opposite handed.

The position of the purge button is also important. If it stands proud and is easy to get to it will be easily knocked against rock in tighter passages, resulting in a loss of breathing gas. A well placed purge button will be away from the areas on a second stage that frequently rub against rock or be recessed so that it will not be activated; the side is good for this.

The hose length supplied with the demand valve will be usable for side mounting for most divers. But it must allow the diver's head a full range of movement without pulling the hoses tight and rotating the second stage in the diver's mouth. If the second stage does get pulled around or takes on an uncomfortable angle in the divers' mouth, then the standard hose can be replaced with the slightly longer hose.

High pressure contents gauge hoses supplied for recreational diving are not ideal for side mount diving owing to the hose length. Although it is possible to loop the unwanted hose around the dive cylinder and still leave the gauge readable, this is not an ideal solution. Pressure gauges should be mounted on short high pressure hoses (150 mm) for ease of hose routeing, reading and transportation underground. These are often sold for use on stage cylinders. Hoses are easily damaged in the cave environment and it may be worth considering the use of hose protectors at all junctions where the highest amount of flex occurs; protection should be regularly removed to check for leaks or damage.

All regulators should have a pressure gauge capable of registering 25% higher than the planned cylinder pressure. Pressure gauges should be clear, robust and compact.

viii.   Instruments

Typical instruments used for UK cave diving are:

- *Compass.*
- *Depth gauge and dive timer.*
- *Computers.*

Compass: A standard scuba compass or a liquid filled walking compass will do for UK cave diving. It should not be part of an open water style console (combined with a contents gauge), instead having its own strap, and be low profile to reduce the potential of snagging. It is worth replacing some types of strap on scuba compasses with bungee or a snoopy loop as they are less prone to failure.

Depth gauge and dive timer: The mechanical analogue depth gauge records depth and the maximum depth it has been taken to since it was last reset. It is used in collaboration with a waterproof watch to record dive time and maximum depth. This system is adequate for most UK cave diving despite its limited functionality. Digital devices (sometimes refereed to as D-timers) that record depth and duration under water have replaced the mechanical depth gauge and watch. They record current depth, duration of dive and maximum depth reached on each dive. They turn on when wet contacts touch the water and a required minimum depth is reached. They can also measure surface interval duration which can be useful if tables are to be used to calculate decompression requirements. In addition some can offer a logbook function that records dive history. Most are sold as sealed units with no battery replacement possible, providing a reliable, robust method for a diver to record dive information. These are more than adequate for most UK cave diving if the diver has a desire to know the depth and duration of a dive during or after the dive. They can also be used as a backup device if the diver moves to more challenging dive profiles. As depth gauges/dive timers which are usually worn on the forearm, come with a moulded buckle-up strap it is worth putting a piece of thin bungee cord through the holes in the strap to form a loop which will prevent loss if the buckle comes undone.

Computers: Dive computers measure depth and duration of a dive in the same way as D-timers, but also calculate the decompression requirements on a dive based on standard diving algorithms. The range of types and the specification variations are vast. For most UK cave dives the diver will not require decompression stops but the dive computer offers the most reliable way of approximating a diver's inert gas loading for the profiles dived in UK caves. There are many features available on dive computers, some of which can be very useful for the UK cave diver, notably audible ascent rate warning, micro bubble tracking and downloadable profile data. Some computers can calculate decompression requirements for different gas mixes (see Ch.7) although trimix diving is rare in UK caves, nitrox is more commonly used. The primary considerations if choosing a computer should be a clear display (possibly backlit), a robust case and strap, ease of use, audible alarms (on ascent rate and decompression) and a user changeable battery. If a diver anticipates that future dives may involve the use of mixed gases a computer capable of calculating decompression information for theses gases may be a good investment. Like depth gauges/dive timers the computer is usually worn on the forearm and the buckles can come undone. The same technique of threading a piece of thin bungee cord though holes in the strap can be used as a retainer or the strap can be replaced with bungee cords.

ix.　　Harnesses

A side mount harness is usually custom built for cave diving to hold the cylinders securely in the desired position whilst distributing the weight around as much of the torso as possible, usually the shoulders and the waist. This not only keeps the cylinders in place and in a streamlined position but also makes surface carrying of the gear less tiring. The harness will consist of a waist band and shoulder straps plus a way of attaching cylinders and other equipment. The waist band on most harnesses also provide mounting points for lead weights; if this is not the case a separate weight belt will be worn. A caver's wide battery belt is best for this, as a diver's quick release weight belt is unsuitable owing to the risk of loosing buoyancy control if the belt releases. There are two methods for mounting cylinders; the British method and the more common American side mount system:

The British method uses a single mounting point consisting of two metal loops on a metal band clamped round the cylinder. A part of the harness waist band is threaded through the loops and secured, along with the diver's lead if the harness is designed to carry it. The diver then puts on the harness and secures the waist buckle. This mounting gives a solid way of holding the cylinders in place but can become uncomfortable on longer dives with bigger cylinders; it is also difficult to remove cylinders mounted this way when underwater as the complete harness must be taken off. The bottle bands are not an off the shelf item and can be difficult to fabricate so that they grip securely and don't provide a snag point for the line.

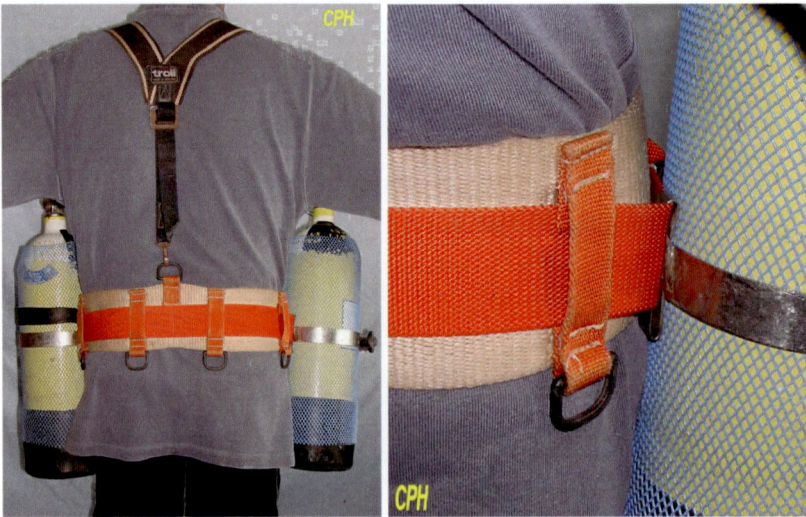

British side mount showing cylinder attachment detail.

The American side mount system uses two mounting points for each cylinder. A karabiner or similar on the cylinder links into a D ring on the harness waist band. A length of bungee or similar is routed from the back of the harness, under the diver's arm to the front D ring. The bungee is looped round the neck of the bottle on the way. This system allows the diver to load the lead onto the harness and put it on before attaching the bottles, thus making kitting up easier and greatly simplifying cylinder removal underwater. The lightweight metal band on the cylinder is invariably a large Jubilee clip. A karabiner or piston grip is fixed to this using a length of webbing or cord. The choice of karabiner is a matter of personal taste; snap links can provide an entrapment hazard if the line enters by opening the gate. Screw gate karabiners and piston grips avoid this problem of line entrapment but both can jam especially when they are worn internally by cave mud. Twist lock karabiners also avoid the problem of line entrapment but care must be taken when choosing them as some have actions which are impossible to operate with diving gloves on. Some karabiners have a hook mouth to carry load, which is not needed for mounting cylinders and should be removed to ease clipping the karabiner into the D rings. The cylinder mounting waistband D rings are positioned on the diver's back so that once in the water the cylinders hanging by the karabiners lie along the diver's side, tucking in under the arms with most of their weight on the waistband. The bungee that locates the neck of the cylinder is mounted in different ways dependent on harness design but the simplest and easiest method is to route the bungee from a D ring in the middle of the back (usually where the shoulder straps cross) under the arms to chest D rings that are linked by a third piece of bungee or fabric. The bungees are attached by piston grips or similar so they can be quickly linked to the harness when it is being put on and when cylinders are being attached. Several methods of securing the cylinder neck are used; some hold the cylinder firmly under the armpit and others allow the cylinder to hang down slightly loosely. The method used by each diver is a matter of choice and trainees are advised to try several different approaches before deciding on one.

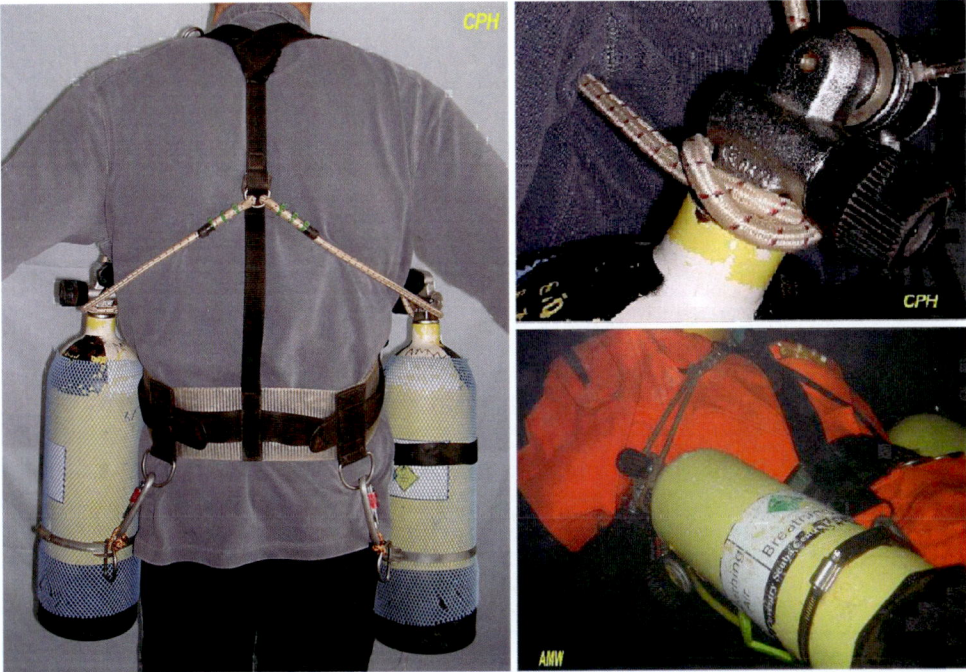

American side mount system with the cylinders behind the diver's arms in the water.

x.   Helmet

The two fundamental purposes of a cave diver's helmet are head protection and to provide a convenient location for mounting lights. Either a normal caving helmet can be worn or a helmet from another sport such as canoeing, skateboarding, ice hockey etc. Which ever is chosen some sort of

…cation is likely to be needed, either to provide vent hole to let air out or provide mounting points for the torches.

Divers are encouraged to use as robust a helmet as possible. The drilling of holes for mounting torches may weaken the integral structure of some helmets. This should be considered when adapting helmets specifically designed for caving or climbing. The chinstrap on a diving helmet must be substantial, and both it and the cradle (if fitted) should be easily adjustable to allow for the wearing of a neoprene hood and its subsequent removal on leaving the water. For extensive caving beyond a sump where a non-caving helmet will be used for diving, it is probably worth taking (and perhaps leaving) a conventional caving helmet.

Torches can be mounted either by using elastic loops (shock cord or strips of inner tube are commonly used) or by cutting off a length of PVC tubing and slitting it to make a clip-type mounting. This can then be clipped or bolted to the side of the helmet.

Typical Helmet configuration.

xi.   Lighting

There is a choice of three types of light; filament bulbs, LED (Light Emitting Diode) and HID (High Intensity Discharge). Whichever type is used, on its own, or in combination with other types a diver must carry a minimum of three lights, with each light having a burn time of at least twice the planned duration of the dive. All are supplied as torches: these are best suited to UK cave diving.

Filament bulbs have several bulb designs but all suffer from short burn times, large batteries, lower temperature equivalent light and poor bulb reliability.

LED lights have long burn times from the smallest batteries and excellent reliability. The output is usually better than the filament lights and larger more high powered models (although expensive) are almost as good as the low power HID lights.

HID lights are the most expensive type of light; most are supplied as umbilical units. They offer the best light output but are very delicate (replacement bulbs are very expensive) and are therefore only suitable for dive sites that can be reached with little or no caving.

The three different types of design make comparing output very difficult; the best method is to see other people's lights underwater. Without this help the best guide is the temperature output of the light, the beam angle and the wattage. The manufacturers list temperature as a way of comparing their lights with daylight; this gives a good indication of the spectrum the torch emits across, the higher the temperature the wider the spectrum. The beam angle is useful when trying to gauge how well the light will penetrate through particulate filled water. A tighter beam will suffer less from backscatter but will provide only a very narrow view of the cave ahead when compared with a wider beam. The wattage of a light is only really good for comparing lights of the same type, but some manufacturers do quote equivalent wattages for different types, although as a rule this is not the best guide.

In most UK conditions, LED based systems give the best compromise between output, duration and robustness.

xii.   Search reel

A search reel is an emergency kit item that should only be used as a last resort in a lost line situation. It should be taken on all cave dives.

The essential characteristics of a search reel are that it should be sufficiently compact so as to be hardly noticeable as an extra item, and that it should be quick and easy to use in typical UK conditions of restricted passage size and poor visibility. The size of the reel is determined by the length of line that would be needed to traverse the entire cross-section of the passage being explored. In most sumps, 15m of line is sufficient.

There are two types of reel in general use; the modified finger spool (worn on the upper arm or at the elbow) and the home built reel (worn on the forearm). Both are designed to hold 15 m of 2-3 mm diameter cord that is held in place on the reel by a snoopy loop. In both cases the line is tied securely to the reel at one end and has a loop in the other end for attachment to belay devices. As the reel will not be used often, the cord should be inspected occasionally.

Two types of search reel (modified finger spool on the left).

xiii.   Cutting tool

Some form of cutting device is an essential piece of equipment that every diver must carry. A cave diver should never dive without at least one, and preferably two, such devices, be it a knife or shears. A combination of the two types can be useful.

An effective cutting tool will be small enough to be carried easily, easy to use and be capable of maintaining a sharp edge. It must be capable of quickly cutting through line. Additionally, if the cutting tool is to be carried close to the diver's compass it should be non-magnetic. Trauma shears have been found to be excellent for the job.

To prevent loss when in use, cutting tools can be fitted with a lanyard that loops around the wrist. To avoid stab wounds it is advisable to grind off the sharp point of knives.

Where there is any possibility of entanglement in wire line, a pair of wire cutters is also necessary.

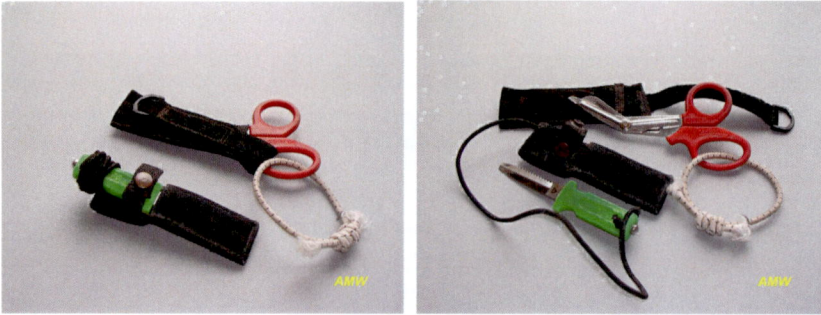

xiv.   Slate

A writing slate serves several functions; it can be used to record several types of data, or as a method of communication between divers. If a diver intends carrying out survey work (see Ch.5.B) a specially formatted slate can be used. Many divers attach their D-timer/computer, compass and knife to their slate to reduce the number of separate straps worn on the arms. A dive slate can be used to record information such as cylinder contents at the start, thirds limit, decompression information, passage directions, dive start time, greatest depth, etc.

There are a variety of slate designs from simple sheet to multi page plastic or waterproof paper books can be used.

All slates will need a pencil which will normally be held on the slate by a tube or loop when not in use and secured to it by a length of cord or flexible tubing. Plastic self-propelling pencils are ideal for this as then don't need sharpening and don't rot. Some method of easily securing the pencil to the slate when it is not in use is advisable. A short length of tubing can be used to hold the pencil and protect the point.

xv.   Necklace

Demand valves must be attached to the cave diver in a way that allows the diver to reach them immediately in an emergency. This may be by the use of neck straps made from static cord, tape, or shock-cord. Both valves can be mounted on a single cord if required and most divers have their own idiosyncratic way of wearing them.

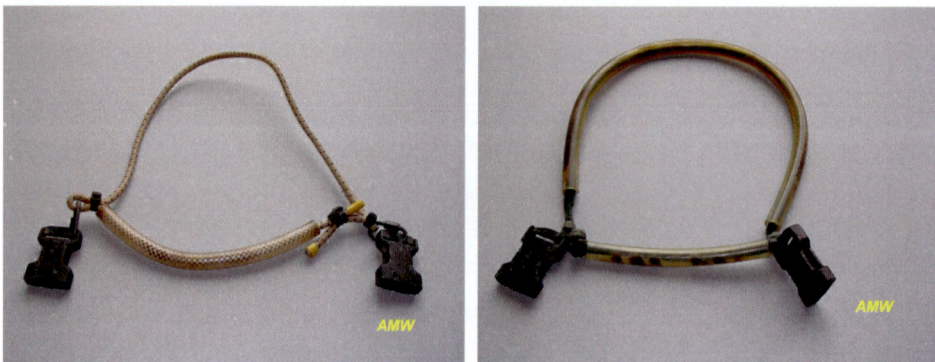

Shock-cord necklace and static cord necklace.

xvi. Ancillary equipment

Glow sticks: Thin chemical light tubes can be used as markers at line junctions or when equipment is staged through a sump (such as staged cylinders). They are easy to carry under an instrument strap or a bungee. When used they can be wrapped around the line and provide reassurance even in poor visibility. Once used, they must be removed from the cave as they are not a natural part of the cave environment.

Instrument reader: In extreme situations, where visibility is absolutely zero, instruments can be read by using a small sealed Perspex tube filled with air or clean water. Light is shone through the side of this while the diver looks down the length of the tube.

Cable ties: For securing knots and belays along the line quickly the cable tie offers a cheap and reliable method. The larger size cable tie is easier to see and manipulate underwater.

xvii. Buoyancy compensator

For backup buoyancy with a dry suit or primary buoyancy device with a wetsuit some side mount harness designs have attachment points for a wing. The normal open water technique of holding the wing between the cylinders and a back plate clearly won't work with a side mount configuration and the harness is fitted with multiple attachment points to hold down the wing to avoid snagging and entanglement. Various types of open water jacket style BCD have been used successfully, although great care is needed to choose a robust, compact jacket that doesn't have line traps and allows the diver easy access to the harness (worn underneath) for mounting cylinders.

B) Equipment maintenance

As cave diving is dependent on equipment thorough maintenance is needed to reduce the risk of equipment failure. Faults can manifest themselves during pre-dive checks, resulting in a missed dive or whilst the diver is underwater forcing the diver to execute a safety drill and turn the dive. Some maintenance procedures should only be carried out by trained individuals but the most common types of equipment failure can be avoided by any competent diver.

The most common form of equipment failure is O-ring failure. Any valve or air tight sealed item of equipment will have one or more O-rings. These will fail owing to dirt, aging, wear, incorrect installation and damage. All dive equipment should be cleaned and inspected after each dive with special attention paid to O-rings. To help the O-ring maintain a seal silicon or Oxygen approved grease is used; this lubricates the O-ring so that it can seat properly. Silicon grease should not be used with silicon components such as diaphragms in demand valves and dry suit dump valves. These can easily be damaged if they come into contact with silicon grease. Threads on demand valves and other metal items of diving equipment are delicate and can be easily damaged by over tightening. Manufacturers have used differing thread types and it is possible to destroy a thread by forcing two dissimilar types together. When a thread is damaged it will be less able to withstand the pressures that will be placed on it when valves are pressurised.

General equipment maintenance should consist of simple procedures covering washing and inspection after each use.

i. Demand valve

Clean after each dive, keeping the valve pressurised during the process. Use water and ensure that the second stage is purged of water before the valve is depressurised. Inspect the hoses for breaks to the surface layer and any bulges or sharp kinks; these can indicate a weakness in the hose. Check along the length of the outer sheath for small bubbles whilst the hoses are pressurised. Pressurised hoses have an inner layer that stops the gas escaping, a middle layer that supports the inner layer and an outer layer that provides physical protection. The outer layer has small vent holes along its length to let gas that has breached the inner layer escape in a controlled manner. Leaks from these holes are an indication of the need to replace a hose. Leaks can also occur at junctions between hoses and the valve sections they link. When these are seen the O-rings at the joint should be checked. If the O-ring is found to be faulty it should be replaced.

Submersible pressure gauges should be checked to see if they read zero when there is no pressure in the valve. If an SPG fails to read down to zero it should be replaced as the inaccurate reading may result in an incorrect gas margin calculation. Faults noted during the dive should also be considered by the diver. A free flow or a stiff breath may indicate that the demand valve needs adjustment or service. This should only be done by trained individuals. All such work should be carried out in accordance with the manufacturer's instructions.

ii.   Lights

Should be cleaned in water and checked inside for any signs of leakage. The O-ring seals should be cleaned, inspected and re-greased before reassembly. On some types of torch the manufacturer's instructions will state that the torch should be stored open. This is to prevent the O-ring becoming deformed. When dealing with filament or HID bulbs care should be taken to avoid touching the glass of the bulb; this can lead to reduced bulb life. All switches should be checked for smooth operation and cleaned as needed.

iii.   Dry suit

Should be cleaned externally using water and dried. Inflation and dump valves should be inspected and serviced if needed. The suit material should be inspected for damage especially around the wrist and neck seal areas. The zip should be inspected and cleaned with a zip cleaning fluid before re-lubricating with bees wax or the manufacturers specified lubricant. Regular maintenance should be carried out in accordance with the manufacturer's instructions. If a suit is found to be leaking it can be pressure tested by the diver and repaired or by the manufacturer or local dive shop.

iv.   Cylinders

Cylinders should be washed in water. After each trip the exterior of each cylinder used should be inspected for significant damage before refilling. Particular attention should be paid to the cylinder tap. This can be damaged by mud in the threads of the DIN fitting, by the DIN fitting being knocked out of round and by damage to the tap knob.

As cylinders are pressure vessels there is a legal requirement to have them periodically pressure tested by a recognised test centre. All commercial filling stations will check for a valid test stamp before filling. All cylinders will be marked with their date of manufacture and this serves as the initial date stamp. When this expires a test centre will mark the cylinder with a stamp showing the type of test it has undergone, the date of the test and who carried it out. There will also be a sticker marking the next due date for a test. The recreational diving industry has two types of test: a hydraulic test and a visual inspection. The legislation at the time of writing requires cylinders to be hydraulically tested five years after the last hydraulic test (or date of manufacture) and visually inspected every two and a half years. During the test procedure the cylinder valve is also tested to see if the threads are in good condition. If a cylinder does not carry a valid test stamp various insurance policies may be invalidated. A filling station can refuse to fill any cylinder irrespective of its test status.

v.   Buoyancy compensator

BCs should be washed in water and drained of any water that has entered the gas cell during the dive. BCs should be stored partly inflated so that the inside of the gas cell is not under strain but is not allowed to fold against itself.

vi.   Electronic instruments

Some electronic instruments will include a battery life indicator as one of their functions. This should be checked and the battery replaced if needed. For some instruments it will be possible to periodically check their accuracy against some datum such as a shot line (for depth).

vii.   Other equipment

Should be cleaned and inspected for damage. Minor repairs should be made before the next dive where the fault might develop into a significant problem. Particular attention should be paid to clips, straps and buckles on fins, mask and instruments.

C) Configuration

Equipment distribution for any diver is important and has led to the development of different configurations for different environments. For the UK cave diver this will typically be side mounted cylinders, helmet mounted lights, instruments and ancillary equipment on the forearms and no buoyancy compensator. This configuration has developed because it allows the diver a streamlined profile, ensuring all kit is easy to reach in restricted passages, whilst keeping the hands free to control the line and carry out other tasks. Some common details have also been developed; there should be no line traps or snag points, equipment should be tight to the diver and not dangle. All equipment controls must be operable with dive gloves on. Any equipment that is large enough to prevent a diver passing a tight spot should be removable.

Each diver will develop a unique equipment configuration although a great deal of similarity will exist between divers. The core of the configuration should be designed so that it will work with the different types of diving suit the diver expects to use and the full range of cylinder sizes the diver has available. Extra dive specific equipment can then be added as needed for each dive. A good core configuration should remain unchanged, allowing the diver to get on with cave diving and not spend each dive testing a new way of doing things.

i.   Core configuration components

- *Harness, lead and cylinders.*
- *Demand valves.*
- *Lights.*
- *Cutting tools.*
- *Instrumentation.*
- *Search reel.*
- *Slate.*

Harness, lead and cylinders: With a side mount harness, a diver is using one piece of equipment to carry the heaviest items, the cylinders and the lead. The positioning of the harness and the way lead and cylinders are located and mounted can have a big effect on the trim characteristics of the diver in the water (see Ch.4.A). They also greatly effect the profile of a diver and how constricted passages are passed. How tightly the cylinders hang on the diver's body is a matter of preference. Some divers like the cylinder to hang slightly neck down; this gives a loose hang that makes the cylinder easier to move around so it can be positioned to allow the diver to pass a section of passage. It also makes the cylinder valve more accessible. The alternative is to secure the cylinder neck tight to the body, creating a slightly more streamlined profile that offers more protection to the valves. Although the cylinders are less manoeuvrable, there is less need to move them owing to the lower profile. The reduced accessibility of the cylinder valves can be overcome by careful design of the cylinder attachment bungees. Hanging cylinders loose using a stage bottle rig does not work well in UK sumps as this increases the diver's profile and exposes the cylinder valves. Lead is typically worn on the waist band of the harness (or in the same position on a separate weight belt) but must be positioned clear of the cylinders. If lead is positioned in between the cylinder and the diver's body, the base of the cylinder will be forced outwards creating a shape known as "flare out" which increases drag. This also makes passing constrictions more difficult and creates a line trap if the diver has cause to reverse. To avoid this, lead is usually worn in front of, or just behind the position where the cylinders lie; both methods give a low profile. Lead can also be placed on the waist band in the middle of the diver's back but this can be problematic in constrictions as it has a detrimental effect on the diver's profile.

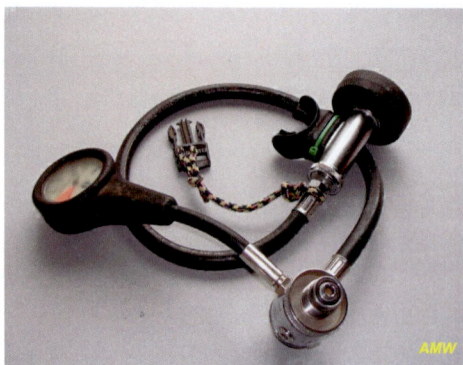

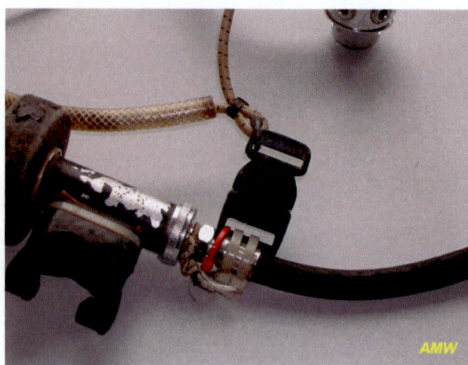

Short contents gauge hose and necklace attached to the second stage.

Demand valves: All demand valves should be fitted with a pressure gauge which should be easy to read, although positioning is a matter of personal choice. The short high pressure hose is either pointed up in front of the diver's shoulder or down along the length of the cylinder. The former provides the better position for easy gauge reading, the latter offers less chance of trapping the line but makes reading more difficult. Each breathing set typically has one second stage. Both the second stages should be clipped to the necklace; close enough so that they don't dangle and create an entrapment hazard but with enough freedom of movement so that they can sit comfortably in the diver's mouth. The interstage hoses should lie flat against the diver's body to reduce entanglement hazards. The "ports" on a first stage will limit the choice of hose routeing; most will only provide one high pressure port for the pressure gauge and then a number of medium pressure ports (sometimes called low pressure ports) for the inter-stage hose and suit/buoyancy compensator inflation hose. When deciding on a hose routeing, trainees are advised to inspect the equipment configurations of several divers.

Lights: Helmets mounting is the most common and practical method of carrying lights for UK cave divers who use small, all in one, units. For sumps with high levels of suspended particles, mounting a light on the back of a wrist can reduce the backscatter problem associated with light sources close to the eyes. Lights should be positioned so that they illuminate the diver's field of vision, allow easy access to switches with gloved hands and do not frequently make contact with the cave passage. To do this, test the point where the torch beam falls; it should be well within the area visible through the mask at the typical distances encountered in UK sumps, up to 5 m. Switches should be exposed but not to the point where contact with rock will operate them. To avoid frequent contact with the cave, torches are mounted on each side of the helmet, the top being the most common part of the helmet to rub against surrounding rock. The weight of multiple lights on a diver's helmet can create discomfort. This is not usually a problem if the diver is using LED light with small batteries but for divers using filament bulb or HID light, the discomfort can be significant. An even distribution of heavy lights can prevent the helmet from being pulled to one side. If the diver is using one heavy light, it should be placed on one side and counterbalanced with all the other lights on the opposite side. When this is not possible owing to the weight of a light, mounting that light on the back of a wrist should be considered.

Cutting tool: Accessibility is the most important consideration for cutting tool placement; it is not important that it be visible to the diver. In constricted passage a diver may not be able to reach all parts of the body, making the arms the best location. It can be positioned somewhere that is easy to get at but may be out of the diver's line of sight. Most cutting tools come with a holder that has a mechanism to prevent the tool falling out accidentally. The chosen position for the cutting tool should not make operation of this mechanism problematic or expose it in such a way that contact with the cave rock will release the tool. If a lanyard is fitted this can either be positioned so that it can be placed around the wrist before the tool is removed from its holder or the lanyard can be permanently looped around the wrist of the hand the tool is used in. With the latter method the cutting tool is released by the opposite hand, making cutting tool deployment a two handed task. Typical positions for cutting tools are on the forearm, the upper arm or as part of a console (again on the forearm). Right handed divers will usually put the cutting tool on the left arm and vice-versa. Backup cutting tools can be similarly located but can also be carried on the helmet, strapped to a cylinder or on the harness.

Instrumentation: Most instrumentation is worn on the forearms within easy view, either independently or as part of a console. As space on the forearms is limited, combining as much functionality in one unit as possible is useful. With electronic instruments this usually means a combined depth gauge/timer/decompression calculation capability. Combined instruments are also useful in that they require fewer straps and therefore reduce kitting and de-kitting times. This is the main advantage of a console which can hold multiple instruments as well as other ancillary equipment. When positioning independent instruments or a console, care should be taken to ensure that line traps are not created, arm movement isn't compromised, the compass is positioned away from possible magnetic materials (cutting tool, cylinders, light) and that instruments can be easily read.

Search reel: A search reel needs to be positioned so that it is virtually unnoticed during a dive unless it is needed. In this case a diver must be able to deploy it blind without risk of loosing it, or getting it tangled with other equipment. For these reasons search reels always have a loop lanyard that is worn around the diver's arm or wrist so that on deployment the reel can either be swung or slid into the hand without having to remove it. A search reel will also have some means of preventing the line from coming off the reel during the dive. The reel must be positioned so that this mechanism isn't compromised. Due consideration must be paid to which hand the diver is happier to operate the search reel with, as it will only be used in the most stressful situations when ease of use is paramount.

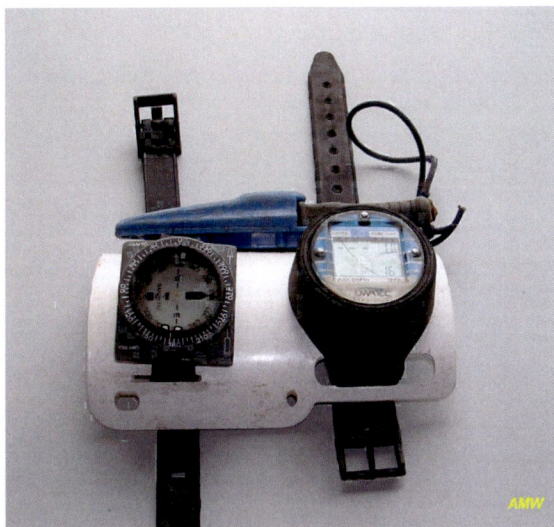

Modified slate as a console.

Slate: A slate is worn on the arm and may not be taken on all dives; the choice of forearm will be dictated by which hand the diver writes with. If the diver is using a notebook style slate it can be conveniently carried in the diver's pocket. If a compass is mounted on the slate, care should be taken to avoid magnetic interference from other items of equipment. If the slate is to be used for survey work there are also other considerations (see Ch.5.B).

ii.   Additional equipment

- *Stage cylinder.*
- *Belays.*
- *Ancillary equipment.*

Stage cylinder: Being able to carry one or more stage cylinders greatly increases dive plan flexibility. When multiple sumps are to be passed or more than one gas type is to be used, it can be advantageous to clip off stage cylinders. The methods used to carry stage cylinders are on the harness or to use a separate item called a bra harness. To clip a single stage cylinder to a side mount harness the crab on the cylinder is clipped to an equipment D-ring on the front/side and the neck and valve are secured through the harness chest bungee. This method requires no extra equipment, doesn't get in the way of the rest of the diver's kit and is easy to use. For more than one cylinder it will be necessary to add extra underarm bungees to secure the cylinder necks as two won't fit through the harness chest strap. Trying to secure two cylinders with only one underarm bungee makes kitting up difficult and unclipping a stage underwater becomes more complicated. When larger cylinders are used with this method it may be easier to side sling (see Ch.10) one set of cylinders rather than using a second set of bungees. The bra harness is made up from two lengths of bungee; one around the waist, the other in a figure eight shape around the shoulders and crossing in the middle of the chest. The stage cylinder is cradled in place by the two pieces of bungee.

Belays: The best place to carry belays is on the forearm, although silt screws won't fit and are best carried on a cylinder secured by snoopy loops. Net bags can be carried under an instrument strap and snoopy loops (see Ch.5.A.iv.) are best carried either under one snoopy around the arm or the cylinder, or on a purpose built holder mounted on the forearm. Cable ties can be tucked under instrument straps or through the snoopy loops holding a light on the helmet. All belays must be easily reachable and secure enough so they won't fall off during the dive or when a single belay is being removed for use. Most belays have a loop attached so they can be larks-footed to the line; these loops can present a snagging hazard and may also catch on the diver's other equipment. To avoid this, the loops must be strapped down with only one being available to grab so that the belay can be deployed. (Please refer to chapter 5 for details of belay types).

Ancillary equipment: Glow sticks and cable ties can be carried under instrument straps, under a torch holding bungee or under a snoopy loop on a cylinder. An instrument reader and torch can also be carried under an instrument strap or snoopy on the forearm strap and if possible secured by a lanyard.

Chapter 4 Core skills

Large chamber with bedding fault and arch exit.

A good understanding of the risks of cave diving is not sufficient without an understanding of the hazards which create the risks. Good technique provides a diver with the ability to deal with the hazards of a sump. A core of techniques must be understood and practised before a diver enters a sump for the first time. This core of techniques must be maintained and updated throughout a diver's career. Whatever the planned objective of a dive, the basic techniques will always be used or be ready to be used; this results in a diver always having a task load. To prevent mistakes being made when a diver is distracted by some other aspect of the dive, the core techniques must be practised until they become second nature. If a diver has a period of inactivity, all techniques should be refreshed in open water before entering a sump.

The core techniques described are the basic abilities required for passing a known sump with an existing line in place. These techniques are the basis for all other activities a diver will carry out in a sump; as such they must become second nature to a cave diver. Divers should practise these core techniques throughout their cave diving careers. This is especially true for trainees, who are advised to master them before entering a sump.

A) Buoyancy

i. Weighting and trim

Good buoyancy and trim are important because they contribute to the diver's level of control in the sump. With neutral buoyancy and horizontal trim the diver presents a low drag profile that makes progress through the sump easier and frees the diver to concentrate on other aspects of the dive. A diver with good control will also have less impact on the visibility, by creating fewer disturbances to deposits. To achieve good trim, a diver must first weight for neutral buoyancy with empty cylinders. Then the distribution of the weight must be adjusted to balance the diver in the water. Moving weight towards the head will create a head down trim and towards the foot will result in a foot down trim. The most influential piece of equipment when adjusting trim is the harness. It (normally) holds both the lead and cylinders; together they provide most of the negative buoyancy. Changing the position of the cylinders along the body is often enough to change the trim. The position of the harness waist band and the lead it carries should be matched to the type of suit being used. If a semi-dry suit is used it will probably have more (positively buoyant) neoprene on the upper body than will be the case with a dry suit, in the former case the waist band will probably need to be higher on the waist than for the latter.

ii. Buoyancy control

Depending on the temperature and depth of a planned dive, a diver will either choose a dry suit or a wetsuit with, or without a buoyancy compensator. Dives carried out in wetsuits with no buoyancy device require correct weighting and trim and an appreciation that gas consumption may rise with increased depth as the diver uses lung volume to maintain neutral buoyancy. In some sumps a wetsuit may be the only suit that allows a sufficiently streamlined configuration, or it may provide enough thermal protect for the planned dive. In both cases it offers the simplest most reliable system for diving in shorter/shallower sumps.

In UK conditions a dry suit is considered to give sufficient buoyancy on its own for almost any dive. When the temperature allows, a wetsuit can be used with a buoyancy compensator. Diving with a buoyancy compensator (a dry suit is considered to be a buoyancy compensator) allows the diver to control buoyancy irrespective of suit compression (created by pressure at depth) and variations in weight when staging equipment in a sump or carrying a load through a sump. Diving with a buoyancy compensator increases a diver's task loading and introduces more potential for something to go wrong, typically from:

- *Diver error.*
- *Equipment failures.*

Diver error: is best avoided by anticipation. Unlike diving in open water where a diver's body maintains a consistent position during the dive a cave diver's body will go through a full range of movement allowing the air bubble held within the buoyancy compensator to move around. This alters the diver's trim and prevents the dump valve from working. This is more of a problem with a dry suit than a wing or jacket style BCD as the air can move along the entire length of the body and change the trim from horizontal to head up or feet up. To correct the latter position the tuck and roll technique used in open water may be possible, space permitting. Or the diver can simply grab a convenient rock outcrop and rotate around it to migrate the bubble in the suit away from the feet. To prevent this happening in the first place the diver must view the passage ahead (if possible) and anticipate trim problems. Air should be dumped early from the dry suit or wing/jacket BCD if gas dumping may become a problem during an ascent. When approaching a descending section of passage the diver should be positioned so as to avoid a head down position which may result in buoyant feet. A further problem that affects dry suit dumps occurs when they operate automatically as the diver rolls to the side, raising the dump valve to the highest point. If the suit has an auto dump, setting it to maximum resistance before such a move will prevent dumping.

Equipment failures: are either a leak in or out. Leaks out of a wing/jacket BCD make the dive more difficult but since the line is usually laid along the floor of a sump a diver with no buoyancy can exit. A leaking dry suit has the additional problem that the diver will now lose some thermal protection and whilst a failed wing/jacket BCD may not cause a diver to abandon a dive, a flooded dry suit probably will. A free flowing BC inflator valve will increase the diver's buoyancy, taking the diver to the roof of the sump and possibly away from the line. If this happens the diver should disconnect the feed hose. If a diver loses contact with the line during a buoyancy failure of this type no horizontal movement should be made (unless the water is flowing strongly), so the ascent will have been vertical and the descent will also be vertical as buoyancy control is restored and the line will be under or close to the diver when the floor is regained. Follow the lost line procedure (see F.iii of this Chapter) if the line isn't regained.

B) Movement

Movement through a sump should be steady and controlled. The many tasks a diver has to carry out during a dive must be done in an unhurried and thorough manner. Visibility must be maintained as much as possible for the outward journey. The diver should take in as much information about the sump as possible. Knowledge of the passage will be invaluable to an experienced caver returning with a reduced field of view. Moving too fast will not only reduce visibility but increase the likelihood of losing control of the line, resulting in entanglement or line loss. The diver's kit will also be more prone to snagging on rocks. The diver should not move too slowly either, in some sumps rolling silt clouds (generated by the diver) can envelop a diver and reduce visibility to zero. Travelling too slowly also exposes the diver to cold for longer and increases the amount of breathing gas needed. The ideal speed is a balance between going fast enough to maintain good visibility and slow enough to avoid exertion which increases the rate of gas usage.

Irrespective of what a diver is doing in a sump, from simple movement to more complex project work with additional task loading, situation awareness is critical. For any diver in a sump awareness of the surrounding passage is as important as the other techniques needed on a dive. Awareness of the passage and the position of the line in it is needed for anticipating problems with buoyancy, line following and maintaining visibility. It can also provide the diver with information used when line laying or searching for a lost line.

i.   With fins

In most sumps fins are used to provide propulsion. A variety of finning techniques can be used; which-ever is chosen should reduce the risk of disturbing sediment. In the US, cave divers have developed a wide range of finning styles which are designed to reduce disturbance to silt deposits and thus maintain the visibility. Most UK sumps are too restricted for these techniques to be used with the same results, but using some of them can go a long way to reducing the amount of silt stirred up as the diver swims. The principle of most of the techniques is either to direct the water moved by the fin stroke away from the silt deposits or minimise the amount of disturbance so that it doesn't reach the silt. Most techniques use a combination of both principles. For normal movement the raised flutter kick provides good propulsion whilst keeping the fins above the body and away from the floor deposits. To reduce the water movement created by this type of kick all the fin stroke can be generated from the ankle. When areas of lower passage with a silt floor covering are entered, the kick can be further modified by placing one fin on top of the other and pushing them together, which directs the water flow backwards rather than up and down. Moving the fins slowly on the non-power part of the stroke also reduces disturbance.

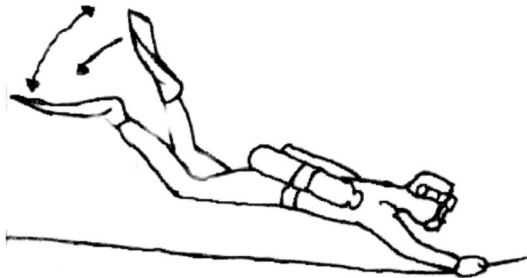

Using shuffle kick minimises sediment disturbance.

ii.   Without fins

In some sections of cave passage, the diver may find it easier to pull on the rock to move through the sump. This can be very good for maintaining visibility if the rock used is clean and the diver moves with enough caution to prevent the disturbance of silt. In tighter sections of passage, this may be the only way of moving; in these circumstances maintaining the visibility will be impossible unless the passage is clean washed. The line should never be pulled. Some dives will be conducted without fins. For these dives the feet can be used against the roof, walls or floor along with the hands. This method will not preserve the visibility, but it is a technique that can be applied to sumps that are too restricted for fins to be helpful. Open sections of sump can be a risk to a diver with no fins. A diver who is neutrally buoyant can become stranded in mid water, unable to reach any rock to pull on. Normal swimming strokes do not provide sufficient propulsion to move a fully kitted diver underwater for normal movement through a sump. If a no fins dive is planned and the diver knows there is an open section in the sump the diver should be negatively buoyant, or be able to adjust buoyancy. A negatively buoyant diver will be able to maintain contact with floor of the sump and the line, which will most likely be routed along it.

iii.   Securing the line

For some tasks a diver will greatly reduce the risks involved by stopping and securing the line. This can be done by holding the line in the hand if the task is short or by wrapping the line round an arm if both hands are needed or if the task will take long enough for the diver to let go of the line accidentally. It is very important to check the direction of travel when stopping. Restarting in reduced visibility can result in a diver travelling in the wrong direction without knowing it until the next line tag is reached where the diver may or may not discover the mistake. A compass can be used to record a bearing if the visibility is good enough, or a line marker can be placed on the line ahead to indicate the direction of travel.

C)   Mask skills (clearing and failure)

A diver's kit must not prevent the use of mask clearing techniques; in particular the helmet must not interfere with the top of the mask. This will not only make mask clearing more difficult but also cause extra leakage into the mask as the helmet moves and knocks the mask, breaking the seal in the process. In UK sumps the diver will not always be in the ideal position to clear the mask and may even find that water is moved into the eyes by some orientations. Anticipation is the best solution, so the diver should take the opportunity to clear even a small amount of water from a mask when it presents itself rather than letting the amount of water in the mask build up.

In the event that a mask fails completely and cannot hold any gas, the diver can swap to a backup mask (if one is carried) or swim out. All divers should be able to swim without a mask but physics dictates that this will not be possible in all body positions. If the cave passage requires the diver to take a nose up position the air in the diver's lungs will drain out and be replaced by water. The only way round this problem is to hold the nose shut with one hand whilst following the line with the other.

The task of changing a mask underwater is made less challenging by having a helmet chinstrap with a buckle in it; without one a diver must remove the demand valve to take the helmet off and put the new mask on. Since this will have to be done blind it will produce extra stress for even the best drilled diver.

Whether carrying out a mask clear or replacement a diver must first secure the line (see Section B. above).

D)   Sinus and ear clearing failure

At a very early stage in their training, all divers learn about the need to equalise pressure in the air-filled cavities of the skull. Problems of pressure equalisation on ascent are very rare, although not totally unknown (e.g. "reversed ear"). On the descent however, it is necessary to transfer gently air into the skull cavities e.g. the valsalva manoeuvre (either by nose pinching or jaw movement), to "clear the ears". This is because the openings into the middle ear and sinuses are restricted and may not allow air through until there is a higher pressure in the nasopharynx compared with that in the cavities. Also the structure of various tissues at the entry to these cavities makes them behave like valves, especially if the pressure differential has been allowed to become too great before attempts are made to equalise.

For this and other reasons (e.g. upper respiratory infections leading to inflammation of the nasopharynx) a diver may find it impossible to clear an ear or sinus on the descent.

In an open water situation this scenario is merely a nuisance which forces the diver to stay shallower than intended or abort the dive. In caves however, it can be a major hazard which has led to a number of divers suffering severe barotrauma, in particular a ruptured ear-drum. The problem is that many caves have saw tooth profiles. Having passed one or more deep points it is usually necessary to return along the same route. Numerous short ascents and descents can cause barotrauma. If a blocked sinus or Eustachian tube occurs on the re-descent to an "elbow" in a sump en-route out, then obviously this is a far more serious situation than if it happens on the dive in.

Ear and sinus clearing problems are more likely to happen if:

- *The water is cold.*
- *The diver is a smoker (loss of lung function and capacity).*
- *The diver suffers from an allergy which results in inflammation of the nasopharynx, e.g. hay fever.*
- *The sump is shallow—the change in volume of air (per unit depth change) is greatest at shallow depths.*
- *The diver has been in a smoky atmosphere in the preceding 24 hours (or encountered any other naso-pharyngeal irritant) i.e. avoid smoky pubs and dusty caving huts.*
- *The diver has recently been suffering from a cold or other upper respiratory infection.*
- *The diver has forgotten to make frequent small pressure equalisations and has "locked" an ear as a result.*
- *The diver has a pre-existing middle ear infection.*
- *The diver is not in the habit of clearing mucus from the nasopharynx that naturally accumulates on longer dives, and spitting it out. (Note that this needs practice but is a very useful skill to acquire. It is most easily done at times when the profile of the sump forces small ascents as expanding air in the skull cavities helps loosen such mucus.)*

If there is a clearing problem on a return descent the most important thing to do is STOP. Once an ear has "locked" it is not possible to force air through the offending "valve" without causing a large amount of damage (possibly also including damage to the inner ear!) Further descent will just make the situation worse. Take a few breaths and think carefully before trying anything.

There may be several options open to a diver in such a predicament.

- *Re-ascend a little to unlock the blockage causing the problem and then re-descend slowly, clearing more frequently.*
- *Return to an air bell to clear and spit out mucus from the nasopharynx.*
- *Exit via a different entrance that does not involve further descent.*
- *Exit via a different route that is shallower (bearing in mind the constraints of gas margins – allowing, for example, a broken line being encountered.)*
- *Continue descending and (very possibly) rupture an eardrum. This is likely to cause severe disorientation for a few minutes as cold water disrupts the normal functioning of the balance organs. Hold the line and concentrate on which hand is on the "out" side. Wait for the disorientation to subside before continuing.*

The latter should not be considered unless there is no other option (e.g. severe time pressure owing to gas shortage).

This list is roughly in preference order but the layout of each individual sump will dictate the best solution to the problem. Well-informed divers who have taken the trouble to familiarise themselves with details of previous surveys or dive logs are more likely to escape without injury. In most circumstances a short ascent (even just from floor to roof) followed by more careful ear clearing on the re-descent will solve the problem. Ear clearing is slightly easier in the head up - feet down position. Also, gentle swallowing may help.

If there is any possibility that an eardrum has actually ruptured it is essential for the diver to have a consultation with a doctor as soon as practicable and follow the advice given.

E)   Breathing supply procedures

A diver's gas supplies should be checked underwater each time the diver submerges. This is to test if the valves work underwater and for any air or water leaks. Take several breaths from each second stage and swap underwater to make sure there is no entanglement that prevents this. Check the SPG readings to see if the needle is moving in an unacceptable way and that the readings are as expected.

Once the dive is underway the diver should swap breathing sets throughout the dive. Doing this will mean the diver will spot breathing supply problems earlier when more gas remains in reserve. If a diver is using uneven sized cylinders with one dedicated to bailout only, periodic valve swapping should still be used, but only using a couple of breaths from the bailout supply. When swapping breathing sets secure the line and note the direction of travel, make sure the second stage when taken out can quickly and easily be replaced (keep hold of it) just in case the other breathing supply fails.

During the dive several failure modes are possible with demand valves:

- *Free flow.*
- *No Gas.*
- *Flooded second stage.*
- *Gas leaks.*
- *Faulty SPG.*

i.   Free flow

Secure the line. Turn off the cylinder tap and turn it on again to see if the valve still free flows. If it does the diver will have to control the flow rate with the cylinder tap. Two methods are possible for this: turn the cylinder tap on and off with each breath or set the cylinder tap to supply slightly more gas than the diver needs and breathe from the low speed free flow that results. If the visibility is good enough it may be possible to inspect the free flowing valve underwater once it is switched off. Check for anything holding the diaphragm open or if the second stage has a breathing resistance adjustment, check and adjust. An airbell, if available, is a good place to carry out such work. When a free flow occurs the contents of the faulty breathing set should be used first to make best use of the available gas supply.

ii.   No gas

Secure the line. Swap second stages, then check to see if the cylinder tap has been "rolled off" against the cave passage or the diver's own equipment. If this is the case, turn it back on and check it works. Also check the other cylinder tap for roll off before continuing. Some activities that have a lot of arm movement can result in roll off and divers should periodically check the cylinder taps through a dive. If the cylinder tap is on and no gas is available check the SPG reading; if it shows other than zero it could be faulty. Swap to the other breathing set and exit. With most valves the diver will have no warning that the contents of the cylinder is about to run out or that the cylinder valve has rolled off. The last breath from the valve will feel different, requiring more of a suck. This can be simulated by turning off a cylinder and breathing a valve down to zero pressure. Becoming accustomed to the feel of the last breath from a valve is a useful skill that all divers should practise.

iii.   Flooding second stage

This can be caused by foreign matter in the exhaust diaphragm, a split in one of the diaphragms or a split mouthpiece or a loose mouthpiece cable tie. If the problem is minor, the diver may be able to continue breathing from the faulty second stage by pointing the exhaust port downwards to aid water drainage. If the problem prevents proper breathing, secure the line and swap valves. If possible inspect the exhaust diaphragm and mouthpiece and clear or repair if needed. As above, air bells are useful for this sort of work. If the cause of the problem is a split diaphragm, it will not be repairable underground and the diver should exit. If an airbell is available it will be possible to swap the good valve onto the cylinder with more gas. As has been noted in (see Ch.3.A.vii) second stages are designed to work the correct way up. Using them with the exhaust valve uppermost may cause flooding. When passing a constriction always ensure that the exhaust port on the second stage is orientated downwards.

iv. Gas leaks

For a slow leak, maximise the available gas by breathing from the leaking valve, leaving the other breathing set as bailout. For a fast leak it may not be possible to control the gas flow. The diver should secure the line and switch off the cylinder. During the exit the diver may have access to an airbell which will allow the good valve to be swapped to the cylinder with more gas, assuming the leak isn't from the cylinder tap itself.

The speed of any leak will vary depending on where it comes from. Leaks from the interstage hose have a greater potential for gas loss than those from the high pressure hose owing to the flow restrictor at the start of the high pressure hose. The most common source of leaks is from O rings. These usually occur when the demand valve is first pressurised. For this reason it is good practice to leave valves pressurised at all times between departing and returning to dive base (see Ch 9.C.iii).

v. Faulty SPG

If during the monitoring of a cylinder pressure gauge it is not seen to be moving, the diver should assume a faulty SPG. The contents of that cylinder are therefore unknown. The diver should exit, continuing to use the same breathing set to maximise the use of the available gas. The second breathing set is held in reserve and should be needed only if the diver has unwittingly exceeded thirds or another fault develops. Note: it is possible for a diver to be reading the wrong pressure gauge. Always check that the gauge being read is from the breathing set being used.

Vertical line in a mainland European cave.

F)   Line skills

Line skills reduce the risk involved in cave diving. A diver must constantly monitor the line and be well practised in the drills required for safe line management.

These drills include:

- *Line following.*
- *Line repairs.*
- *Lost line drills.*
- *Dealing with entanglement.*

i.   Line following

In UK conditions the visibility can change very suddenly; for this reason contact (or very close proximity) with the line should be maintained at all times. This increases the risk of entanglement in the line, or snagging of the line, thereby potentially re-routeing it into an impassable section of passage. Following a tight and well routed line that allows a diver to pass restrictions whilst still maintaining the body at a safe distance from the line reduces the risks. When a line is loose and has belays that are far apart, the risks are greatly increased. Even lines that started as ideal can present increasing levels of risk with age. Belays and line can break or become loose. To follow a line, a diver should hold the line at arm's length away from the body; this reduces the risk of entanglement and snagging. The line should be held in the hand so that it will not be pulled away from contact if the diver enters an area of low visibility. On no account should the diver pull on the line. Pulling the line can dislodge belays and move it into a tighter part of the passage, away from the line's original route. When a line crosses the passage, forcing the diver to change hands, the line should be held at arm's length. To further reduce entanglement risks the move should be planned so that the line is in front of the diver at all times. This has the added advantage of making entanglement easier to sort out if it does happen. When diving in zero or low visibility using two hands to follow the line provides additional security. One hand remains stationary holding the line whilst the second follows the line forwards along to a comfortable point that does not bring the diver into contact with the line. The first hand is then brought along behind the second hand and the process is repeated. Extra care will be needed at belays and junctions because they will have more than one line. The line used to secure belays should be different from the guide line and should feel different allowing identification of the correct line by touch. This may not always be the case and if a diver has any doubt one hand should be used to secure the known line and direction of travel, whilst the other hand is used to determine which line goes to a belay. At junctions the diver should again secure the line and direction of travel with one hand whilst using the other hand to search for out markers on the line. Although this technique will bring the diver closer to the line and increase the risk of entanglement, if used carefully it can greatly reduce the risk of line loss especially at belays and junctions. When using this technique care is needed to avoid pulling on the line.

When passing a line junction a diver should use a personal marker to mark the route out. This should be identified as personal to the diver. When encountering other divers' junction markers, great care should be taken not to disturb them.

ii.   Line repairs

When broken belays are encountered on a lose line they should be replaced so that the line is drawn tight. The original site of the belay should be on the route of the line but if it is not any new belay placement must take into account good routeing. If on the way into a sump a diver finds a section of frayed line the diver must decide if it is still strong enough to be trusted. If not, the frayed section should be replaced, either then, if spare line is being carried or as a task on a later dive. The search reel line is not generally suitable for frayed line repair, as it will not be thick enough to resist abrasion over a long periods and it should be kept available for a lost line situation. If a diver finds the line is broken, a lost line drill should be performed to find the other end. If this is unsuccessful the diver may have to reline the remainder of the sump. Any sections of line found and judged to be in good condition when doing this can be included in the relining. Any line in poor condition or un-belayed must be removed from the sump. (For knotting and belaying techniques see Ch.5.A.)

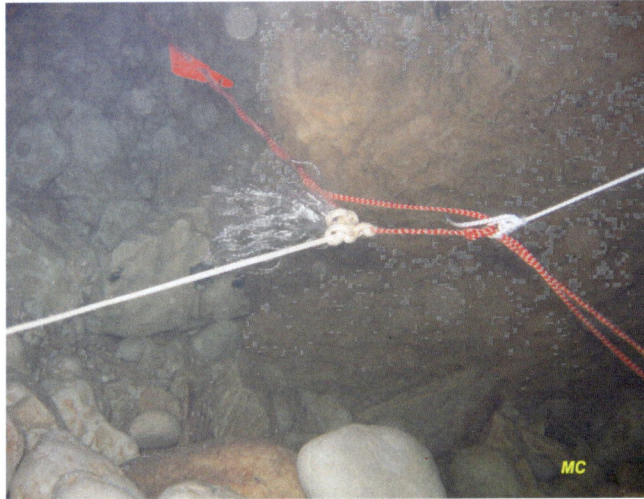

Belays and junctions present an increased risk.

iii.   Lost line drills

The line can be lost in several ways. The line can be unbroken but can become unreachable in an impenetrable part of the passage. The line can be broken, presenting the diver with a gap to bridge to the continuation of the line. A diver can lose contact with the line in poor visibility, when carrying out another task, or when swimming off the line to inspect some feature. The first thing a diver should do is stop and orientate. The method used will depend on the nature of the line loss. When the line is unbroken but in an impenetrable part of the passage, a compass or line arrow can be used.

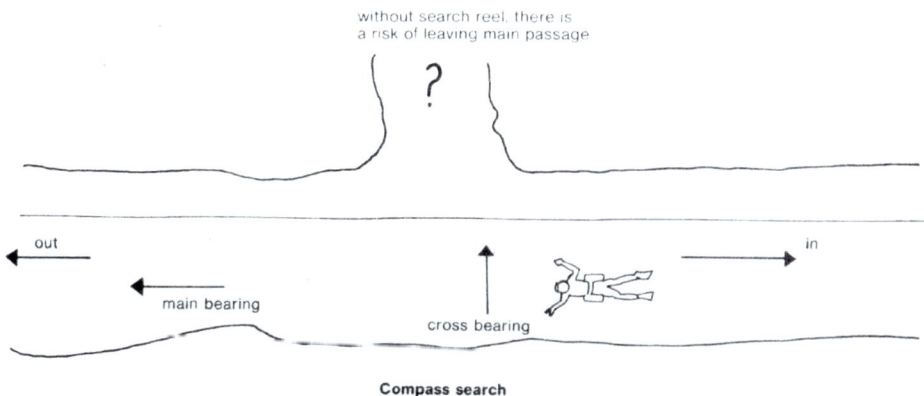

Compass search

If the line is broken the same compass or line marker system can be used. When the line has been lost completely the compass may work if the visibility is good enough, or the direction of travel can be fixed by placing a hand on the floor of the sump pointing ahead. The second stage is to relocate the lost line. If the sump has a flow that can clear the visibility, the diver may then wait before starting a search in the hope that as vision returns the line can be spotted. If this fails or there is no flow, the diver must search for the line.

If the line runs through an impenetrable area a line reel (main or search) can be tied onto the line and laid out around the obstacle in an attempt to regain the original line on the other side. If the line is broken, the search for the other end can use the broken line or a line reel (main or search) depending on the amount of slack available. In sumps with no flow, the two ends of line may be close together.

Otherwise, loose line will move with any current to the limit allowed by remaining belays. Buoyant line will float up to the roof. Situation awareness will help the diver choose the best area to search, by reeling out and moving in increasing arcs whilst trying not to reduce the visibility.

When a diver has completely lost contact with the line, the search will be more stressful as the diver has no connection with the surface and therefore will have no route out. Working from the position with one hand on the sump floor and assuming that any visibility improvement hasn't allowed the line to be spotted, the initial search can be made by hand. In most lost line situations the diver will not have strayed far from the line and this method can search a large area of passage. Using the hand on the floor as a fixed point the diver moves across the passage extending the other hand along the floor to the wall (or to the limit of reach) and up to the roof (or the limit of reach) before returning to the fixed hand. If the line hasn't been found the fixed hand is swapped over and the other side of the passage is searched in the same way. If the line still hasn't been found the drill can be repeated. When the diver is confident that a thorough search of the passage has been made to the limits of this method the search reel must then be deployed. This is a technique that adds extra risk to an already stressful situation. Deploying a thin line close to a divers' body in zero or very low visibility conditions can result in entanglement. The technique must be practised. The first step is to choose a suitable belay appropriate for the sump conditions; a lead weight works well in most cases. This belay must be solid enough to take a light strain as the diver will want to keep enough pull on the line to prevent it from forming coils and becoming a hazard. The search reel can then be deployed and attached to the belay before it is placed. To help with orientation a second belay can also be placed close to the main belay, purely to indicate the direction of travel as noted earlier. The diver can then move away from the belay paying out the line whilst keeping it from becoming slack. Several search patterns are available to the diver and one should be chosen that covers the last known position of the diver relative to the line. The sump conditions are a good indicator of where the diver has previously been. Clear visibility means the diver has probably moved away from the area the line was lost in. If another part of the line is not present the diver may have ventured into an unlined side passage away from the original route (see diagram below.) If the line isn't regained as a result of the first search the search area must be widened, either by reeling out more line, going in a different direction or by moving the belay a short distance along a known bearing. If the last method is used a diver should make notes if visibility allows to construct a mini survey of the section of passage to facilitate a thorough search. When divers are working together it may be possible for a diver who has lost the line to attract the attention of any following divers, or block the passage in the hope that they will be guided back to the line.

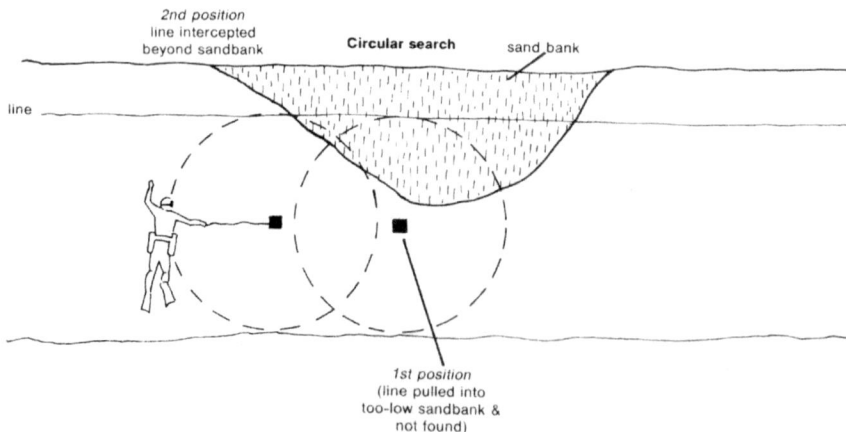

2nd position
line intercepted
beyond sandbank   **Circular search**   sand bank

line

1st position
(line pulled into
too-low sandbank &
not found)

If the diver regains the line by one of the above search methods, a calculation of available breathing gas reserves will need to be done. The diver must then assess the actions needed to reduce any hazards found or created. For a poorly routed line the diver may consider leaving the alternative line in place as a temporary measure (if it is properly belayed) and plan to come back another time to reline the section. The same choice is available if the diver has bridged a broken line. In both cases the state of the line must be publicised for the benefit of other divers who may visit the site. When the diver has lost and regained the line, there will probably be a strong desire to exit. If the diver has enough gas the search reel should be reeled back in before an exit is made as it presents a risk to other divers. If gas reserves are tight, the reel can be tied off to the line for later recovery; this is not ideal as the diver then has no search reel for a lost line situation. If gas reserves are tight the diver may not have time to carry out such a search again. Lost line searches are by no means infallible. If the diver is unable to relocate the line with search drills then a study of the passage conditions along with compass bearings taken on the way in are the unenviable alternative. Divers will have to judge for themselves what the correct actions are in this situation.

iv.   Entanglement

Becoming significantly entangled in the line, especially thicker UK style line is rare. It is more likely to occur with thinner line which tends to stretch as it tightens making it much more difficult to unravel. When an entanglement is felt, the first thing to do is remain calm and immediately stop; pulling harder on the line will normally make matters worse. In most cases a piece of equipment will merely be snagged by the line or caught on the cave passage. Simply reversing and going forward again may be enough to free the diver. If this fails, locate the line ahead and follow it by hand along the body to find the offending snare; usually one of the demand valve components, a cylinder tap, the harness or a fin strap. Remove the line from the ensnaring item and if possible move to arm's length from the line before continuing. If the line is found to be free from the diver but an entanglement is still felt equipment may be caught on the passage. Maintain contact with the line with one hand and search all the equipment with the other. When the offending item is found, free it and stow it away before continuing. If attempts to remove the entanglement are unsuccessful, the line may have to be cut. Since cutting the line will introduce additional hazards, this should only be done once the diver feels it is the only available option. The first step is to secure the line out. If there is enough slack, make a loop on the way out side, tie an overhand knot, insert an arm through it, and clip into it or attach your search reel. Note: if it is not possible to tie a loop in the main line, the search reel can be attached by wrapping the smaller search line several times round the main line and locking off with a knot. On hawser laid line, it may be possible to thread the search line through the strands of the main line, separating them by turning the main line against its natural twist. Only when firmly linked to the exit can the diver start cutting the line. It may need cutting on both sides of the tangle. Ideally, belay the loose end or join the broken ends together. If the search reel was attached, then the diver can reel this out to join the two broken ends together. Once free of the break, it should be possible to swim down the line until the next belay is reached and proceed normally. If the lines were not rejoined, great care must be taken to avoid re-tangling in the slack line after the cut is made. If the way out is downstream and it is not possible to belay the line, the current may wash the loose line into the diver, possibly causing another tangle. In this case the line should be coiled in front of the diver until the next belay where it can be tied off. If a diver has plenty of air and some line, the break should be repaired. Attempting to repair the line is very important if other divers are still on the wrong side of the break. If this is not possible, and the way out lies downstream, it is worth trying to belay the line as near to the cut end as possible so that the line does not float downstream. This makes it easier for other divers to pass the break and prevents the line washing downstream and causing a serious and dangerous obstruction. If enough slack exists, it may be possible to simply rejoin the line. Pass the cut end through the overhand loop already made and knot it substantially, ideally with a double fisherman's knot. Alternatively a short section of search reel line can be used to make a repair, especially if others divers are on the wrong side of the break. There is a certain onus on a diver who cuts a line to repair it. If this is not possible, every effort must be made to publicize the fact that the line has been cut so that the situation will not endanger other divers.

In some sumps previous divers have left reels in-situ at the limit of exploration, which presents a possible entanglement hazard if the stored line should spill off. When a line spill occurs, the line will be moved downstream by any current or spread cross the passage in a static sump creating a net. Line swept downstream can either be reeled in or secured by belays before later removal. When the line hasn't been moved along the passage, allowing it to gather together in a small area, the hazard is much greater. When line is found in this condition the diver should stop and secure the line out, then reel in and secure the lose line before any other activity is undertaken. The line can be wound onto a reel or gathered by hand and secured by a snoopy loop or cable tie. If the diver has planned on removing lose line then an alternative method such as a tackle bag or H frame may be available. In poor visibility a diver may not be able to see spilled line across a passage ahead and may swim into it. As the line is slack the diver will probably be unable to feel the entanglement until well inside the area of spilled line, with possible multiple snag points and the potential to create more with every movement. Once the diver has recognised the situation all movement should be kept to a minimum to try and reduce further entanglement. The entangling line should then cut into sections short enough to avoid further snagging, the thinner the line the shorter the lengths owing to greater flexibility. Cutting line in this way is a time consuming task and to make best use of the available breathing gas, no attempt should be made to gather the cut line. The diver must focus on cutting all of the entangling line as time will be needed as more snags may occur when the diver moves again after clearing one set of snags. Care should be taken not to cut the out line by mistake, as the diver may not have sufficient breathing gas reserves to carry out a lost line search once clear of the entanglement. When clearing entanglement any sediment present will most likely be disturbed, quickly reducing visibility. Divers should not forget the importance of knowing the direction of travel whenever they stop.

G)   Use of instrumentation

i.   Depth gauge and dive timer/computer

Information such as depth and duration of the dive should be checked throughout the dive and compared with information gained from pre-dive research. This can help a diver estimate progress into a sump. Maximum depth and dive duration should be noted down on a slate on all dives that may require decompression. Some dive computers/dive timers have an audible ascent rate alarm which provides   warming of to rapid an ascent for a diver in low visibility conditions.

ii.   Submersible pressure gauge (SPG)

Check frequently; unexpected readings can indicate a problem. On a stage cylinder with the valve switched off read the SPG before turning the valve back on as a leak test. If the SPG shows a large increase when the valve is turned on there could be a problem with the demand valve.

iii.   Compass

The most common application for the compass is to check the direction of travel by frequent reading. This information can also be compared with bearing from pre-dive research to estimate progress. In the event of line loss and recovery the compass bearing last read can be reversed to find the direction out.

iv.   Read the line

Although not an instrument the dive line can provide the diver with information. Tags may indicate the in and out directions along with distance from dive base. Different colour lines can be used to indicate main lines and branch lines at junctions. If present, out tags at junctions indicate the exit line to dive base. If the line markings are done in accordance with best practice some information can be gained in zero visibility by touch alone. (See Ch.5.A.)

H)   Removal and replacement of kit underwater

As kit can become tangled and snagged on the line and cave, all equipment that is not in the field of vision should be removable underwater. It may also be necessary to remove cylinders to allow a diver to pass a constricted section of passage. The choice of clip is important when designing a configuration that will allow easy removal of equipment underwater. All clips should be quickly and easily operated with dive gloves on. Stopping to remove equipment creates an increased hazard of line or direction loss. The line should be secured before equipment removal is commenced. Removal of some equipment will alter the diver's buoyancy; cylinders and lead weights will produce the biggest change. It is then important to hold any heavy item once it has been removed unless the diver will be within easy reach of it and the line when pinned to the roof. Removing a helmet can be made less stressful by having a plastic quick release buckle in the chin strap. The buckle can be undone allowing the helmet to be removed without having to remove the demand valve from the diver's mouth. If the diver has to put equipment down once it has been removed to carry out some other task, the item should be clipped to the line to avoid losing it as the visibility decreases.

I)   Underwater transport of kit

Several methods are available for moving equipment under water, the two main methods are:

i.   Tackle bags (empty and full)

For carrying equipment beyond sumps and even in sumps the standard caving tackle sack is ideal, as long as the equipment is tolerant of getting wet and being exposed to pressure. An empty tackle sack can be wrapped around a cylinder and secured with snoopy loops. Care must be taken to ensure all the straps and cords are on the inside of the roll and do not create a snagging hazard. Full tackle sacks can be carried on the diver's back if the sump is big enough to give the diver clear passage. The shoulder straps on the tackle bag must be clear of all the other equipment and must allow removal of the bag. Where the passage is more restricted, the bag can be hand held, or clipped to the chest for larger sections of passage. Using a haul cord as a tether to prevent the loss of the bag may be an advantage if the bag has to be put down in a poor visibility sump.

ii.   Equipment boxes/tubes

For equipment that needs to be kept dry and will be potentially damaged by pressure the best methods of transportation through a sump are rigid boxes and tubes. Each box will have a maximum working depth rating. This will be very dependent on the condition of the seal, which must be kept clean. Boxes can be mounted on the harness waist band or by the standard caving method of a sling over the shoulder. Tubes can be attached to the waist band (front or back) and towed through the sump. As rigid boxes contain air they should be trimmed for neutral buoyancy, either by weighting (internally if possible) to reduce buoyancy, or by attaching rigid foam or empty sealed tubes to the outside of the box to increase buoyancy. Another method is to put the box and a weight into a tackle bag. Items which are either positively or negatively buoyant will be difficult to move through a sump and occupy a large amount of the diver's time and energy.

J)   Task Loading

Being able to cope with stress caused by high levels of task loading is an important skill for the cave diver. The individual skills needed in a UK sump are each relatively simple; but when they have to be carried out together by a diver who is under time pressure, errors can occur. A diver who has developed and practised skills so that tasks are carried out in an un-hurried, orderly manner will be less prone to making mistakes.

i.   Time pressure

Task loading problems are increased by time pressure. When a diver is forced (or feels forced) to do things quickly, there will be a temptation to cut corners; this can create additional problems. Time pressure can take two forms:

- *Immediate.*
- *Continuous.*

Immediate time pressure: Comes about when something goes wrong and a diver has to respond immediately to the situation. This may take the form of an interrupted breathing supply or a lost line etc. The normal response to these situations is an emergency drill. A diver who is well practised in these drills will find them easier to execute quickly. An un-drilled diver may make a mistake when dealing with the situation. In the case of an interrupted breathing supply, the diver may swap to the second supply but fail to secure the line or note the direction. Thus, further problems are created owing to the diver not carrying out all the tasks at the correct time.

Continuous time pressure: Acts on a diver throughout the dive. A diver may be so rushed when carrying out drills that require good visibility that may quickly deteriorate. With a limited supply of breathing gas a diver may feel rushed to carry out the normal diving tasks and carry out all the tasks in the dive plan. Time pressure can result in a reduction in the frequency of the routine tasks all cave divers should perform, or the complete omission of some tasks. To save time, a diver may travel quickly through a sump without observing the passage or taking time to inspect the line. This may leave the diver less able to deal with a problem encountered on the return journey in reduced visibility.

ii.   Task integration

Once a diver has mastered the individual core skills (see Ch.4) for basic cave diving, further practice will be required so that they can be carried out simultaneously. If a diver has to carry out each task separately, time pressure will be increased. If the tasks can be integrated less time will be needed to execute them all. Developing integrated skills also develops a routine that a diver can follow automatically which reduces decision making by the diver. A diver who does not have to think about each action on a dive has time available to think about the dive itself. This creates the potential for a more productive dive.

The routine that each diver develops will be dependent on the individual equipment configuration. The same drills will be needed by all divers and they will need to be executed with the line in either hand. Most of the drills are dependent on visibility; integrating the drills with the movement of the line of sight is therefore important. Inspection of both the passage and line should become second nature, as should regular instrument reading. Most routines will be easier to carry out when the diver is stationary. The method the diver uses to secure the line must be considered as part of the routine and should be designed so that it does not increase the difficulty of the tasks the diver needs to do. This may result in a different method being applied for securing the line on each side of the diver, depending on where the diver wears instrumentation.

Once a diver has developed a routine, it should be practised before it is used in a sump. When the routine is fully established, it should be consistently used; modifications can increase task loading thereby negating the benefits. A consistent equipment configuration will help to support a consistent core skills routine.

iii.   Reducing task loading

For inexperienced divers, task loading on a normal dive can be a significant problem. A cautious approach can reduce the chances of an inexperienced diver making a mistake. Good visibility sites should be chosen for the early dives and the diver should travel slowly. This will give the diver more time to execute the various drills, without being pressured by an imminent reduction in visibility. Dive plans should also be simple and clear. If a dive has too many objectives, task loading will be increased and extra time pressure will be placed on the routine drills.

For inexperienced divers, equipment testing dives are very common. Although everything should be tested before it is taken into a sump, the first dive in a sump may highlight a previously unnoticed problem. For this reason the first time any item of equipment is taken into a sump should be considered a test dive. This on its own may be enough task loading on top of the normal routines and the diver should resist the temptation to make the plan more complex.

Task loading can also be reduced by limiting time pressure. If a diver feels less pressure to get things done there is less chance of a mistake. One simple way to do this is to take more breathing gas. With more time available a diver will feel less continuous time pressure.

When a diver is fully competent at dealing with the task loading created by the core skills, others can be added to the dive plan and tested in an open water environment. This should be done gradually, allowing the diver to develop ways to integrate the additional tasks with the standard routines. Both carrying equipment in the hands and surveying are excellent ways to develop task loading skills. Divers carrying out these tasks should maintain an awareness of how well they are executing the routine drills. With practice, a diver's ability to cope with task loading will improve.

Chapter 5 Exploring and recording sumps

Offset line (belayed at line tag) routed through boulders to guide the diver through the widest section.

For some, cave diving is a method used to reach dry passage beyond a sump, it being the only way to get to a section of cave; alternatively the flooded passage may provide an easier route than many hours of arduous caving. For others, diving will provide a chance to explore and map new passage both flooded and dry.

The core skills discussed in the previous chapter underpin both line laying and sump surveying techniques. To be proficient at these skills a diver must be able to cope easily with the task loading imposed by these core skills. The Group's Qualified Diver Practical Examination tests trainees' ability in both areas to assess if they are capable of line laying and surveying using safe and up to date practices. It is therefore important for all trainees to study these activities even if they never intend to lay new line or survey a sump. Skills learnt at this stage will help to develop wider knowledge as well as improving a diver's understanding of the sump environment.

A) Line laying techniques

It is important that good line following skills are learnt before line laying is attempted. Only by understanding line following can a diver lay line that will be safe to follow. A poorly laid line is a hazard not only to the diver laying it (both on that dive and all future dives at that site) but to all other divers who might enter the sump. Trainees are advised to practise line laying in open water conditions or as a re-lining project in one of the larger, easier sumps before attempting it in more challenging or unexplored passage. Line laying is a high risk cave diving activity, requiring maximum awareness and a methodical approach.

i. Risks and benefits of using a line

The benefits of a well laid line significantly increase diver safety. The line not only guides the diver through a sump in all levels of visibility from good to zero, it also allows the diver to find the best part of the passage cross section to travel through. By routeing the line next to (but not through) the widest point of a constriction the diver is giving future divers a marked path through the sump avoiding obstacles, one of which is the line itself. A well tagged line will reduce diver stress by indicating clear exit directions not only at junctions, but along single lines through a sump where direction and distance markers can be a great help. A well laid, tight line is also a benefit for survey work. Risks associated with line in a sump are due mainly to entanglement.

Entanglement hazards are most common when a line has been laid loosely with insufficient belays or has been damaged, creating loose or broken line. Other causes of entanglement are poor kit configuration, inadequate line management as well as poor general diving skills. Constricted passage and line reels left over from previous exploration attempts can also present a hazard. The false sense of security a line may give can result in a diver neglecting best practice, such as not noting compass bearings or simply following the line without being aware of other aspects of the sump environment, aspects that may tell the diver that a mistake has been made.

A well laid line in a silt floored passage avoiding a bedding on the left, giving the diver a route to the right.

ii.   **Line Preparation**

a.   **Properties, types**

Choice of line is important. There are a number of characteristics that a line must satisfy according to the nature of sump.
These are as follows:

- *Strength.*
- *Abrasion resistance.*
- *Diameter.*
- *Buoyancy.*
- *Colour.*
- *Texture.*
- *Ability to knot.*
- *Construction.*

Strength: Most synthetic lines are more than strong enough for cave diving, given that it is normally difficult to shock-load the line. Although a line of only 2 mm diameter will hold the weight of a fully kitted diver in the open air, it will probably have unsuitable abrasion characteristics and is prone to tangling and catch on equipment.

Resistance to abrasion: This quality is perhaps more important because even the gradual movements of a diver or the water can have a sawing effect where the line runs over sharp projections. For this reason, it is unwise to use line of less than 3mm diameter in UK conditions. In turbulent sumps, lines of even 6mm can be broken after only one flood. For extreme conditions short sections of metal chain have proved almost indestructible.

Diameter: Time and experience have suggested that 4mm diameter line is a good compromise for British conditions. It is strong, it can stand up to short-term abrasion, and a reasonably sized reel can hold enough line for most exploratory dives. On deep shafts, sumps with high flow, poor visibility or well-travelled sumps, 5 to 6 mm lines are recommended. As well as improved abrasion resistance, the greater the diameter of the line the easier it is to feel in poor visibility; its more rigid quality means there is less risk of looping, spilling, or ensnaring. The limiting factors on the maximum diameter of line are its weight, the length that can be fitted on to a manageable reel, and the effort needed to cut it in an emergency.

Buoyancy: For British conditions, a slightly buoyant line is preferable. Such line is less prone to silting up and encourages the diver to keep in mid-water, preserving good visibility. A fully laden reel should be just negatively buoyant, so that it does not float if dropped or placed on the floor. Positive buoyancy can be a big problem with thick synthetic lines (e.g. Polypropylene.) Part of the problem is poor wetting of the line, causing tiny air bubbles held within the weave, particularly in shallow sumps. Nylon is negatively buoyant.

Colour: Most synthetic lines can be easily obtained in a variety of colours and the use of different coloured lines can considerably aid navigation. Similarly, where there are one or more junctions or side passages, the use of a single colour of line down the main passage and different colours of line on side passages can make such junctions considerably safer and individually distinctive. Whatever colours are used, they should be bright enough to be seen distinctly in the often brown and tannic waters of the sump.

Texture: How rigid or flexible your line is will affect its handling on and off the reel. Rigid lines do not gather up and loop so much in front of a moving diver's hand and so tangles are easier to avoid. More flexible lines hold knots better and will be easier to loop through natural belays. For the diameter used in UK sumps Nylon line is considered rigid and Polypropylene line is considered flexible.

Ability to knot: Rigid lines are easier to tie knots in underwater because they can be felt more easily and do not flop about. However, because they have more of a plastic memory they are more easily untied, and may even untie themselves. Polypropylene needs some care, and knots which present the maximum integral friction must be used (e.g. double Fisherman's rather than single Fisherman's or reef knots and figures-of-eight rather than an overhand knot). As with knots in caving rope, the loose tail from the knot must be long enough to prevent the knot untying. If tied above water, this tail should be taped down with a few turns of insulating tape or secured with a cable tie.

Construction: There are two types of construction for commonly used line, hawser laid and plaited-no core. Hawser laid line is twisted multi strand which the diver can open to place tags and markers on the line. This is the most common type of construction for thicker lines. Plaited-no core is multi strand plaited that must be stretched taught when laid. This is the commonest type of construction for thinner lines.

The line most used in UK cave diving is 4 or 6mm hawser laid Polypropylene.

b. Line tagging

Before any line is wound on a reel, it must be measured and tagged at regular intervals. This can be done by placing two pegs in the ground 5 or 10 m apart and wrapping the line between the pegs. All the tags can then be added at the chosen separation and the line is kept taut for winding on the reel afterwards.

If a light-coloured plastic tape is being used, distances can be marked on the tape with an indelible pen making initial survey and navigation much easier. This is especially true in poor visibility, where there may be little else to relate to. Plastic insulating tape is the easiest material to use for tags and is simply attached by pushing one end between the strands (in hawser-laid line) and then sticking the tape ends together. This avoids slippage or loss. To avoid slippage of tags when using plaited lines, the line must be bound tightly with tape for about 5 cm before the tag is attached. A strongly contrasting tape/line colour combination is important.

Dual tagging, with two colours, or the placement of direction arrows are advised. Yellow and black tags are often used. The yellow tag is attached on the entrance side (way out) and the black tag on the cave side (way in). In such circumstances, the diver knows in which direction to swim out as soon as the tag is reached. In caves with more than one entrance careful consideration must be given as to which direction is out. Line arrows can be used to indicate the way out at regular intervals. Major sub-divisions should be marked in different coloured tape, e.g. using a different coloured tag every 50 m. As a general rule, tags should be placed every 5 m. For larger sumps 10 or 20 m is sufficient. Cable ties can be used as an alternative to insulation tape for tagging lines where the diver does not wish to record the distances on the tags, as is often the case when adding short lengths of line to a sump. If the diver wishes to record the distances, insulation tape can be applied over the cable tie to form a secure tag; alternatively plastic squares can be fastened with the cable ties. To indicate direction, three cable ties can be attached to the line. Two close together 5 mm apart and one 40 mm away can show the out direction. The tags close together would be on the in route.

iii. Line reels preparation and usage

a. Types of line reel

Several different designs of line reel can be used in UK sumps, not all of which are of a design that is conventionally thought of as a reel. Divers should understand the strengths and weaknesses of each design. This will allow the most appropriate reel to be selected for the planned dive.

The basic types are:

- *Standard reel (spool).*
- *Plastic bottle.*
- *Lead weight block.*
- *Derbyshire tube.*

The standard reel: Should be easily transported and robust enough to withstand cave conditions. It must also have simplicity of construction and operation. The design of reel will be subject to the type of line being laid. A few commercial reels for UK cave diving are available although home building is common. Spools are typically up to 30 cm diameter and 20 cm wide. The diameter of the spool core should not be too small (5 cm minimum) or the last few metres of line will be difficult to unwind. A re-wind knob should be attached to the opposite side of the reel to the handle. The position and size of the handle are crucial. The handle should be as near to the centre of gravity of the reel as possible, to minimise leverage on the wrist. The handle needs to be large enough to be gripped with a gloved hand and have sufficient clearance from the spool to avoid snagging. Some means of attaching the reel to the hand or harness should be fitted to the handle. UK cave reels are normally made of stainless steel and the more robust plastics, as both are hard wearing and neither will corrode when left in the water for prolonged periods.

The main advantages of a standard reel are:

- *Can hold a large amount of line.*
- *Easy and quick to use.*
- *Can be used one-handed.*
- *Reeling the line back in is easy.*

The main disadvantages of a standard reel are:

- *It can be difficult to manoeuvre in tighter passages.*
- *Unless weighted, it can be buoyant when loaded with line.*
- *If the line is not kept tight, it can easily spill from the reel.*
- *An unsecured reel left in a sump can spill line, creating a hazard.*

Standard reel with lock detail

Plastic bottle: Typically a 1 or 2 litre soft drinks bottle can be filled with line which is fed out through the neck. Holes will need to be put through the bottle at the opposite end to the neck to prevent air becoming trapped as the diver starts the dive. Some form of securing loop can be fitted through the sidewall of the bottle to make transportation easier. The line is pulled from the bottle with one hand as the diver progresses, holding the bottle in the other hand. If the line has to be reeled back in, the diver can coil the line around the outside of the bottle.

The main advantages of a plastic bottle reel are:

- *It is easy to carry to the sump.*
- *It is unlikely to snag and spill line (unless line has been wound on the outside).*
- *Compact design makes it useful in constricted passage.*
- *Easy to use.*

The main disadvantages of a plastic bottle reel are:

- *It has the buoyancy characteristics of the line.*
- *Reeling back in creates the potential for line spillage.*
- *It can hold only a small amount of line.*
- *Care is needed when loading the reel to avoid tangles when the line is extracted.*

Lead weight block: Reels are constructed from a lead block with snoopy loops to hold the line. A loop can be added to clip the weight onto the diver's harness or the weight can be carried in a bag. The line is tied to the block and looped concertina style under the snoopies. The line is pulled from under the snoopies in a controlled manner.

The advantages of a lead block line reel are:

- *Very compact.*
- *The block can be used as a belay.*
- *The small amount of line carried reduces the potential for entanglement.*
- *The block can be used as a mobile belay whilst a diver inspects several parts of a boulder choke or dig.*

The disadvantages of the lead block reel are:

- *It can hold only a very small amount of line.*
- *It is heavy to carry to the sump through dry passage.*
- *Reeling in is difficult.*
- *The reel should be used two handed to avoid spilling all the line at one time.*

Derbyshire tube: Reels are constructed from a short length of scaffold pole (typically 30 – 40 cm in length, depending on the nature of the site where its use is intended). The ends of the tube must be carefully filed smooth to avoid cutting the line. A 10 m to 15 m length of line is first tied through the tube, forming a loop. The line is then secured onto the tube backwards and forwards below snoopy loops such that short sections of line can be pulled out as small advances are made in difficult terrain. As this reel is intended for difficult diving conditions, often involving low visibility, the use of thick line is advised. The reel is best carried underwater by hand or in an SRT bag so that it does not snag and have the line accidentally pulled from it en route into the sump. If too much line is laid from it (e.g. when the diver needs to try several different directions) the excess can simply be wound round the outside of the reel. If the length of the scaffold tube is known, it can be used to test the size of low beddings. Once all the line it carries has been laid, the scaffold pole acts as a direct "drop weight" belay or as a silt screw. If used as a drop weight, the tube should be aligned with the direction of current so that it is not rolled away from where it was placed by the diver. If the current is likely to be strong enough to move a tube even when properly aligned (possibly in a flood) additional belays can be used and/or the tube can be placed in the lee of a large rock. The loop of line tied through the scaffold pole provides a safe attachment point for the next section of line to be laid on a subsequent dive. This loop also provides an attachment point for the next line reel if it must be left in a sump for future use.

The advantages of the Derbyshire tube are:

- *Can be used as a belay whilst digging or at the end of the line.*
- *It can be left in place between dives.*
- *The line will not spill off it.*
- *Compact design for constricted passage use.*

The disadvantages of the Derbyshire tube are:

- *Two handed operation to withdraw line from it.*
- *Limited amount of line can be carried.*
- *Careful preparation of the reel is needed to avoid sharp edges.*

- *As the reel often becomes a belay it may only last one dive.*

b. Line reels (configuration/carrying)

There are several options for carrying a line reel in a sump, depending on the reel, dive plan and the preference of the diver. Line reels can be carried in the hand, tied to the wrist with a loop lanyard or clipped to the harness. If the distance to be carried is short or the aim of the dive is to inspect and repair the line, then hand holding the reel will be a good method. Although it does occupy one hand, the line reel is easy to deploy and can be manoeuvred to avoid entanglement and snagging. For longer sumps or in situations where the diver wants both hands free, wrist mounting is a good compromise. This can be achieved using a loop built into the reel or by belaying the outer end of the line to the rim of the reel creating a loop which can serve as a wrist mount. Deployment is still quite easy as the reel remains attached throughout the process; although it is less controlled, it is mounted within view, making entanglement and snagging problems less likely. The free movement of the reel can create problems with visibility in silty sumps. When a reel is to be carried through a longer section of sump or the dive plan assumes that the existing line is in good condition, the reel can be clipped to the harness, usually to a D-ring on the waistband, either hanging free or sitting above the cylinder with the handle between the cylinder and the diver's body. This method keeps the diver's hands free and does not increase the clutter on the diver's forearms, and if the reel sits well it won't greatly increase the profile. Deployment can be easy if the D-ring is placed for easy access and a good lanyard is used to make securing the reel easy during the process. There is a greater risk of entanglement and snagging owing to the reel being out of view. The clip used to secure it should have a gate that can be locked to stop the clip being snared by the line as the diver moves through the sump.

c. Loading line reels

Choose the line length to suit the planned dive and gas margins. Choose the reel to suit the type of passage and the dive plan. The chosen reel must have enough capacity for the amount of line to be carried but still be manoeuvrable in the sump passage. Line reels must not be overloaded as spilled line is an entanglement hazard. They must also allow the diver to attach the line on the reel securely to existing line in the sump.

Whilst it is possible to join line underwater using knots, the practice can often be minimised by good planning. A simple method of joining lines, (see Ch.5.A.v.a) without tying knots underwater, has been developed for man-made fibres. To use this method, special line preparation is necessary when the line is being loaded onto the reel. This preparation is best done before the line is tagged if accurate distance measurements are to be taken from the line for survey work using the simple method. (See Section B.i of this chapter.)

A loop is tied using a double figure eight about 2 metres from one end of the line. The loose end (tail) is used to secure the line to the reel; the loop is used for the final belay and for attaching the next length of line. At the other end of the line a loop is then tied that is big enough to allow the diver to pass the line reel through it. Distance tags can then be placed onto the line using the two loops as the ends of the line; the tail is not included as it will be cut.

When the line has been prepared, it is secured to the reel using the tail; this must be long enough to allow it to be easily cut by the diver when the reel is empty and the end of the line has been securely belayed. The length of the tail will vary with reel size/design. Next the line is wound onto the reel, trapping the first loop. With stiffer lines, always lay the line out on the ground before the dive to remove any twists and to counteract the line's plastic memory. Then wind it in neatly so that the line does not spiral into coils when laid in a sump. Note that with the standard reel design the line should be wound onto the reel by rotating the reel, not by wrapping the line around a static reel, as this will lead to twists. Once all the line has been loaded onto the reel, the terminal loop must be secured to the reel so that it will not come free and create an entanglement hazard for the diver. The method chosen for this will depend the type of reel being used.

a)

loose end

loop large enough
to pass reel through

b)

loose end tied off

insulating tape
secures end loop

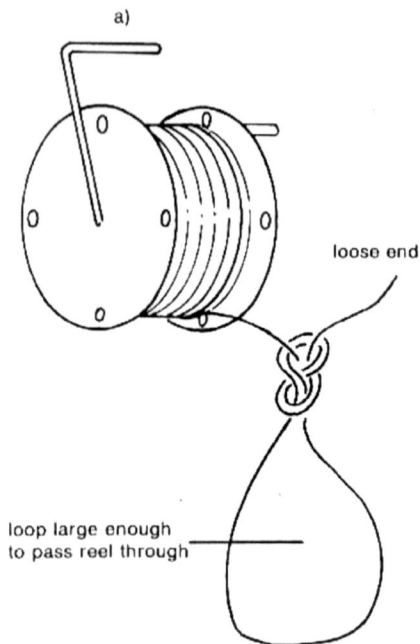

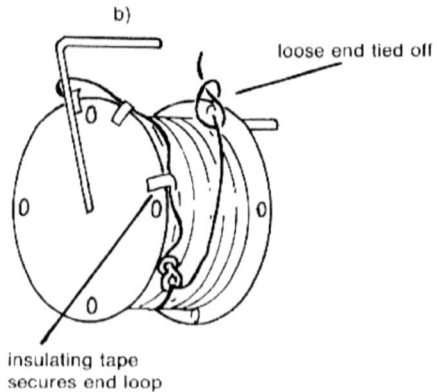

*Forming a loop at the end of a new line
to attach to an existing line.*

iv.   Belaying line

Good belaying is essential for line laying. This is especially important in low, meandering beddings where the line may pull into places too narrow to negotiate on the return. The hazards of rifts should not be underestimated as these can pose the same problems as beddings. The line must be carefully placed using plastic pipes to avoid line traps.

The main types of belays are:

Natural belays
- *Eyeholes.*
- *Rocks and flakes.*

Artificial belays
- *Snoopy loop.*
- *Lead weight.*
- *Plastic pipe.*
- *Cable tie.*
- *Net bag.*
- *Buoy.*
- *Self drilling bolts and pitons.*

Natural Belays: As with dry caving, using natural belays is sensible, cave-friendly and good practice.

Eyeholes: Eyeholes provide one of the best underwater belaying aids as it is virtually impossible for an eyehole to fail. It is easiest to form a loop in the line, which is passed through the eyehole. The reel is taken around the other side and passed through the emerging loop, which is then pulled tight. No knots are required, but a cable tie can be used to secure the belay in case the line breaks on one side.

Rocks and Flakes: Wrapping the line around large rocks or flakes can be a good technique for securing the line, especially if locked off with a knot or cable tie. Consideration should be given to the quantity of line used for such belays during later surveying. Placing rocks on the line is a useful technique but must be regarded as temporary. Such belays should be replaced at the first opportunity. If the line is wrapped around a loose rock, it should pass over the top of the rock, which allows the hand to follow the line in zero visibility. Sometimes rocks can be used as chock-stones to trap the line in cracks. A bight should be tied in the line and placed around the chock-stone before it is lodged into the crack as the line could be hard to follow if merely placed behind the chock stone. Rock belays have the advantage that they can be moved around the sump by the diver to provide a belay point where it is required.

Artificial Belay: There are various types of artificial belay commonly used when no natural belay is available.

Snoopy Loop: They are extremely easy to make and use and have no effect on buoyancy. Snoopy loops are made by carefully cutting a car inner tube into loops approximately 2 cm wide. A clean cut is important as the slightest nick or hole may start a tear when the snoopy loop is stretched over a rock. A length of line about 30cm long is passed through the rubber loop and then tied to form a second loop by a double-fisherman's knot. The traditional method of use is to larksfoot the snoopy loop line onto a loop tied into the main line. Another method is to omit the loop of line and larksfoot the snoopy loop directly onto a loop tied into the main line. To form a belay the snoopy loop is first tied to the line and then stretched round a suitable rock or flake projection with the line routed on the outside of any flake or on top of any rock to make it easier to follow. If no rocks are available where one would make a good belay the diver can easily move one from another part of the sump.

Snoopies are easily dislodged, especially when applied to projections. If opposing projections can be found this can be avoided and the line tension can have the effect of holding the belay in position.

Lead Weight: Lead weights are reliable and permanent but expensive and heavy. The latter point is the most important, especially if the diver does not have any means of variable buoyancy control. When diving with a wetsuit, three or four 1kg weights are usually the most that are carried. Otherwise the diver will be too heavy on the way in or, even worse, too light on the return. Lead weights are typically used when a reliable belay is needed and no solid rock feature is available.

Plastic Pipe: Plastic pipe belays (often referred to as 'bog pipe belays' or 'silt screws') when well placed become good permanent belays. They are made by cutting sections of 2-4 cm pipe into 20-40 cm lengths. Either a hole is drilled or a large v-shaped slot is sawn close to one end. A short loop of line is threaded through the hole and tied with a double Fisherman's knot. It is attached, before placement, in the same manner as a snoopy loop. If the diameter of the pipe and size of the slot are large enough, the loop of line can be omitted and the main dive line can be larksfooted through the slot in a similar fashion to attaching the line to an eyehole. On silty or gravel-floored passages they can be used in a similar way to ice screws. The line is larksfooted directly to the pipe or loop of line and the pipe is twisted into the floor as deeply as possible. In sumps with stable silt banks, this can be regarded as a permanent belay. If the silt banks are mobile in floods, it should be replaced with a lead weight or net bag at a suitable opportunity. In low beddings, rifts and cracks, the pipes can be used as stemples and hence carrying a variety of lengths is a good idea. If well placed, this is a permanent belay.

Cable Ties: Cable ties are strong and 200x3.6 mm ties are ideal for this purpose. They can be used to secure the line to natural features and any artificial belay when the extra distance given by the attachment cord is unwanted. The cable tie can be secured to the line by passing it through a loop tied in the line or by feeding it through the twists in hawser laid line.

Net Bags: Net Bags are used in passages containing small pebbles or stones that can be placed inside the net and the drawstring tightened. This is then larksfooted to a loop tied in the main line.

Buoys: Small buoys are not generally used but are effective in kicking-water air bells where no natural belays are available and the diver does not wish to use a bolt; a plastic sealable container of around 5 L is ideal. If the airbell is off the main line route, a jump line, preferably of a different colour or thickness, can be laid. The main line should be tagged on the out side of the junction. Allowance needs to be made if the cave could flood and lift the buoy, as the line belays may be pulled off. Hence it is difficult to maintain the correct tension and avoid slack line. Ideally, the air bell jump line should be run horizontally away from the main line before rising up to the air bell so as not to cause an obstruction. It is also best to use a floating line such as polypropylene for the same reason.

Self-Drilling Bolts and Pitons: Bolts and pitons are rarely used owing to the time needed for each placement. Bolts are sometimes used as a first belay at the start of a sump or in a kicking-water air bell. Bolts have been used successfully in passages where very high flow is experienced and a more substantial belay is required. They are sometimes useful in low squeezes where precise positioning and tensioning of the line is essential. Another common use is during decompression diving, e.g. belaying the decompression line at the head of a shaft or for anchoring equipment.

v.   Aspects of line laying

A well laid line will be secure and easy to follow. The risk of entanglement and snagging will be reduced by good line tension and routeing. A diver following a well laid line in zero visibility will be guided through the easiest part of the passage without the line having to be held too far away from or too close to the diver's body and equipment. Line junctions will be tagged so that a diver can identify the exit line by touch alone, even when wearing thick gloves. Belay points should be solid enough to withstand flood conditions without being moved. At each belay the line should be tied so that it cannot pull through several belays if it breaks. Usable air bells in a well lined sump will be fitted with jump lines to allow a diver to retreat to a place of safety if necessary.

The basic procedures of line laying are:

- *Establish a secure base belay.*
- *Lay a tight, well belayed line.*
- *Where possible belay at line tags (makes surveying easier).*
- *Secure the line at belays, so that if it breaks it is loose only to the next belay.*
- *Belay to prevent the line getting pulled into low beddings/tight rifts.*
- *Avoid rub points.*
- *Place jump lines to air bells.*
- *Lay line for the best visibility.*
- *Route the line to avoid entanglement, particularly in tight sections.*

a.   Start belay or attaching to the end of a line

At the start of a new sump, it is very important that a good permanent belay is found. The belay should ideally be placed out of reach of non-divers. Nowadays, it is very rare in the UK for a diver to lay line from base in a virgin sump and it is more likely that the end of the line will be reached some distance into the sump. During the journey to the end of the sump, the existing line should be inspected and repaired as necessary. At the end of the line the ongoing passage should be visually inspected before the new reel is attached (and before the visibility is lost). The lines can then be joined using the loops placed on the ends of each line when they were loaded onto their reels (see Section A.iii.c of this Chapter). At the end of the existing line there should be a loop at the final belay; this is used as the attachment point for the new line on the reel. The long loop secured on the reel is first unclipped and then passed through the end loop in the existing line. The reel is then passed through the long loop forming a larksfoot in the long loop that connects into the loop attached to the last belay of the existing line.

Attaching the reel will probably reduce the visibility; new line laying can start in the direction chosen during the earlier visual inspection. Once the diver has moved from the area disturbed during reel attachment, visibility available for continued line laying will depend on the flow conditions, the type of sediment in the passage, the size of the passage and the ability of the diver.

b.   Laying line

When laying line, the diver must maintain control of both the line on the reel and the line just laid but not yet belayed. To reduce the risk of entanglement the diver should keep a slight tension on the line being laid (enough to feel the previous belay) whilst holding it away from the body and also keep tension on the line being fed off the reel. The method the diver uses to do this will depend on the type of reel being used and the conditions in the sump. The line can be fed directly off the reel (the diver holds the reel at arm's length and keeps the line tight by applying friction to the reel) or by using one hand to feed the line off the reel and keep it tight whilst the reel is held (again with friction applied to the reel) in the other hand. The one handed method is best suited for spool type reels in larger sumps with good visibility that will remain to some degree despite the actions of the diver. The one handed method can allow the diver to move faster through a sump but with less control over the line. The two handed method can be used with any type of line reel and allows the diver to have better control over the tension on the line. This enables the diver to reduce the risk of entanglement in more constricted passage and where visibility may be reduced quickly by the diver. The two handed reel method will reduce the speed at which the diver can move. When the diver chooses to place a belay, the line on the reel must be secured so that it does not spill. For some reel designs, the line is held in place by bungee; these reels can be put down as long as the diver maintains contact with the line throughout the belaying process. For spool reels the diver will have to secure the line to the reel before it can be put down; this can be done by looping the line around the reel handle or by placing a snoopy around the line. Once the line has been secured, the reel can be put down but again the diver must maintain contact with the line. In sumps with silt deposits, a buoyant reel can be an advantage as it will float up towards the roof whilst the diver is placing a belay and not disturb any of the silt on the floor.

There is no set rule on how often belays are required as this depends entirely on the nature of the sump. Belays are required less often in larger, clear sumps and more often in smaller sumps, especially if the visibility is poor or the sump is in a bedding plane. Typically belays might be placed at intervals of less than 10m in low, poor visibility sumps and at larger intervals in bigger clearer sumps. Belays should be placed at every turn or when the distance between belays on a straight run has become too large. In the latter case, if possible, place the belays at the tags as this will aid later surveying. In most instances, the more belays the better: should the line be broken then the distance between the broken ends is smaller. There is also less chance of the line pulling into low sections.

The line is normally laid along the floor, as roofs and walls tend to be complicated by solution pockets and cross rifts. The floor is full of useful navigational aids. Deposits of silt display ripple marks and together with bits of flood debris and the movement of particulate matter in the water can indicate the direction of flow. In static water, or where there is no other indication of direction, scallop markings are a useful clue (the sharp edge points downstream). Pebble deposits can indicate a change of flow direction or a rise or fall in passage depth. In very bad visibility it may be better to follow one wall, feeling for low beddings and belaying the line wherever possible. It is very important to look into any clear areas ahead before visibility is destroyed by the diver's progress. If the sump suddenly ends in a blank wall, look above; the continuation might be an ascending shaft, or go back several metres and see if there is another way on at a different level.

When laying line through constricted passage, there is the potential to create an entanglement hazard. To avoid this, line should be routed to allow the diver to use the widest part of the passage, with the line running parallel and within reach. If the passage shape does not allow the line to be routed away from the diver, the line can be run through a hose pipe. The rigidity of the hose pipe reduces the entanglement hazard.

In large clear sumps, following a wall and the floor may also be psychologically better as it removes the disorientation associated with free swimming in the centre of a large passage, out of sight of the walls and floor.

In some sumps, there can be advantages to laying line in the roof of the sump.
These may be:

- *Decompression advantages (deep sumps with large passages).*
- *Sumps with mobile floors.*
- *On slopes.*

In low passages, avoid swapping from one side of the passage to the other, as this will necessitate crossing the line on subsequent journeys and an increased risk of entanglement.

If thick line is used, it should be kept reasonably taut but not stretched tight. A small allowance for line shrinkage should be made to prevent the belays being pulled off when the line contracts. Sufficient belays should be used to allow the line to run as tautly as possible without pulling into awkward sections. When pausing to perform a task, or to belay the line, any slack should be wound onto the reel and the line kept as taut as possible behind the diver.

If thinner line is used, it should be stretched tight between belays, typically along one of the walls. As the line is stretched no allowance for shrinkage needs to be made. At belays, the line is often belayed by wrapping it around a flake projection and placing a snoopy over the wrap. Although this is fast, it has certain disadvantages as the line is prone to damage and if the belay should come off, slack line can be generated. A better method is to avoid potential abrasion problems by using a conventional snoopy loop, cable tie or weight. If this is done the line should be knotted around the belay to stop the line tension being lost.

In addition to providing navigational aids, the walls, floor and roof of the cave also provide natural belays. Whether or not they later prove to be unnecessary, it is sensible to secure the line to any suitable rocks, flakes or eyeholes that the passage offers. If potentially mobile belays are being used, care is needed in paying out the line. Dubious stone belays should be replaced at the first opportunity with lead or other permanent belays.

Diver on a well belayed European line.

feed out with
one arm outstretched

stones - if right shape,
wrap line round

leading (no natural belay)

net bag filled
with small stones

sand bank

sand bank

Line belaying through a sump.

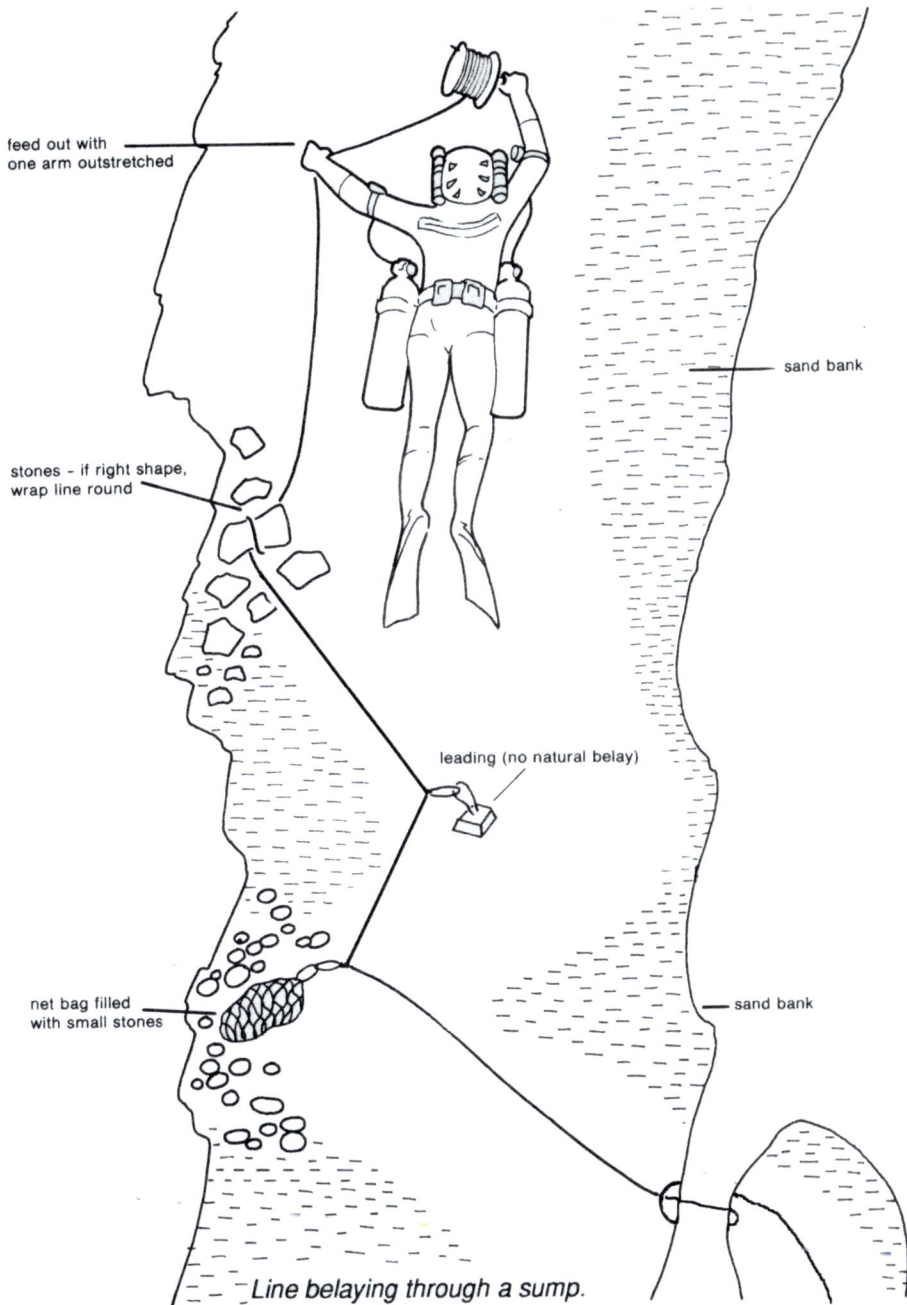

c. The final belay

When all of the line on the reel has been used or the diver is unable to make further progress (owing to gas supply limitations, reduced visibility, shortage of belays etc), a secure final belay must be made. If the end of the line has been reached, this can be done using the loop tied in the end of the line when the reel was loaded (see Section A.iii.c of this Chapter). Once a secure belay has been placed, the reel can be detached from the line by cutting the tail between the loop and the reel. To ensure that the line is not lost while belaying, put the loop over one forearm, or clip on with a karabiner, and do not remove it until the line is belayed and the reel has been cut off. Do not cut the line too close to the knot such that it can come undone.

When the diver has to stop line laying before all the line on the reel has been used, the diver must choose to either leave the reel in place or belay the line, cut it and remove the reel. Leaving a reel in place creates a possible entanglement hazard and should only be considered if the diver is sure the reel will not spill the line if left in place for a long period (years) and the reel can be securely belayed. The fabric of the reel must be of a type that will not corrode in the water and the line should be secured onto the reel such that it will not come off due to the effects of flow through the sump. If the diver cannot be sure that the reel will not present a possible hazard on future dives (possibly to other divers), then the reel should be removed. This is done by first tying two loops into the line; belaying the line at the loop further from the reel, securing the line onto the reel using the loop closer to the reel and then cutting the line between the two loops. The line out should be secured during this process in the same way as described above.

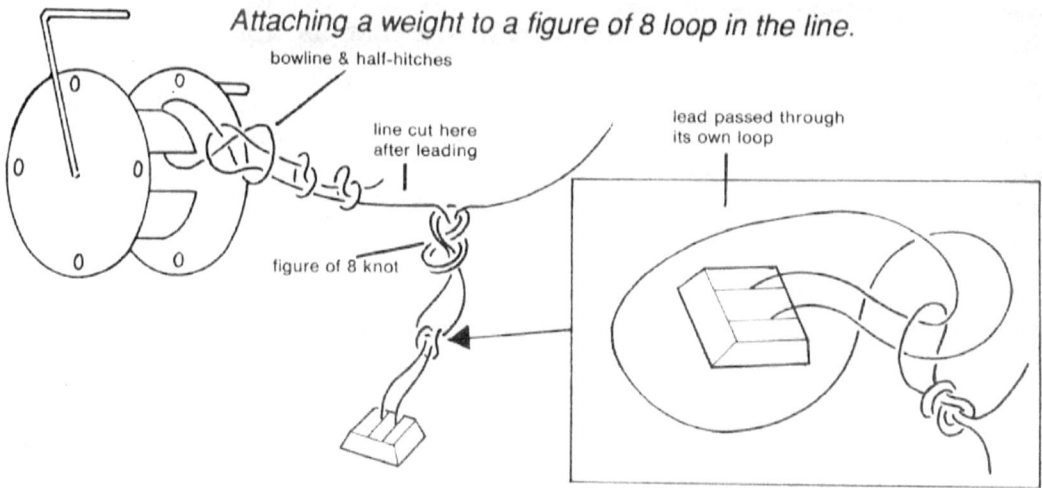

Attaching a weight to a figure of 8 loop in the line.

bowline & half-hitches

line cut here
after leading

lead passed through
its own loop

figure of 8 knot

d.   Line junctions, junction markers and air bell jump lines

The majority of sumps in the UK consist of one route through with no side passages or air bells, but in the more complex sumps both these features are common. To reduce the chances of a mistake, all line junctions must be clearly marked with an out tag. This must be usable by a diver wearing thick gloves in all levels of visibility. In addition the point where the lines meet must be secure so that one line can't slide along another and so that the joint will not fail if a line is broken.

Normal line tagging is not considered a sufficiently good method for marking an exit line from a junction since all lines to and from the junction will have tags. The best method is to attach a plastic out arrow to the exit line close to the junction point. Arrows must be big and clear enough to be identified in zero visibility using only touch; they must be firmly attached to the line by a knot or cable tie. This form of permanent junction marking is preferred to, but does not replace, the personal junction tags that divers can use; (see Ch.4.F.i) rather the diver should rely on both methods along with their own caving skills.

When setting up a junction or placing an airbell marker, a knot should be tied in the main line to create a loop that the other line can be linked into. If the line is too tight, the branch line can be larks footed around the main line and cable tied to prevent it from sliding. Alternatively the larks foot can be passed through the weave of the main line (if it is hawser laid). The out tag as described above is then placed on the exit line and the branch line is run out for a short distance and belayed to protect the junction point from being moved about by the branch line. Line laying then continues as normal. If a jump line to an air bell is being set up the main line is knotted in the same way and the jump line is run out, typically to a buoy belay in the airbell. It may be necessary to add another belay near to the junction to prevent the main line being pulled about by the jump line attached to a buoy belay when water levels change. It is very important that an out tag is added to this type of junction because a diver dropping down from an air bell can be easily disorientated, especially in poor visibility.

e. Safety

Safety during line laying is of paramount importance as there are many dangers which face the diver. The most likely danger is for the line to pull into an impenetrable bedding area. This can be avoided by good belaying, as described above. Unstable gravel slopes pose a hazard. Falling rocks are also an additional hazard either in boulder areas or in the roof of larger passages. The hazards of a boulder choke are self-evident in that the diver can be trapped by rocks disturbed when air replaces water around a rock. This sort of event is difficult to foresee and only careful examination of the roof can identify this hazard.

vi. Base-fed line laying techniques

Base-fed line laying is not often used in modern cave diving but under certain situations has some advantages over a diver-controlled reel. It is a useful method for initial, short penetrations, to see if a sump is "going to go". This is usually when a passage appears low or silty, making line reel management more difficult. If, during a base-fed dive the passage is found to be continuing the diver should return to base and use a diver-controlled reel, with belays, for future dives. Base-fed line techniques can also be used by two divers working together in a sump. One diver stays on the main line, controlling the line and the second diver searches or investigates a side passage. With practice this method can be used to carry out quick searches of multiple leads in a sump.

Base-fed line laying, as its name suggests, involves the line being controlled from a fixed base with the line attached to the diver around a wrist. Normally, base-fed penetrations are carried out feet first without fins. Most important is that the diver is only as safe as his attendants; a complex system of signals has little place in cave diving and the number of signals can best be limited to the so-called 'SUD' system, as follows:

1 = "S" = stop
2 = "U" = up (or take in slack line)
3 = "D" = down (or pay out line)

plus something distinct, e.g. 6 pulls, to mean "sump passed" and continuous tugging to indicate emergency.

The attendant will control the line from base, feeling the diver's movements all the time, paying out and taking in the line in response. If a system of signals has been agreed upon, the signal should always be returned by the person receiving it to show that it has been understood.

vii. Line removal

One of the most significant hazards a diver can face is loose line in a sump. This may occur owing to flood damage, bailer twine or rope washed in from surface streams or old line reels left in a sump deteriorating and spilling their contents. To reduce the risk to the divers visiting the sump all loose line should be removed as a priority.

For divers planning to remove loose line from a sump the choice of method used will be dictated by the nature of the line. If the line is tangled a tackle bag should be used (weighting the tackle bag can make this process easier to manage); larger tangles can be cut into sections to make stuffing easier. If the line is loose but not tangled a robust H frame will allow the diver to wind the line in quickly before visibility is reduced. The line is then secured with a snoopy or a cable tie. If a diver plans to remove an old reel from a sump a tackle bag can be used to hold the line securely on the reel as it is transported out of the sump, although care is needed to prevent spillage of the line when the reel is stuffed into the bag.

Whichever method is used, clearing tangled line in poor visibility can be extremely demanding and divers should be aware of the potential to cut or reel in the sound line.

viii. Conclusion

Whatever the conditions underwater, line laying is one of the most important skills that must be learned by a cave diver, whether or not exploration diving is anticipated. If a section of line is in an awkward position, or if a belay has been pulled off, or if the line is broken or badly worn, an attempt to repair or replace it must be made.

B)   Underwater cave surveying

An awareness of the directions taken by a cave passage is fundamental to safety in cave diving. It is vital that every cave diver should become familiar with the use of a compass very early in the training process. The production of an electronic or paper survey from routine "direction monitoring" information is not difficult and is a useful skill for cave divers to acquire. Underwater surveys are a valuable aid to continuing exploration, to the study of cave systems by scientists and as evidence when conservation measures are required or SSSI protection is being considered. In deep sumps, an accurate knowledge of the dive profile is vital for determining optimum gas mixtures, for the production of custom tables and for planning the details of the decompression phase of future dives. A good survey can prove extremely useful in the event of a rescue involving sumps, especially when information it can provide is required in an urgent situation.

Trainee cave divers who have never really been interested in surveying may find some of the following information a little off-putting. Don't attempt anything too ambitious to start with. A good first step is to practise on the surface, e.g. belay a 50 m loop of line in a field, survey it, draw it up and see how far apart the initial and final stations are. The size of the error divided by the total length of the loop (multiplied by 100) gives the "percentage misclosure", a valuable indicator of accuracy. Next, go into a dry phreatic cave (i.e. most similar to the passages in a sump) and find a horizontal loop to lay a carefully belayed line around, then survey it using the same techniques - there is no time pressure, so a good understanding can be developed. When this has been mastered, have a go in a sump, which has a well laid line and an existing published survey for comparison of results. Next, carry out a survey in a sump which has not yet been surveyed very well. This will be useful original work and may result in the discovery of new leads. All divers should get into the habit of surveying any new line laid. Laying out line may be very exciting on a personal level, but is not very interesting to the general caving community unless there is a survey to show where the passage goes.

Two methods of sump surveying have been developed for UK conditions: the basic method and the special method. The basic method utilises the standard equipment routinely carried by divers and can be done relatively quickly. The second method is used if a more precise survey is required. This uses specific survey equipment, takes longer and as such will usually be the main focus of a dive plan.

i.   Equipment

Before embarking on a survey, it is very important that the line be tagged at suitable intervals (usually every 5 or 10 m) before it is laid in the sump (see Section A.iii.c of this chapter). The tagged line is normally the guideline laid on the original exploration dive. This must thus be belayed without slack or it will lead to errors in subsequent surveys. If when laying the line, belays can be attached to coincide with the tags it greatly improves precision when measuring distances.

a.   Basic method

The instruments used for the basic method are normally carried by all divers for safety reasons, whether or not surveying is intended. They consist of:

- *Slate (as described in Ch.3.A.xiv).*
- *Diver's compass.*
- *Depth recorder.*

Slate: Prior to the dive the slate may be marked with a table for readings of distance, bearing and depth. This will help to keep the data clearly aligned, help fit more data onto the slate and reduce the chances of confusion when the slate is read after the dive.

Compass: A standard liquid filled diving compass is good enough for surveying in UK conditions. The resolution is typically limited to 5 degrees, but using an instrument capable of giving more precise readings is slower.

Note: although reading an instrument beyond its resolution is not ideal practice, experience has shown that doing so with a compass can result in more accurate surveys with less than 2% misclosure errors. This technique should be practised and tested in a sump that has a loop so that misclosure errors can be calculated.

Depth recording: All depth gauges used for UK cave diving are suitable for basic method surveying. They all have sufficient resolution for the accuracy required. If a dive computer or digital dive timer is used, it must be in freshwater mode.

b.   Special method

For the more accurate special survey method more precise measuring devices are needed. Although the same data for distance, direction and depth form the core of the survey, different equipment is used to take the measurements. This consists of:

- *Survey board and pencil.*
- *Plastic/fabric tape measure.*
- *Electronic depth recorder.*

Survey board: For more accurate surveying, a dedicated survey board can be constructed from a sheet of heavy-duty Formica or similar material, upon which the compass can be mounted. This can be held in front of the diver, and the edge of the board held close beside the line. The dive line is more precisely aligned alongside the longer edge of a survey board (compared with the relatively short edge of a typical dive compass), hence improving precision. There is more space available on the board for descriptive recording and additional instruments can be mounted if required. If this is made at standard A4 size it can be easily photocopied after diving to make a permanent record of the original information written on it whilst underwater. All such boards must have an attachment point to prevent loss underwater, or allow them to be safely clipped to the dive line whilst the diver is occupied by other underwater tasks. If carried underwater whilst clipped to the diver, such boards may cause line entanglement or the information on them may be accidentally rubbed off, so it may be better to carry them by hand whilst swimming along. It is also possible to construct both standard arm mounted slates and larger survey boards with multiple pages secured by shock cord "hinges" and page restrainers. These allow a much greater area on which to write, but the aspirant designer of more complex slates should always bear in mind the increased possibility of line entanglements. A survey slate or board should also have a mounting point to hold a pencil when it is not in use. The pencil itself should be attached to the slate or board by a lanyard that is long enough to allow the diver to write clearly across the whole area of the writing surface.

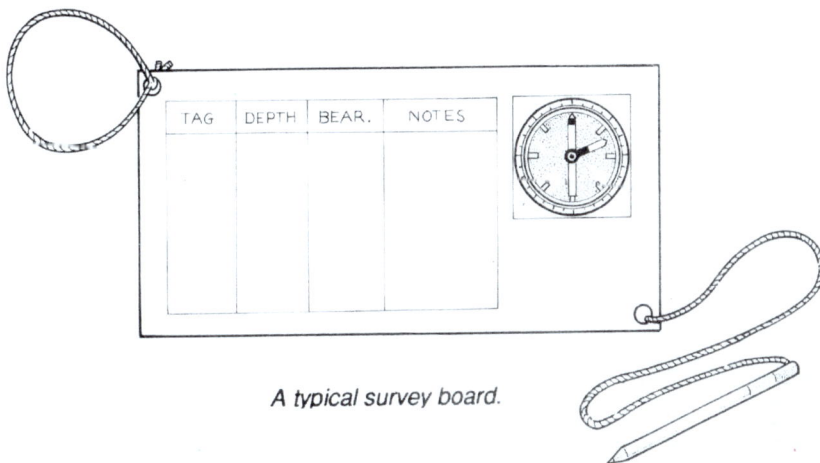

A typical survey board.

Plastic/fabric tape measure: More accurate survey leg lengths are measured with a plastic/fabric non stretch surveying tape fitted with a couple of clothes pegs. The pegs are attached to the diving line at a survey station before reeling it out to the next station. Once the distance is recorded the tape is pulled to detach the pegs (i.e. there is no need to swim back and forth). It is then reeled in before repeating the process over the next survey leg.

Depth recorder: For the special survey method only digital depth recorders offer sufficient resolution. As with the basic method dive computers and digital dive recorders have to be in freshwater mode.

ii.   Recording data

Experience has shown that, with a minimum of effort and a basic knowledge of surveying theory, it is possible to produce reasonably accurate surveys of sumps. The basic method is a compromise between speed and accuracy. Attempts at improving the accuracy tend to require a much more complicated and time-consuming technique, slowing the diver down so that a law of diminishing returns applies.

As with "dry" cave surveys, the aim is to produce a centre line onto which details of the passage are added. The former is more important than the latter; even in mediocre visibility it is possible to emerge from the sump with a list of bearings, distances and depths from which a survey of reasonable accuracy can be drawn. In UK sumps it may not always be easy to include much passage detail after a single dive; this can be added bit by bit later as familiarity grows over subsequent dives. If the diver has some prior experience of working on ordinary cave surveys, this makes things much easier (and provides one example of why a caving background is useful for aspiring cave divers).

To start a survey, the first station chosen should be the final station of any previous survey in the dry part of the cave, if working inwards from a dive base. More often the diver will be surveying back along a new section of line just laid. The "final" station of this survey will then be the point where that day's new line was laid from, which, if in dry passage, should correspond with the end of any previous survey. If the locations of previous survey stations are not known, choose an easily identifiable (permanent) feature and describe it in detail in the notes so that it can be tied in later, even if the dive line is destroyed by floods. It is useful if this station coincides with sump level, although at certain sites with fluctuating water levels this is obviously less meaningful.

All subsequent survey stations are chosen when the line changes direction (be it left, right, up or down) or some significant feature (belay, side passage etc) is encountered. At each survey station the following data is collected:

- Distance.
- Depth.
- Bearing.

Both distance and depth will have to be taken at the survey station to be accurate. Bearings will also be more accurate if taken at a survey station when the diver is stationary. The disturbance to visibility in the sump created by the diver may dictate that only forward bearings can be used. Deteriorating visibility will also limit the amount of time available to take the readings and write them down. When a reduction in visibility prevents the diver from taking all three readings at the survey station, the bearing can be taken whilst travelling along the leg to the next survey station, where it can be written down. A bearing taken by a diver on the move is likely to be less accurate than one taken when the diver is stationary. It is perhaps better to collect data with reduced accuracy than to collect incomplete data and end up with gaps, although missing information could be collected on a subsequent dive.

For the basic survey method: the diver will use the line tags as indicators of distance and estimate the survey leg length by judging how far from the previous tag the end of the survey leg is. The depth is recorded by placing the depth recorder next to the survey station. The bearing is taken by aligning the compass with the dive line. Care should be taken to ensure that the compass is sufficiently level to allow free movement of the needle.

For the special survey method: the diver will use the tape measure to establish the length of the survey leg. The tape is clipped to the dive line at the start of the leg with the clothes peg. The tape is then rolled out to the next survey station where a reading is taken. The depth is recorded by placing the electronic depth recorder next to the survey station. The bearing is recorded by aligning the long edge of the survey slate with dive line. Care should be taken to ensure that the compass is sufficiently level to allow free movement of the needle.

The data are written down in columns on the diver's slate. The method of data recording used by a diver must be consistent. Mixing different methods of data recording invites confusion when the data are read after the dive. The data recorded in this way will be enough to draw a line survey of the sump, providing useful directional and profile information.

On subsequent visits to the sump the basic line survey can be enhanced by recording information on passage cross sections, floor sediment type and any notable features. This can be done with the diver's slate, but the special survey board provides more space for information. If the visibility in the sump is good on the first survey dive then an attempt should be made to record as much passage information as possible, as collecting information on separate dives can lead to confusion between survey stations (but always beware that task loading may itself result in confusion, which can result in any data collected becoming unintelligible).

When any survey dive is over, great care should be taken to protect the data on the carry out of the cave. A second copy of the data should be taken either with a camera or in a waterproof notebook.

iii.   Errors

There is no such thing as a "good" or "bad" survey. No survey performed using the technique described will ever be 100% accurate. It does not matter what standards have been achieved as long as the published survey gives some indication of the expected accuracy. Ordinary cave surveys often have a B.C.R.A. Grade but this is perhaps less meaningful on a cave diver's survey since these grades were not designed to include underwater methods. One answer to this problem is to quote instead the instruments used and / or the typical "misclosures" of loops obtained. For example if, when the data is plotted for a survey of a 100 m loop of line, the final station is 2.4 m away from the initial station (which it ought to coincide with) then the misclosure is 2.4%. If the diver fully understands the process then many of the errors can be minimised and misclosures of less than 5% should be fairly easy to achieve. It is important that divers practise both the reading and making of underwater surveys to ensure that errors arise only from the limitations of the instruments rather than from poor technique.

Errors occur in each of the three measurements:

- *Directional.*
- *Distance.*
- *Depth.*

Directional: The main source of error is directional. Both the lining up and the reading of the compass require care. Most diving compasses are calibrated only to the nearest 5 degrees, so most bearings have to be estimated if greater resolution is wanted. Although day to day calibrations are probably not necessary, both the observer's ability to read the compass and the instrument itself should be checked periodically against a known true bearing. The difference between the true bearing and the recorded bearing is the correction factor which must be applied to all observations made. The diver should also be aware of errors caused by the proximity both of magnetic and/or magnetised items of equipment. Steel cylinders, knives etc. should all be checked, as should the potentially strong magnetic fields created by the bright diving lamps now in widespread use. Watch out also for compasses being deflected by the presence of naturally occurring ferrous minerals in the rock. Also, it is well established that long survey legs exacerbate directional errors. It is therefore perhaps wiser to split any sections of line more than about 20 m long into two shorter legs for the purposes of surveying. Finally, it is worth mentioning the apparently common mistake of reading the compass at each tag, rather than (correctly) at each deflection of the line. This can introduce very serious errors.

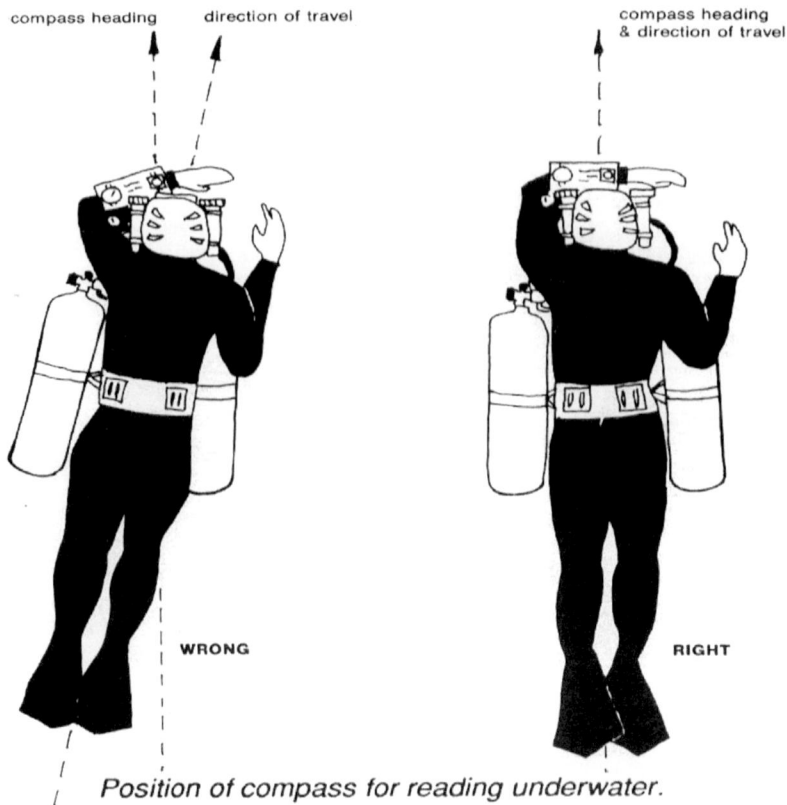

compass heading   direction of travel   compass heading & direction of travel

WRONG   RIGHT

Position of compass for reading underwater.

Distance: Distance errors should be fairly small. Experience has shown that when divers guess the distance of untagged lines they have laid, they usually over-estimate. For this reason it is now standard practice always to lay properly tagged lines on all exploration dives. When tagging the line, the total distance from the start of the line may be written on every tag to avoid confusion underwater. This is just as important for accuracy of surveying as for swimming the right way out after a lost line emergency (once the line has successfully been relocated). The total distance of any point in the sump is therefore known, allowing a useful check on estimates made while underwater. The hand-over-hand estimates of distance are a potential source of errors. Divers should constantly monitor these; e.g. if two legs between a couple of tags 10 m apart were estimated as "5 m" and "4 m" then a rapid alteration to, say, "5.5 m" and "4.5 m" would be an intelligent correction which could be carried out by the diver at the time (assuming no line had been used up in belaying around rocks). Such a compromise correction would be quite accurate if both legs had similar bearings - if their bearings are very different, then it might be worth using up extra gas going back to recheck (but watch gas margins!). Distance errors can also arise because synthetic lines may shrink (by as much as 10%!) when bathed in water (i.e. the sump). Pre-soaking lines before tagging (as with nylon SRT ropes before cutting to length) may therefore be worth considering. Station position errors can be minimised by frequent, careful belaying of the line (thus avoiding having to pick imprecise stations where the line has accidentally been caught on some rounded projection).

Depth: Mistakes in levelling are usually very small in sumps, provided that an accurate depth gauge/dive computer is used. Unlike a clinometer error in a dry passage, a depth gauge error is not transferred to all subsequent stations. The two ends of the sump will always be at the same level and a diver's survey will always show this. Note however that water surfaces in air bells may be below sump level. Very occasionally the water surface in an air bell may be above sump level. A "strange" depth gauge reading in an enclosed air bell may not therefore be incorrect! It is also worth mentioning that as modern dive computers can record the depth to +/- 10 cm, they can actually be used for measuring passage heights (by subtracting the ceiling depth from the floor depth).

If possible, loop closure should be carried out as an error check, as mentioned above. An artificial closed loop can of course be engineered by surveying back along the same line - or simply by taking back bearings if visibility allows. If a loop has been created by surveying through a sump to connect both ends with part of the dry survey in a cave then an important decision must be made about whether to bias the error correction more through the underwater data or to spread it throughout the whole of the above water and below water data. The more appropriate approach to this problem may not be as obvious as it appears. If the dry survey is done to a high grade and the sump was surveyed quickly by an inexperienced diver, then it is perhaps most sensible to assume that the above water survey is correct and adjust the underwater data to make them fit! However, many aspects of divers' surveys actually make them more reliable than dry surveys. Apart from more accurate levelling than is possible with a clinometer (see above) the total distance of the underwater traverse can be verified since there is a continuous measured line through it. Although a standard cave diver's survey might be expected to include misclosures of typically around 3% there are examples of very carefully conducted underwater surveys giving misclosures as small as 1%. In such circumstances it may be more meaningful to bias any corrections towards the dry cave survey data as the underwater details may well be more accurate!

iv.   Drawing up a survey

As mentioned above, it is wise to transfer pencil notes to a proper notebook (or photograph them) at the dive base before packing away the gear. In this way the diver has two copies of the data (i.e. at least one should survive the journey out!) and has the chance to consider any confusing items as soon as possible whilst the dive is very fresh in the memory. Other useful information can be recorded at this stage, such as date, visibility, water level, calibration data, etc. If the slate version of the data does survive the carry out then a direct record can be made by photocopying it before cleaning—in this way the actual notes made in the sump can be preserved for cross checking if necessary.

Before drawing the survey, all numerical data should be reduced to co-ordinates in the usual way. Alternatively it is possible to use the old fashioned method of constructing the line survey on (squared) paper with a protractor, ruler and pencil, although this gives a less accurate result. However there are plenty of "dry" cavers with the necessary skills who will help if asked. It is a simple matter to adapt a computer cave survey programme to accept depth information rather than clinometer readings. There are also several readily available shareware programmes which will do this directly (e.g. the excellent software known as "Survex", for a copy of which contact the BCRA Cave Surveying Group). The line survey can be presented either as a plan, or elevation, extended elevation, or all three (depending on the intended use of the survey). The extended elevation is a method of presentation often used to portray sumps. It presents the elevation as if all the bearings for each survey leg were the same (in plan view of this would look like a straight line), thus the full distance of each leg is shown. This converts the survey into a dive profile which can be used for calculating dive times, gas requirements and decompression plans. For deeper/longer sumps the extended elevation is invaluable to future divers.

BECK HEAD STREAM CAVE UPSTREAM SUMP
CLAPHAM, N.YORKS.

Plan, BCRA Grade 2, July 1994

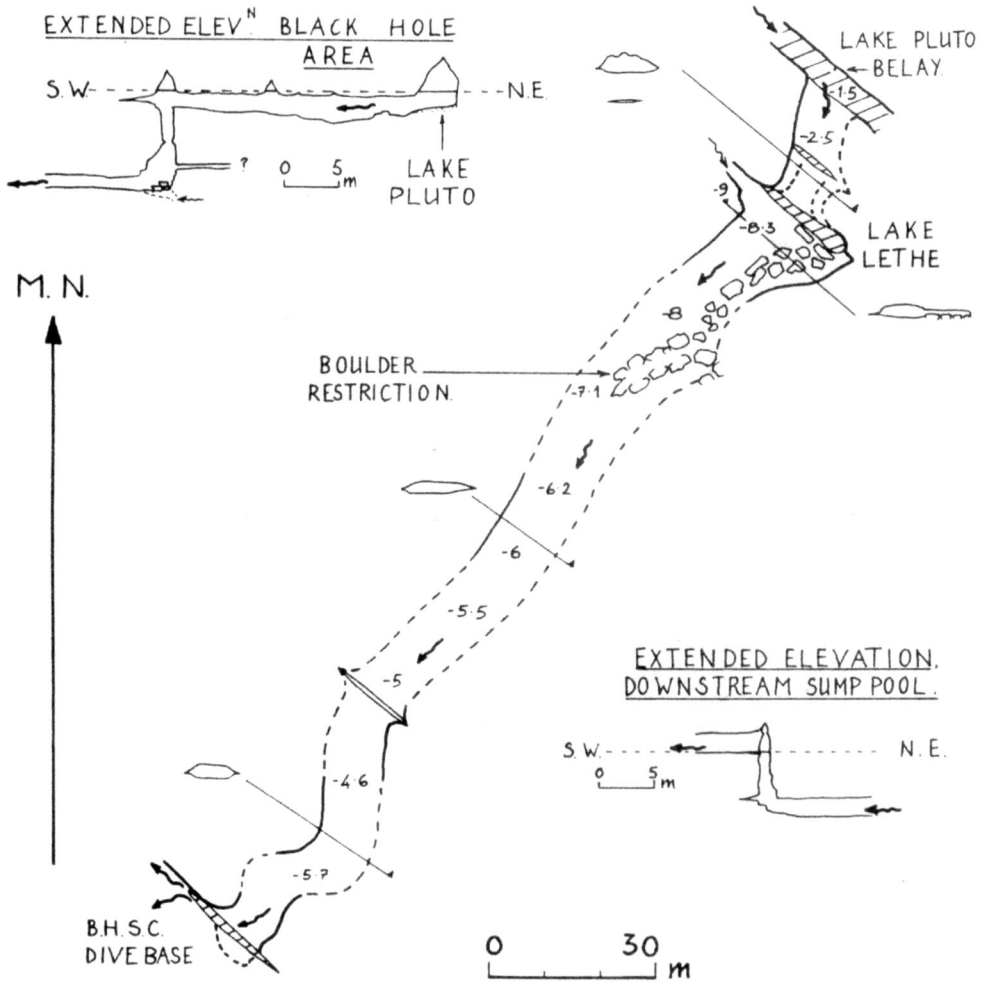

EXTENDED ELEV.^{N} BLACK HOLE AREA

S.W. --- N.E.

0 5 m

LAKE PLUTO

LAKE PLUTO BELAY

-1.5

-2.5

-.9

-8.3

LAKE LETHE

-8

M.N.

BOULDER RESTRICTION

-7.1

-6.2

-6

-5.5

EXTENDED ELEVATION, DOWNSTREAM SUMP POOL.

S.W. --- N.E.

0 5 m

-5

-4.6

-5.7

B.H.S.C. DIVE BASE

0 30 m

The next job is to add whatever passage detail is available. Do not draw in the walls unless they have definitely been observed and their distance from the centre line estimated—major leads have been ignored because of this in the past. In the early stages of a cave diving project this may mean that the survey might only consist of a centre line at first, but this is to be expected in British conditions. Interpretation of passage detail can be added bit by bit as the sump becomes more familiar to those exploring it. Any other useful information can be added as it becomes available, e.g. cross joints (take bearings if possible), side passages, permanent stations, radiolocation points, depths (on the plan), faults, decompression points, direction of current, flow markings, dip of the limestone beds, floor deposits and so on, depending on the scale of the drawing. The position of the diving line in the passage is often worth showing if the route taken by the divers is not obvious or straightforward. Adding cross sections may also be useful, to show how the passage shape changes. Don't forget to make it clear which direction the passage was viewed from when it was sketched and whether they are drawn at a larger scale than the main survey.

It is very important to label the survey clearly. It should have a title, scale, grid north arrow. This will vary slightly from the magnetic north which a compass responds to; check a recent O.S. map to work out the difference or obtain the current "magnetic deviation" from the British Geological Survey website. If the survey only has a magnetic North then it must include a date so that grid North at the time of survey can be established at a later date. Include some indication of its likely accuracy, typically using the normal survey grade system. A detailed underwater survey is more clearly drawn without the cross hatching which cavers normally use to depict sumps. Any symbols used should also be accompanied by a key; there is currently no international convention on symbols for use in flooded passages. However, as most of the features found above water also exist in sumps (e.g. sediments of assorted particle sizes, joints, bedding planes, large isolated boulders, and even formations) it makes sense to stick as far as possible to the agreed UIS symbols. One symbol which isn't needed is that indicating a draught, but direction of water flow and indeed layering of water masses are well worth including. There is a huge range of interesting features which the observant diver can record, and which can be usefully portrayed on the final drawing.

Having completed the drawing, there is one other vital step which is too often forgotten: making sure that the survey notes are stored safely and accessibly. Nothing should be thrown away, no matter how tatty and muddy. A very common mistake is to throw away or simply lose the original data once the survey has been drawn. The pages of a dry cave survey notebook or the photocopies of actual slate notes should be filed carefully away. Copies of the data should be made and stored in more than one place. Useful repositories are regional cave registries and the larger caving club libraries. The CDG library would be a good place for copies of sump survey notes. It may be appropriate to make the data available on a website (as well as, but not instead of, other methods of storage). Perhaps the best option would be to support the initiative to establish a national archive for cave survey data. This will have varying levels of security which can be specified by contributors. For further information contact the BCRA Cave Surveying Group. Wherever the copies of the data are kept it is worth publishing this information, e.g. in a dive log, so that people will be able to find it in future.

v.   Surveying beyond sumps

If time and the frequency of visits allow, dry passages beyond sumps should ideally be surveyed to BCRA Grade 5. This is not always possible, so faster methods may be necessary. Obviously, there is a trade-off between accuracy and time spent surveying but it is usually preferable to have a reasonable survey of all parts of a dry extension than a really precise survey of just a bit of it. A good compromise is to perform a Grade 2 (pace and compass) survey, with some of the stations later radio-located to correct errors. A Grade 2 survey can be done by a solo diver using standard equipment being carried for the dive. With practice, angles of inclination can be estimated fairly well, which improves the accuracy of any plan produced.

If radio location is not possible (owing to lack of availability, excessive depth, proximity of mineral veins or lava beds containing ferromagnesian minerals) and a full Grade 5 survey is impractical, the diver can produce a solo survey using a short piece of diving line. A measured 10 m length is cut from the reel and tied to a lead weight (from the diver's weight belt). The diver lays this out along the floor, takes a back bearing, then pulls the weight in before repeating the process. Shorter distances can be estimated quite well by folding the line into half, or quarters or indeed any other fraction of 10 metres. As mentioned previously, angles of inclination can be estimated or better still avoided by using the line and lead weight as a plumb bob to create vertical legs. This technique approximates to BCRA Grade 3, mainly because the compass can be aligned more reliably along the line than is possible when trying to sight along to the next (as yet undetermined) station in a Grade 2 survey. Alternatively a higher grade survey can be produce by multiple divers beyond a sump using standard caving survey techniques.

Radio location in a dry passage beyond a sump used to create a loop closure for surveying.

vi.   Availability of surveys

Most British cave divers who make surveys submit them for publication in the Cave Diving Group Newsletter. Another useful source of these surveys is in the regional sump indices, produced by the CDG on an occasional basis. All the UK caving areas are covered, and there are also some which describe underwater caves overseas. Surveys in these publications are not always very detailed as they are generally small. Accounts of more important discoveries made, along with larger scale surveys, are sometimes prepared for the journals of caving clubs of which the divers concerned are members. The most reliable source of information is undoubtedly by direct contact with the surveying diver(s), who may be able to supply larger drawings and the original data.

Chapter 6 Specialist skills and equipment

Temporary boulder support.

Once a diver has mastered the core skills used to dive a known sump and developed the line laying and surveying techniques used to explore new passage, some specialist skills and equipment may be needed to carry out project work. These skills may be aimed at collecting information in addition to what has been learnt from survey work or to apply scientific and digging techniques underwater. Information gained from these activities is important; it also represents a heavy commitment in time, effort and resources from the diver. Publishing this information so that it is not lost and at the same time becomes available is to the advantage of the wider caving community.

Information gained from published surveys and from other activities can be extremely valuable in a rescue. Active divers, with good local sump knowledge, will be the best candidates to attend a rescue call out involving flooded passage.

A)   Compressors

There are two types of compressor used for diving operations: low-pressure (LP) and high-pressure (HP). LP compressors have a working pressure of between 6 and 10 bar and are used for surface supply work. Owing to the nature of UK cave diving, surface supplies are rarely used. The high-pressure type is used to charge diving cylinders.

A compressor has several basic constituents: power source, compressor, filter units, air intake, supply whip and pressure relief valve.

i.   The power source

The power source can be one of three types:

- *Petrol engine.*
- *Electric motor.*
- *Diesel engine.*

Petrol engine: The unit most commonly used for compressors up to 200l/min is a petrol engine; it has the advantage of being light, reliable and relatively cheap, so it is suitable for use on portable compressors at diving sites.

Electric motor: Found in fixed installations; the larger compressors need a three-phase power supply. Electric units have the advantage of requiring little maintenance, have no exhaust fumes and are relatively quiet.

Diesel engine: Found on some portable compressors, usually those between 150 and 250 l/min, and on most fixed compressors above 200 l/min. They are economical, reliable, and are durable owing to their normally lower speeds, but have the disadvantages of weight and cost.

ii.   The compressor (HP)

A typical HP compressor will be a unit of multiple stages, using either air or water-cooling. The output, measured as the volume of free air, is directly related to the displacement of the first stage. The further stages only increase the output pressure.

Piston-type compressors require lubrication to the bearings and the pistons, as in a car engine. They require special non-toxic lubricating oil as recommended by the manufacturer, as some oil (as mist or vapour) is bound to contaminate the compressed air.

Air is heated by compression, so cooling is arranged between each stage and after the final stage. The cooling may be by air or water; the former is usual on portable units.

Also, water vapour is condensed by compression and further by cooling, so a water trap and drain valve will be included.

iii.   Filter unit

Filters clean the air after it has been compressed. Particles in the air and any impurities introduced by the compression process itself must be removed or reduced to a safe level, so that it can be breathed with no ill effect.

The filter system will be designed to remove:

- *Particles.*
- *Vapour.*
- *Contaminants.*

Particles: Are removed by a filter pad. A filter unit may have several filter pads to ensure separation between different filter materials and to clean any particles introduced by the previous layer.

Vapour: Is removed by a mechanical trap and/or a granular bed made of water absorbing material. The vapour is removed before the air is cleaned of contamination to prevent the contaminant filter being exhausted rapidly.

Contaminants: Are absorbed by a layer of activated carbon. Oil vapour (from the compressor) that has passed through the vapour trap is removed by the contaminant filter.

Some impurities will pass through a compressor filter. These include exhaust gases from petrol and diesel engines. Air from a compressor should not be considered to be clean just because it has been filtered.

The filter unit must be carefully and regularly maintained; to neglect this is dangerous. Some filter units use replacement packs; in all cases follow the maker's instructions. Where replacement packs are not used, replace the component parts in accordance with the manufacturer's instructions.

iv. Air intake

The air intake will contain a filter; this must be cleaned or replaced regularly. When setting up a compressor to pump absolute care must be taken to ensure that no exhaust fumes from petrol or diesel engines can pollute the air intake.

v. Relief valves

A working compressor should never be left unsupervised during pumping to ensure that cylinders are not over pressured. An additional safety net is provided by the relief valve; always check that it is set no higher than the filling pressure of the cylinder being filled—i.e. do not charge 200 bar cylinders through a relief valve set for 300 bar.

Compressors in operation with air intakes well away from the exhaust gases.

B)   Water Tracing for Divers

A detailed description of the various methods of tracing water from sink to resurgence(s) is beyond the scope of this manual; general information is widely available in existing caving literature. Cave divers, however are in a unique position as they can obtain far more comprehensive results (dry cavers do not have access to submerged hydrological junctions). Divers may also want to conduct their own tests in totally submerged systems. There are special problems to consider when using dye tracing equipment under water.

It is perhaps worth considering why cavers perform water tracing experiments. In most situations such work can provide useful information about two main aspects of water flow:

- *Proof of a connection between sink and resurgence(s).*
- *Estimates of average flow rate under the conditions of water flow when the test was conducted.*

The most important thing to do, right from the outset, is to obtain permission to conduct the test. This may involve contact with (variously) the Environment Agency, the local Water Authority, landowners (at sink and resurgence), or statutory conservation bodies if the cave is a Site of Special Scientific Interest (SSSI). It is worth going to some effort to get this right, otherwise when the results are published they may inadvertently create written evidence of wrongdoing.

i.   Water tracing agents

Water tracing agents are many and varied. They may be dissolved in water (dyes) or consist of neutrally buoyant particles (spores). In general they should be non-toxic, cheap, invisible to the naked eye, non-degradable, not absorbed by naturally occurring substances and easy to detect. There are standard formulae for working out how much of a particular agent to use.

ii.   Theory

Working in sumps with dye tracing materials has its own difficulties that may not be appreciated by non-divers with whom you are co-operating. A significant phenomenon to be aware of is water layering. It is well known that discrete water layers exist in sumps and that these often cannot be seen. For example, at the confluence of two passages the denser water will sink to the bottom of the passage further downstream, with the less dense water rising above it. If a detector is positioned on the floor in the denser water the dye may be flowing in the layer above; the detector may thus be negative even though dye has flowed down the same passage. This may help to explain some strange results obtained in the past. To be thorough, detectors should really be placed at several levels in a submerged passage.

Another problem to bear in mind in low flow conditions is that the detecting agent can actually move "upstream" into inlets by diffusion in static water layers trapped in the roof of long horizontal passages. A further complication occurs if the agent has to be released underwater in a sump. It is very difficult to avoid contamination of the diver's equipment and this may then contaminate detectors elsewhere in the cave, or even in other caves entered at a later date. The risk of self-contamination can be minimized, especially if a strong current exists, by facing downstream when releasing the agent and waiting for a pulse to sweep it away. In low flow conditions the use of a remote release system may be preferable. For reasons given above, the interpretation of water tracing results involving sumps needs special care.

iii.   Techniques

On first consideration the technique is simple—some kind of water tracing agent is poured into the sink and an attempt is made to detect it at one or more resurgences. In many cases, attempting a visual sighting will be unwise. It can be time consuming, more costly, involve unnecessary toxic concentrations and may upset local people, possibly resulting in widespread access problems. It is far better to leave the detecting devices at all potential resurgences for later collection and processing (the type of detector depends on the water tracing agents used). This technique allows a much more discreet operation with obvious advantages. Note that it is highly advisable to place some detectors for a period of time and then process these "blanks" before the main test is conducted. This is to check that there is no substance already in the water that could cause confusion, either occurring naturally or contamination from a test carried out by someone else.

Care is needed when installing detectors in sumps. There is potential for confusion so each one should be clearly numbered and its location written on a dive slate as it is placed. If another diver removes them later then there is no doubt about which detector is which. They should normally be attached to the diving line to avoid difficulties in retrieving them in poor visibility – this may not apply in cases where flood damage to lines is likely. It is often worth installing several detectors at each sampling point as they are easily lost or damaged in flood conditions and can be removed one at a time during a long term test. Choose specific detector locations with care, e.g. in the lee of a boulder rather than directly in the main current. Bear in mind also that a detector may be positively buoyant when it is installed and will float in the optimum position, but negative when it has become saturated and all air within it removed.

A special type of detector which has been developed for use in sumps is a large net to catch Lycopodium spores. Great care is needed when positioning these. Lead weights are useful, as is a good supply of inner tube loops or string for guying the nets in the correct position. On collection underwater, the whole net should be carefully placed into a large plastic bag that is then sealed; otherwise all the spores may be lost on the outward swim. Ideally, nets should be recovered in order, by different divers, working upstream.

When removing detectors, replacements should always be installed in case the dye has yet to flow past that particular sampling point. If multiple detectors were originally placed then just one can be brought out on each subsequent dive. At the processing stage beware of the concept of a "weak positive" – a detector is either positive or negative, the technique is not really quantitative. If there is the slightest doubt then the result must be recorded as negative and the test repeated, perhaps with a carefully considered increase in the amount of agent used.

Dealing with detectors in sumps is much more time consuming than in non-sumped passage. In addition there may be factors that prevent diving and thus delay in the recovery of detectors. If a series of tests are intended, for example, in a systematic attempt to define a catchment area for a major resurgence, it may be preferable to perform a multiple test using several different water tracing agents at the same time. This of course would require several different types of detector at each sampling point. Very good co-ordination is required between all participants involved. The test should be regarded as a major exercise requiring careful planning and management. In the long run it may well require less effort than a series of separate tests and because each tracer is released simultaneously, each individual sink is tested under identical water conditions. Thus the results may be more meaningful than if each test was carried out separately.

iv.   Recording results

Whatever the results of the test, even if apparently unsuccessful, it is very important that they should be recorded for the future benefit of others. Often, useful work has been done only to be lost from the records. The details of how the test was performed are every bit as important as the overall findings. There is a wide range of possible places for documenting the details of a test such as club or national caving journals, or the CDG Newsletter. The private records of individual caving clubs are another possible repository for information, perhaps with a brief note published in the CDG Newsletter or national journal referring the reader to that club's librarian. Failing to record information about water tracing may cause it to be lost to the wider caving community.

C)   Digging

The "Golden Age" of cave diving in the UK is over. There are now relatively few sites in this country that have not been well examined by several generations of cave divers. Although new discoveries continue to be made (sometimes even in the popular sites) cave divers have to work hard to find unexplored cave passage. As a general rule, the more remote the dive base, the less carefully the underwater passages beyond will have been inspected. Those divers who are able to organise carries (on a frequent basis) are more likely to be rewarded with unexplored passages. New discoveries will also continue to reveal the occasional new dive site.

Traditional cave digging techniques are now being adapted for underwater use. Changes in diving equipment and techniques have allowed divers to spend longer underwater with more time to carry out tasks. Digging underwater has many advantages compared with conventional dry digs. For example, the current often washes away some of the fine material, underwater digging can often be done when conditions prevent direct exploration elsewhere, flotation techniques are possible (e.g. airbags on boulders, airlifts for gravel etc.) and water lubricates drill bits very efficiently.

There are of course certain disadvantages in sump digging. Work might only be possible in specific water conditions (high flow is usually best) and normally only one person is able to work at the dig face because of disturbed sediment reducing visibility further back. Cylinder duration can limit the time available for work—especially if the site involves significant depth. Some restricted dig sites can be very hard on diving equipment. Care is needed regarding selection of digging equipment for use underwater, for example compressed air devices do present a risk of hearing damage.

i. Choice of project

Choice of project should be based on information that identifies the potential for further passage, accessibility and the type of techniques needed. Information is available through various literary sources and divers who have experience of the site. The level of support the dig will receive should also be considered. Dig sites require frequent visits and the normal system of access may not allow for this. It may be necessary to arrange special permission for access.

There are other factors to bear in mind when choosing a potential dig site. Perhaps the most important of these is water flow. As long as there is a good current, it does not really matter if it is a downstream or upstream dig. In the former, silt clouds will be sucked conveniently into the unexplored area beyond but if the water is coming towards the diver it will always be clear in front (though the journey back to base may be a dark experience). It can be a great advantage to choose a site which is best worked during high flow conditions, so it acts as a back up project for when visibility elsewhere is worse than expected.

ii. Safety

Special care is required when digging underwater. It is very easy to become absorbed in the work. Care should be taken to follow normal cave diving practice, particularly with regard to gas monitoring. A totally different approach to gas management is needed. A modification of the standard "thirds rule" (see Ch.2.D.iv.b) often used. Physical exertion after a long duration dive, even at relatively shallow depth, should be avoided. Consider leaving the heavy tools on site until the following day.

The dig itself may pose special dangers that are not immediately obvious. Roof stability is often difficult to ascertain. Limestone underwater is supported by water; this support will reduce suddenly when the air/water mixture caused by exhaust bubbles comes into contact with it. Delicately balanced slabs may fall down even if they have not been disturbed directly. A further problem may occur when divers spend any length of time at a dig site; gas pockets will form in any roof cavities and a hanging boulder may become totally surrounded by gas. This lack of support may cause the hanging boulder to move. One possible solution is to use a rebreather. It should be noted that artificial air pockets which develop during digging activities should not be breathed. They will contain less Oxygen and more carbon dioxide than normal. These gas pockets can be used to read instruments or repair equipment when the under water visibility has been reduced. For safety reasons the diver must continue to breathe from a regulator after surfacing.

If there is a need to dig upwards through boulders, the situation must be assessed to see whether this can actually be done safely. If there is a solid bedding plane that the diver can hide in whilst prodding with a scaffold pole, it may be possible to encourage some collapses in relative safety. Conversely, if total protection from falling boulders (bouncing sideways?) cannot be guaranteed then the best advice is to try somewhere else. If upward progress is possible in safety, some sort of shoring will usually be necessary. Scaffolding is convenient to use and is easily available, but must be erected properly. A diver should not undertake a project that involves scaffolding or other shoring without being practised in these techniques in a dry caving environment. Steep slopes of mobile gravel or pebbles also represent a hazard. Small disturbances can cause these to collapse and they are sometimes impossible to stabilise.

Another point to consider is line laying, both up to and within the dig. The line from the dig site back to base must be secure so that it can be relied on in zero visibility. The line in the actual dig needs very careful laying; keep it on the same side all the way and slightly away from the actual route the diver must follow. This will reduce the hazard of the diver becoming entangled whilst moving digging spoil backwards in reduced visibility. Large reels in digs can also present a hazard. Another method such as the lead weight, Derbyshire tube or the plastic bottle technique (see Ch.5.A.iii) can be used to reduce this hazard. Alternatively, base fed line may be used. Beware also of the line being chopped where boulders are being rolled around.

Diving equipment configuration is an important element of safety. Divers should ensure that the equipment is suitable for the duration of the planned dive. Some form of dry suit zip protection is desirable - a zip flap or even wearing a full oversuit. Greater equipment redundancy may also be planned such as carrying a spare mask. The ability to remove bottles underwater is very useful to allow the diver to exit back through squeezes passed whilst digging. The American sidemount system (see Ch.3.A.ix) is the most suitable. Wear and tear on equipment can be higher than in normal cave diving. Proper post dive inspection of equipment is therefore more important than normal.

Divers should always attempt to leave a dig site in a safe condition. Diggers have a responsibility to those that may follow, who may or may not know of the work being carried out at a particular site. If a site is left in a dangerous condition following digging, then it must be advertised in the CDG Newsletter.

iii.   Environmental considerations

Any cave digger should try to pursue their project responsibly. As well as having a moral duty to minimise damage to the cave environment, there is now a risk of breaking laws for which the penalties can be severe. An excellent source of information is the NCA's "Cave Conservation Handbook" (ISBN 0 9525520 1 9) published in 1997. The regional caving councils will also advise. If the potential dig is a Site of Special Scientific Interest then you MUST consult English Nature (EN), Countryside Council for Wales (CCW) or Scottish National Heritage (SNH) as appropriate. These bodies are familiar with such requests from cavers and are usually very helpful.

A site with potential archaeological importance may be scheduled as an Ancient Monument (SAM or Scheduled Ancient Monument). Some caves have this designation and as such are also protected legally. In such cases it is necessary to consult English Heritage, CADW (in Wales) or Historic Scotland.

Unfortunately, it is not always obvious that a site has been scheduled as an SSSI or SAM but it is your responsibility to find out. Advice on the status of any site can be obtained from the NCA or by contacting the statutory conservation agencies directly. Projects in SSSIs are usually approved without undue restrictions. EN, CCW and SNH do not want to discourage cave digging; indeed they usually recognise the value of this activity in opening new sites of scientific value. Digs in SAMs are more problematic owing to the nature of archaeological deposits.

If digging in an area that can be accessed by the general public, consideration should be given to minimising the impact of your work, particularly spoil storage.

iv.   Methods for different materials

a.   Specific Techniques

There is a large range of equipment and techniques available to the underwater digger. Most of these are adaptations of those commonly in use by dry cave diggers. The nature of the material causing the blockage will very much influence the approach to the problem:

Very fine sediments: Mud, silt and clay can present special problems since moving it normally results in dense silt clouds or even blackout. If there is a strong current however, just lying there wafting the floor with the hands will sometimes be enough to encourage the flowing water to transport the sediment away. Care should be taken when digging upstream, that it is not being deposited again in tight sections that must be passed on the way out. If the water will not shift this material then scraping it into bags for emptying elsewhere may be the best option. If the material is compacted, it can be loosened with a bar.

Sand: Much of the advice given immediately above also applies to moving sand. One particular danger is the ability of sand (in particular) to behave in a thixotropic manner. As progress is made it can "flow" in behind the diver, potentially blocking the way out - frequent checking is the only safeguard. Sand can also be scraped into bags for disposal, or moved to one side in bedding planes; a small improvised rake can be useful for this. If a dig site is just below the surface a method for moving a lot of sand in a short space of time is to use a pump; but it must be one designed for handling solids mixed with the water. A suitable cage fitted over the inlet of the (non-collapsible) suction hose is vital or larger particles will cause a breakdown. It is important not to try to suck up too much material at once or the pipe may become blocked. Beware also of getting a hand stuck on the end of the inlet hose; it is wise to have a side inlet pipe that can easily be opened by a quarter turn valve to allow release.

Gravel: Materials with particles the size of gravel or larger do not generally reduce visibility as much as those already mentioned. Scraping piles of gravel into bags for dumping elsewhere is probably the most effective approach. Some pumps will also cope with particles of this size. Small accumulations of gravel are therefore fairly easy to shift. When a strong current (in flood) flows steeply uphill it may leave dangerously unstable slopes of gravel or pebbles. Any disturbance may cause many tonnes of this material to slump suddenly. If the exit route involves a low arch at the bottom of the slope, entrapment is a possibility for a diver on the other side of it. Shoring is probably impossible and the only safe option may be to admit defeat. One very effective device for shifting large volumes of gravel is an "airlift". This consists of a rigid vertical pipe with a short flexible section on the bottom with a cage on the end into which air is fed (from a compressor on the surface). The air bubbling upward creates a rapid upward flow inside the tube that carries sand and gravel with it. A curved section of pipe at the top allows the outfall to be directed away from the dig. These are best used at sites that are very shallow with only a short distance between the dig and the compressor. It would be theoretically possible to use a small one supplied with air from diving cylinders, and which could be used a long way into a sump. Beware however that, just as fast as the material is being sucked up at the dig face, it is being emptied out again further back (and possibly filling in the route back to base).

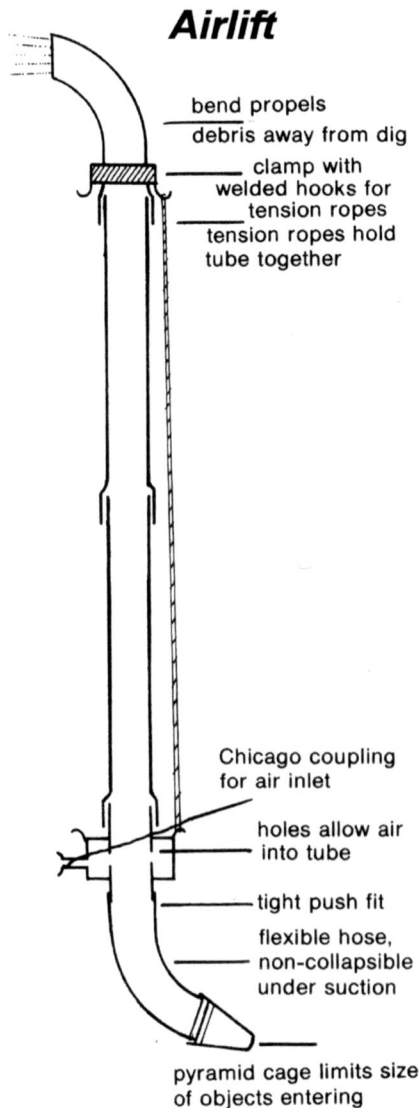

Airlift

bend propels debris away from dig

clamp with welded hooks for tension ropes

tension ropes hold tube together

Chicago coupling for air inlet

holes allow air into tube

tight push fit

flexible hose, non-collapsible under suction

pyramid cage limits size of objects entering

Pebbles and cobbles: Particles of sediment in this size range indicate very rapid water flow in flood conditions. Normally there will be little, if any, fine material deposited here so even fairly energetic digging may have no adverse effect on visibility. This, and the ease with which cobbles etc. can be picked up for packing into bags or a digging boat commonly used in dry digging, makes for fast progress in certain situations. Careful stacking of such material is needed because of its tendency to roll about. If a pile collapses into a low restriction it could block the route out - and this may not be noticed until it is time to return. Bagging up this sort of material in mesh bags helps stabilise the spoil heap.

Boulders: If a passage with a solid roof is blocked by rocks, especially ones that can be lifted by hand, quick and easy progress can be made. If there is a need to work upward in boulders then a greater degree of planning and equipment may be required. As mentioned earlier, scaffolding can be used effectively underwater for shoring but must be installed properly. A description of the safe use of scaffolding is beyond the scope of this Manual; seek expert advice. Plenty of different sized lengths need to be available to select from, together with both 90 degree scaffold clips and "swivels". Timber should be avoided for shoring; its buoyancy makes it difficult to handle and permanent submersion will cause rotting. Wherever boulders need to be moved, it is useful to have available a couple of short bars for levering, and a lump hammer and chisel are handy for trimming rocks when they will not quite fit through small gaps. The use of short scaffold tubes underneath boulders as (transverse) rollers or (longitudinal) sliders can be an advantage. Rolling boulders can be a hazard that can cause damage to a diver's equipment and can also trap a diver. Moving large boulders in dangerous situations should really only be contemplated by experienced cave divers who are totally happy digging in sumps, to allow full concentration on the work to be carried out. Plenty of practice beforehand (through a normal cave digging "apprenticeship") is invaluable. Never work under unsupported boulders; if the project cannot be pursued safely then abandon it (and warn others via the Cave Diving Group Newsletter). Before starting to move the boulders, a plan for spoil storage is needed. If there is insufficient space to store the boulders, the site will have poor potential. The space chosen for stacking will rapidly diminish if great care is not taken to put down each and every rock carefully in the optimum position. Try to build up piles of rocks safely; overlap them (like brickwork) to promote stability and try to save places at floor level for when you encounter really big rocks which cannot be lifted. Long narrow flakes can be used to bind piles of rocks firmly together as used in dry stone walls. If solid front walls are built then smaller material can be dropped in behind and is then safe from collapse. If the boulders are too heavy to be shifted by hand then there are numerous devices which can generate enough force to drag or push them. A scissor jack can be used to push rocks sideways out of the way. Placing a ringbolt in a boulder with a short chain of steel karabiners clipped on allows a crowbar to be used to give a mechanical advantage when levering against crevices in the floor or walls. Simple ratio systems using ropes and pulleys can be used, but are difficult to set up underwater. There is a variety of wire cable winches available. These usually require solid bolt anchors to be fitted and, if they do not have a method of releasing them when under tension, they must be attached to a bolt by a short sacrificial rope loop which can be cut with a knife. Inserting caving bolts underwater is very easy, but a heavier than normal lump hammer (e.g. 1 kg) will be found more effective. Some consideration needs to be given to the dangers of a flying cable in the event of bolt or cable failure. Laying a tackle bag over the wire (to slow it down) and having backup (non-tensioned) bolt belays are both methods to reduce this hazard. The pulling power can be doubled by using a "snatch block" pulley on the boulder. For moving the very largest boulders a chain block is needed. Unfortunately, these are very heavy and therefore difficult to transport a long way into a sump. For safety reasons they also need far more substantial anchor points than can be provided by the normal cavers' self-drilling bolt belays.

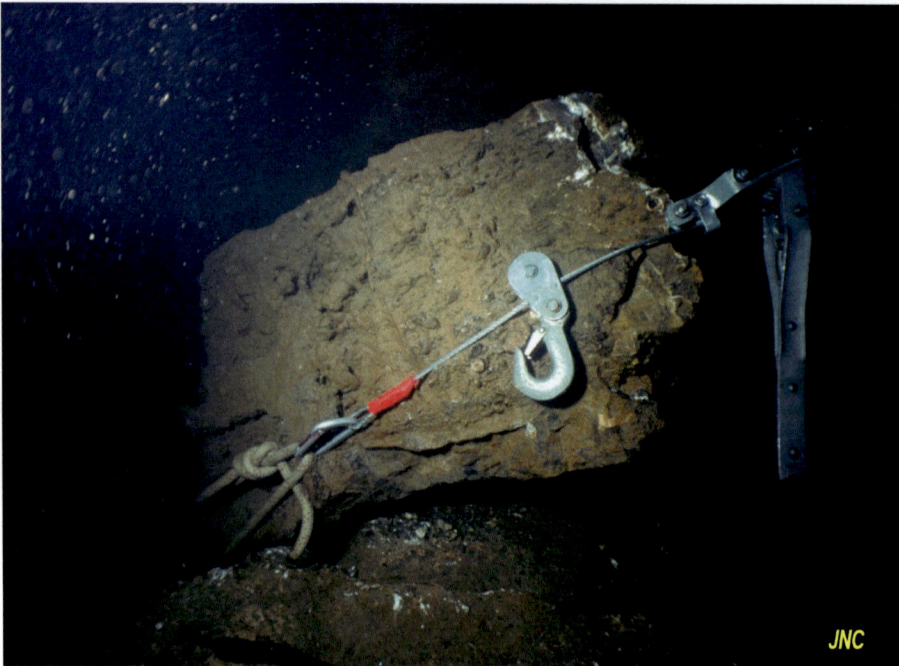

Moving rocks by winch requires careful pre-dive planning.

One alternative to the use of some of the heavy equipment suggested in the paragraph above is to get trapped air to reduce the effective weight of the rocks which need moving. This could be as simple as using ratchet straps to attach plastic drums to boulders which are then filled with air from the diver's breathing regulator (paying due regard to air margins). These should be attached in such a way that the filler cap is at the lowest possible position, so that the maximum amount of air can be blown into them. Open water style lifting bags can be used if there is sufficient headroom, but caving tackle bags lined with plastic bags (bin liners) are just as effective. The best designs of lift bag for cave use are low capacity with a wide body and a narrow mouth. Multiple bags are more controllable and require less height to use than one large bag with the same lift. It is important that divers do not get underneath the rock in case of failure. If a lift bag collides with the cave wall or roof during a lift, gas may be released from the bag and buoyancy lost. If there is an aven or high roof cross joint just back from the choke, a horizontal pull can be achieved by attaching airbags to a rope running horizontally through a pulley on a floor level belay. As the bags are filled they will lift and pull the rope through the pulley providing a side pull on the rock secured at the other end. Once the rock starts moving however, it can be difficult to control as the bags gain lift as they rise and the gas inside them expands. Considerable planning will be needed for this task to ensure that none of the divers involved will be trapped by any of the rock's possible final positions. Whenever a diver is using lift bags, the amount of buoyancy they provide must be controlled. Rocks can sometimes be stuck in mud and will therefore need more force to break them loose than will be required to lift them when they are free. This can cause the rock and bags to ascend rapidly and collide with a wall or the roof.

Bedrock: Solid limestone (or very large immovable boulders) may need to be broken up before moving. Flakes of rock and chert projections can be broken by the use of a hammer. Even more effective with flakes is the additional use of several wedges (e.g. chisels or feathers) hit in succession along the back of the flake. Plugs and feathers can be used to break off corners or split boulders. This requires several holes to be drilled (time consuming) and if the boulder will not split (because hammer blows are less powerful underwater) then the plugs and feathers cannot be recovered. In thinly bedded limestone great sheets of rock can sometimes be levered up or small boulders split where there is no room to swing a hammer effectively.

b.   Other approaches

Sometimes there are alternative ways of tackling an underwater obstacle. One obvious idea worth considering is whether the water can be removed to allow the dig to be conducted in the dry. One method of doing this permanently might involve digging a channel through sediments at the downstream end of the sump (but see "Environmental Considerations" above.) If flow is low then an electric submersible pump can be used. There are also several types of hand pump available, some of which are very effective. Any sump with an incline downward from its downstream end could be considered for siphoning. The tube used should be rigid enough to avoid collapsing and, as with all sump "emptying" methods described, a watch should be kept to ensure the sump does not fill up quietly and trap anyone on the wrong side.

v.   Spoil storage

Any spoil removed from the dig face needs to be moved as far as possible from the dig area. If not, the risk of it being moved back into the dig face is present. This can be due to the water flow washing material back in or by causing spoil to settle and move. It is less of a problem if the flow is from the dig area although in flood conditions the flow can have large eddy currents in it. If the flow is towards the dig face spoil will have to be moved upstream against the normal flow direction to a point where it is less likely to be washed back. Putting spoil the other side of a slope or down an alternative route at a junction can reduce the amount of backwash. If the dig face is in a descending passage, spoil can fall or roll back in to the dig area if not moved far enough away. In the case of rocks, cobbles and boulders these can be moved back along the passage and into a larger area of passage or into under-cuts. If a large amount of hard spoil is moved, it can be used to make dry stone walls in the sides of the passage. Care should be taken not to make an unstable wall. Loose spoil can be put into sand bags (sand bags should be of a man made fibre so they will not degrade and contaminate the environment) and then moved into larger passage or pushed into under-cuts. Whatever method is used be careful not to block the exit.

D)   Scientific cave diving

Pioneering divers took much more interest in the scientific aspect of the sump environment than many of those that followed. Developments in cave diving technique over the next few decades were aimed largely at the safe exploration of dry cave passages that lay beyond sumps. Cave divers in the UK would rarely have regarded themselves as scientists, although many were instrumental in mapping extensive cave systems that lay beneath the limestone hills of the major caving areas in the country. This added significantly to an understanding of the drainage network configurations in such Karst environments and helped reveal the hitherto unexpected complexity of such phreatic river systems.

The development of safer cave diving techniques has enabled cave divers to take a more refined interest in their subterranean surroundings. Under water caves provide one of the more faunally significant of cave habitats, with much of the food budget of cave systems being brought in by drip water or flowing streams and ending up within the phreas. Even in the early days of cave exploration, it was apparent that the divers shared the water with a diverse community of micro-fauna, several species of which proved to be trogloditic (genetically cave-adapted.)

Cave diving scientists throughout the world have recently been very active in original research and exploration in many sub-aquatic caves. There is a whole field of study in the phreatic zone of British caves waiting for interested cave divers with a scientific bent to come along.

i.   Biology

Underwater caves can be loosely divided into three types: freshwater, anchialine and marine. Marine caves have for some time been regarded with interest by biologists as containing species that might otherwise be less commonly found in more accessible areas of the open reef or sea floor. Marine caves often contain reversing tidal currents, and act effectively as underground tidal creeks. These currents can carry the sustenance for life far into the cave passages, allowing studies of the zonation and community structure of reef organisms to be made in comparative ease in an environment very similar to both the interior of shallow coral reefs and to darker depths in the surrounding seas.

Anchialine caves are "bodies of haline waters, usually with a restricted exposure to open air, always with more or less extensive submarine connections to the sea, and showing noticeable marine as well as terrestrial influences" (Jan Stock.) Although this is an extremely broad generalisation, these caves usually lie at or below the mixing zone between fresh and saline waters. Their isolation from both the freshwater cave environment and the marine environment (by both distance and degree of salinity) mean that in many cases a specialist fauna has evolved to fill the peculiar niches available in this isolated and stygian habitat.

The fauna and flora of freshwater cave systems are often a good indicator of water quality, and here hydrology and biology may link together in their ability to monitor pollution. The possibility of cave divers being able to locate and monitor pollution within an underground aquifer by improving the accuracy of sample distribution in less accessible areas of underground cave systems is one which has implications for the Third as well as the First World.

ii.   Geology

Caves provide excellent three-dimensional geological exposures without many of the problems affecting geological exposures on the surface. Accurate surveys of underwater caves can provide much geologically relevant information and simple, accurate geological observations made by non-specialists, such as the occurrence and orientation of fault breccia zones, changes in the colour of the passage walls etc. can be very helpful to the geological community. Rather than trying to identify geological material underwater, accurately located and orientated samples can be passed on to specialists for identification.

Karabiner used to show scale in picture

iii.   Hydrology

The study of phreatic passages by non-diving cave scientists has mainly been confined to drained relict conduits. The drawbacks of this approach have been neatly summarised by Lauritzen et al (1985): "This situation is a direct parallel to the case of anatomists dissecting a dead body rather than studying the living organism".

Cave diving provides the opportunity to study phreatic caves directly. Simple measurements and observations provide the cave science community with useful data to help understand both the processes occurring in active phreatic passages and to interpret correctly the evidence from drained relict conduits. Future advances in Karst hydrology will require considerable input from cave divers and cave diving scientists.

iv.   Techniques

Accurate note taking is a vital aspect of cave diving science. The simplest methods are generally the best. The use of a pencil and slate, usually with a pre-drawn grid ready to record the data, is the easiest and most successful method. As the diver's note taking can be erratic and affected by environmental factors, such as the cold and poor visibility, a prepared recording system on the diver's slate will minimise the risk of misinterpreting the records after the dive. The use of shorthand and abbreviations mean notes should be transcribed as soon as possible. A direct photocopy of the diver's slate should also be kept with the notes, so reference can always be made to the original records. It is advisable to supplement notes with a debriefing immediately after the dive and to keep a record of the debriefing with the notes made underwater.

Trying to undertake complex tasks on top of the already considerable stress load of cave diving can cause problems even for the most experienced diver. Task loading is a factor well known to produce errors in performance. Breaking down even a relatively simple task into a number of simple stages, often undertaken on separate dives, is the best strategy to avoid task overload on the diver. Tasks must be designed so they can easily be accomplished in the time frame of the dive and having a 'plan B' in place for every dive can allow some useful work to be achieved on an otherwise unproductive dive.

At all times ensuring the diver's safety is paramount. Cave diving safety should never be compromised and non-divers should take care to avoid putting a diver in a situation where there is pressure (on the diver) to complete a task which may compromise the diver's safety.

To conclude: this Manual does not require every cave diver to be substantially interested or expert in scientific matters that are peculiar to flooded caves. But a willingness to help out with observations, sample taking and other such tasks at the behest of a scientist is incumbent on us all.

E) Sump rescue

Caving is a hazardous sport and when something goes wrong the local volunteer cave rescue organisation (CRO) will be called out to rescue a caver in difficulty. The techniques used by the CRO have been developed from many years' experience to aid cavers in dry passage. Unfortunately some incidents happen in or beyond sumps and the CRO have no techniques for these incidents. It is up to the cave diving community to provide the diving skills needed for in—and beyond sump—rescues.

i. Cave diving rescue organisation in Britain

The CDG has no constitutional role in cave rescue. If divers volunteer their services to cave rescue teams then they do so as individuals. There are many cave rescue teams in the UK, all of which are represented on the British Cave Rescue Council. Sections of the Group do hold occasional rescue practices in conjunction with the local CRO branch. It is the aim of these practices to train divers for rescues specific to the region; this manual can only cover the subject in very general terms.

UK cave diving conditions are often very difficult with frequent bad visibility, many underwater restrictions, and an increasing number of long and deep sumps in remote locations. All of our main caving areas have long sumps with extensive dry passages beyond, in which conventional caving accidents are a real possibility. Two meetings, in 1986 and 1988, brought cave divers and cave rescuers together for the first time at national level, to work jointly on the serious problem of how to rescue injured persons through long and difficult sumps. The first meeting served mainly to highlight the main aspects of this problem. The second one concentrated on practical aspects of such work and examined the progress made in tackling the problems previously identified.

All rescue work in the UK is the responsibility of the police. Once alerted they are able to call on a variety of resources and specialist teams. In the event of a cave rescue, the police immediately contact a local cave rescue controller who then takes charge of the operation. Where cave divers are involved, an agreement exists that the divers concerned have the final say in what can or cannot be achieved by them.

There can be no hard and fast rules about the right or wrong way to perform a cave diving rescue. Individual circumstances will demand different specialised methods in each case. Those called out must be prepared to make important decisions on the basis of their own experience and judgement of the particular problems inherent in the situation, and to call for additional help and experience if necessary. Underwater cave rescues are at the extremes of cave rescue techniques.

Any diver on the call out list is advised to have current First Aid training as any casualty will be completely cut off from all medical help except that offered by divers. The same is true of dry cave rescue skills, because the CRO will be unable to get to an injured or trapped caver beyond a sump; only the rescue divers can get there and must therefore be competent in dry rescue techniques. The local CRO is the best point of contact for both types of training.

ii. Call out procedure

A list of named divers to be contacted in the event of a rescue call out should be maintained by each section. Divers living further away can also be contacted to be put on `standby' (it could be advisable for them to make their way to the site); their equipment may be of use, even if they themselves are not required to dive. In the case of a prolonged rescue operation backup divers may be needed. Each section should have a contact procedure agreed with the local CRO.

Before a rescue operation can be initiated in any caving situation, it is very important to carefully assess the circumstances and conditions. This is especially important when the extra hazard of water takes a role in the event. The water involved may be either in a passage which is normally flooded (a sump) or, alternatively, normally dry passage flooded owing to adverse weather conditions. A major factor to consider when deciding on the form that the rescue will take is whether the cavers involved are divers or non-divers.

iii. The role of divers

Each local CRO will have a procedure for divers to follow once they have been called out. This may involve going straight to the site and reporting to the controller or reporting to the rescue depot before going to the site.

At the site, the diver's equipment will be transported to the sump by the CRO along with any additional equipment from the CRO stores that may be needed, such as extra cylinders. The CRO will set up communications near the sump so that a dive controller can talk to the rescue controller. The job of dive controller will be done by a diver if possible, but if no diver is available a member of CRO will have to take on the role until a diver becomes available. The controller will note down who is diving, when they went in and out and how much gas they had going in, as well as what they were tasked to do and the results of the task.

It is important that all divers on the call out list are familiar with the diving equipment held by the rescue stores and the kit of other divers on the list as they may end up diving on some of it. In addition divers should be conversant with the use of the CRO communication equipment and be practised in the role of dive controller.

The rescue controller will brief the divers on the nature of the call out; this will dictate the course of action that the divers take. The choices are limited but to apply them to a specific cave will result in complications, any rescue plan will need to be thorough and flexible. The dive controller is responsible for making sure the plan is implemented by the divers, briefing each diver on what is required on the dive, debriefing them on their return and modifying the work required of follow-up divers to compensate for problems encountered.

iv. Rescue scenarios

The types of situation divers can expect to face are limited and fall into clear categories, each requiring a different rescue plan:

a. Non-divers

- *Supply to non-divers trapped by flooding.*
- *Removal of non-divers through flooded passage.*
- *Removal of an injured non-diver through flooded passage.*
- *Recovery of a body of a non-diver.*

b. Divers

- *Removal of an injured diver through a sump.*
- *Search for an overdue diver.*
- *Recovery of a body of a diver.*

a. Non-divers

Typically when cavers are overdue and trapped by flood water, the first job is to dive through the flooded passage (if possible) and search beyond for the cavers. If they are located, then a decision must be made to either supply them until the water levels drop or dive them out.

Supply to non-divers trapped by flooding: On finding a caver or group of cavers stranded by floodwater, the decision must be taken whether it is safer to try and take the cavers out of the cave or leave them until the water level drops. This decision is normally taken by the rescue controller, if time allows. If there is no immediate need for them to be evacuated (e.g. injury), it will be necessary for a supply of food and a source of warmth to be provided in case of a prolonged stay. In cold damp conditions, exposure can set in very quickly without the person concerned being aware of what is happening. Watertight rocket tubes make good carrying containers for food, etc. Some of the larger or more complex caves have permanent rescue `dumps' containing supplies and even in some cases telephones connected to safe areas of the cave where trapped cavers are likely to be.

Removal of non-divers through flooded passage: If the cavers are located in an area of the cave where it is not possible to sit out the weather, diving equipment will be needed to move them. The non-diver should be equipped with only essential kit to avoid any further confusion or alarm. This would include a single bottle and valve, mask, lights plenty of neoprene and fins if appropriate. A clear, concise explanation of what is going to happen and what is expected must be given. It is very important to stress that the valve MUST be kept in the mouth and breathed through, not through the nose. It must be stressed that the (non)-diver MUST NOT let go of the line. The (non)-diver should be placed between two divers who can act as guides through the sump. This is only advisable if the area to be passed is roomy and not too long. Careful consideration should be given to providing a more substantial line than divers normally use as an untrained diver is more likely to pull on the line.

Removal of an injured non-diver through flooded passage: If a non-diving caver is found to be injured beyond a sumped passage, their removal through the flooded area must be seen as a high risk undertaking and considered as a last resort. Any possible 'on the spot' first aid should be administered and the casualty should be strapped into a stretcher if unconscious. A full face mask should be provided as this will not need to be held by the casualty to maintain an airtight seal. If the casualty is conscious a standard valve and bottle can be used. One diver must be responsible for ensuring that the mouthpiece remains in the patient's mouth at all times throughout the dive; instructions to clear ears should also be given. Even if a caver appears to be unconscious it is still important to give a brief explanation of what is happening. Often the ability to hear remains after the ability to respond is lost, and panic induced by not realising the reason for being strapped down and the face being covered etc. could have a detrimental effect on the casualty's condition. In the case of a caver who is conscious, it is better to immobilise the injured limb(s) with splints and use standard cave diving gear.

Recovery of a body of a non-diver: The requirement for recovery of a non diver's body can be for two reasons: A caver who has been caught by flood water and washed into an area of sumped cave or, a caver who has drowned whilst crossing an area of water.

In the first instance this would require a diver or diver's (site dependent) to locate and recover the body. The body would be located (see choice of search pattern below) and should then be moved with care through the flooded passage. If it is possible two divers working together is the best solution one keeping in contact with the line and acting as a guide for the other moving the body.

In the second instance the body would most likely be in water that has an air surface. In this case a line can be used. This is attached to the body and a surface party can then haul the body clear of the water.

b. Divers

Again the most likely call out will be an overdue party or individual; the initial response will be either to search in a sump or pass a sump to search dry passage beyond. Information from this initial search will form the basis of the rescue plan.

Removal of an injured diver through a sump: If a diver is injured on the far side of a sump, diving out may be possible with the assistance of other divers. Having administered appropriate first aid and moved the injured diver to the sump using dry cave rescue techniques (see below), assistance should be given to kit up the injured diver with minimum equipment. The cylinders with the most gas should be selected from those available and given to the injured diver. If the sump is large enough, it may be possible to 'tow' the injured diver. This may be the best option if the injury prevents finning; this method will need extra exertion by the towing diver and will increase gas consumption. It is still important that the diver being helped maintains contact with the line. It is advisable to have a diver in front of and behind the injured party to guide and assist where necessary. It is important that the condition of the injured diver is assessed constantly for any signs of deterioration. A more seriously injured diver will need to be placed on a ridged stretcher and transported out. Unfortunately, passing some sumps would not be possible. There will then be a need to use a less riged stretcher or in some cases no stretcher whilst the casualty is towed. This must be seen as a last alternative.

Search for an overdue diver: A search for a missing diver or divers needs careful planning. It is obviously better to use divers who know the sump for the search. It is very important that the search is carried out in a methodical manner to reduce the risk of failing to search any area of the cave. Each rescue diver should be allocated a specific area/sump. This should not only ensure that all areas are checked but also that valuable time is not wasted with two rescue parties checking the same area. All `nooks and crannies' should be checked, however unlikely they may seem. It is possible that if a diver has become lost in a sump and located airspace off the main route, the diver may be awaiting assistance. (It is important for the search diver to continue to breathe from the demand valve when surfacing in an airbell. The air in the bell may not be breathable.) If the diver's equipment is working normally and air supplies allow, after initial checks of the diver's health and ability, the diver should be guided back to the line. If the available gas is inadequate, the choice will be between the search diver handing over a breathing set or going to collect another breathing set. If the later choice is made, a line must be installed with marked junctions between the lost diver and dive base. The decision to hand over a breathing set or collect another one will be based on the condition of the lost diver (hypothermia) and the amount and condition of the gas in the airbell, as well as the number of cylinders available at dive base. It is important that the risk to the search divers is always considered. If the missing diver has suffered equipment failure, the situation must be approached with care. The available Oxygen in a small airspace can be used up fairly quickly and if the stranded diver sees an available source of gas in the search diver's equipment then panic and desperation may overcome rational behaviour. Uncontrolled removal of a diver's regulator must be avoided at all cost, especially in a restricted sump where confusion could result in neither diver having adequate gas supply with tragic consequences. When searching for a missing diver, large gas margins are needed to allow for longer search periods and the emergency provision of gas in a situation similar to the above. If the missing diver is not located within the sump then any dry passage beyond must be explored in the same methodical manner. The search must continue until the missing diver is located. If the search parties locate the body of a missing diver, the risk involved to the search divers in retrieving the body must be considered. There is a precedent of a body being found, but left when retrieval proved too difficult without endangering the safety of others.

Choice of search pattern

Solo: Use when only one diver is available, or the sump has only one route that is restricted enough to allow the full section of the passage to be searched whilst maintaining contact with the line.

Pair: Use in single route sumps where the passages (or parts of the passage) are of wide enough section to prevent an effective search whilst maintaining contact with the line. One diver maintains contact with the line, whilst the second diver searches the cross-section, contact is maintained between the divers with high power lights or the diver on the line using base fed line techniques. The search line may be attached to a diver on the in situ line, or to the in situ line itself. This technique requires practice.

Multiple solo: Use in sumps with multiple possible routes which have small sections, allowing the passage to be searched whilst the diver maintains contact with the line. This search method requires very good record keeping by the dive controller, clear instructions to the searching divers and accurate reporting of dives from returning search divers.

Multiple pairs: Use in sumps with multiple routes through large enough sections to prevent the searching diver from maintaining contact with the line. The technique is the same as pair searching but with the control problems of multiple solo search patterns.

Recovery of a body of a diver: Recovery of a dead cave diver. This could be for two reasons: Recovering a body from a sump or, recovering a body from dry passage beyond a sump.

In recovering a cave diver's body from a sump (see choice of search pattern above) it is necessary to record as much detail as possible of the bodies location/situation. A record of the cylinder contents, any computer readings, status of lighting and the position of the line should be made; some or all of this information may be required by the coroner. The removal techniques are dependent on the sump (length and depth) in deep and/or long sumps some buoyancy compensation may be required.

The recovery of a body from beyond a sump can allow some preparation before moving the body. A body bag should be used to reduce the entanglement hazard created by the body. When a body has to be moved through a long/deep sump some form of buoyancy compensation attached to the body will be useful to reduce the physical workload on the divers.

<h4>v.   Rescue of injured party through dry passage only reachable via a sump</h4>

If a diver becomes injured beyond a sump, non-diving CRO members will not be able to reach the casualty; only divers. It is therefore important that divers on the call out list have a good grounding in cave rescue techniques, so that the injured caver can be moved through the dry passage to the sump. The local CRO is the best place to organise this training. This will typically involve an induction day followed by attending training and practice meets. Unfortunately, the techniques used by the CRO rely on a ready supply of equipment and manpower; neither will be available to divers trying to move a casualty beyond a sump. Self rescue methods underpinned by the principles used by the CRO are more likely to be possible.

<h4>vi.   Points to remember</h4>

- *An adequate supply of cylinders must be available. These should be as large as practical for the job in hand. If possible, the facility for refilling these should also be available close by.*
- *During a long rescue, divers should be rotated so that each diver dives for the minimum number of trips.*
- *On the journey to the sump, the divers should if at all possible go in empty handed with non-divers carrying their gear. This will leave them as fit as possible for the dive.*
- *If the non-divers are unused to carrying diving gear, they should be given instructions as to the need for care e.g. not dropping cylinders and not banging regulators heavily. This may be obvious to the cave diver but not necessarily a non-diver.*
- *On each rescue/recovery operation the divers at the scene decide if the tasks can be carried out safely or should be abandoned.*
- *All body recovery activities should only be carried out after proper consultation with the appropriate authorities on site. Not doing so may lead to the loss of evidence.*

Chapter 7 Awareness of mixed gases

Open circuit and rebreather divers on mixed gas.

This chapter has been written to meet the requirement of the CDG training standard to gain an understanding of mixed gases (see Appendix 1: CDG Documentation). As such the information contained does not provide sufficient detail to support a mixed gas training program. It is intended to provide only general background knowledge of the subject.

The information in this chapter is aimed at developing an understanding of the limitations of air as a breathing gas and when an alternative gas or combination of gases would be more appropriate. It is hoped that by using the information in this chapter, prospective mixed gas divers will be able to make informed decisions when deciding between alternative training routes.

A) Limitations of air

Air is the most commonly used gas in UK cave diving. The factors that limit its use on deep and/or long dives in other environments still apply to sumps, however in most UK sumps the depth or duration of immersion is such that the limitations of air are not encountered. Despite this there can still be advantages to using other gas mixtures. In a small number of UK sumps the limitations of air can be reached. At these sites a diver will have to use mixed gas diving techniques.

Air has four limiting factors:

- *Oxygen toxicity.*
- *Narcosis.*
- *Work of breathing.*
- *Decompression duration.*

Owing to the effects of Oxygen toxicity deep diving on air can result in convulsions and blackout with the inevitable risk of drowning. The depth at which this can happen is variable dependent on the individual, workload and environmental conditions. Because of the shallow nature of most UK sumps this is not normally a problem.

Commercial training agencies specify different depths at which Oxygen toxicity becomes an unacceptable risk. In all cases the risk increases with depth. To overcome this problem gas mixes can be blended with less Oxygen than air (20.9% at sea level), thereby reducing the risk of Oxygen toxicity at depth. Oxygen toxicity is dealt with in more detail in section F of this chapter.

Narcotic effects become problematic at much shallower depths than Oxygen toxicity. Narcosis can bring about a significant and detrimental temporary effect on a diver's mental capacity. Unfortunately the full extent of the reduction in mental capacity may only become fully apparent when a diver encounters a difficulty. Problem solving when "narced" (affected by narcosis) becomes more difficult; it takes longer and is more error prone. In severe cases the diver will be unable to cope with, or maybe even understand the situation. For a cave diver operating in an already challenging environment, with heavy task loading, difficulties and subsequent mistakes brought on by narcosis are an additional unwelcome hazard.

The factors that bring on Narcosis are related to:

- *Depth.*
- *Environmental conditions.*
- *Susceptibility of the diver (on that day).*
- *Relative narcotic effect of the breathing gas.*

Of these the last is the most influential. Air contains Nitrogen which is considered to be a moderately narcotic gas. Replacing some or all of the Nitrogen in air with Helium which has no narcotic effect reduces the risks posed by narcosis at depth. Work of breathing increases with depth as the higher ambient pressure makes the breathing gas denser and more difficult for the diver to inhale and exhale.

This increased work rate can be a contributing factor in occurrences of:

- *Oxygen poisoning.*
- *Narcosis.*
- *Decompression sickness.*
- *Increase in gas consumption.*

The solution is to breathe a less dense gas mixture at depth. Conveniently gas mixes containing Helium are less dense than air. Since the narcotic effect becomes a problem at a shallower depth than work of breathing, a diver using Helium to avoid narcosis should not suffer from increased work of breathing.

Long or deep dives will require decompression irrespective of the type of gas used. This can result in a diver being stationary in the water for a long time, so becoming cold and bored while off-gassing occurs. By replacing the Nitrogen or Helium with Oxygen during the decompression phase of the dive, the time in the water can be shortened. This is known as accelerated decompression. It is the most difficult mixed gas activity to plan for and execute.

B) Training and preparation

Before contemplating deep mixed gas cave diving, it is absolutely essential that the diver is completely "at home" both in the sump, and with the diving equipment to be used. Only then can problems be dealt with quickly and instinctively. The "incident pit", used to describe how a series of small problems can grow into one big one, is exacerbated by time pressure at depth.

Since mixed gas diving does not form part of the CDG training programme, the UK cave diver wishing to train in mixed gas diving, should have the following experience as a starting point:

- *Several years active cave diving exploration experience, including regular line laying.*
- *Completing a mixed gas training course with one of the training agencies.*
- *Familiarity with multiple cylinder configurations, including staging cylinders.*
- *The ability to undertake solo dives without feeling stressed or intimidated.*

Simply having attended a commercially organised open water based course, should not, in itself, be considered sufficient background to begin cave diving with mixed gas. Such a course will provide useful training for mixed gas use in open water and complement practical experience gained in the cave environment; it cannot deal with the special requirements of planning and carrying out a cave dive. To use mixed gas effectively in a cave diving environment a diver will have to apply safe cave diving practices and equipment configurations to the mixed gas plan. Commercial training agencies do offer mixed gas cave diver training courses but this will be based on a back mounted cylinder configuration. The practical skills learnt from such a course will have to be modified for a side mount configuration for UK cave diving.

The deep mixed gas diver should be totally autonomous; the concept of the diving "buddy" is irrelevant in this situation. Even though some psychological advantage may be gained from the company of another diver, there is very little that one diver can do to help another in the event of an emergency. Normal margins are unlikely to allow enough for gas sharing in a stressful situation at depth. An unconscious diver cannot be brought to the surface until the rescuer has completed the required decompression schedule. All UK cave divers should be self sufficient in all aspects of their dive plan and dive practice. This becomes more important as multiple gas mixtures add complication.

Whilst some types of mixed gas diving (Nitrox) can in some way be argued to improve safety for a diver, the serious nature of deep cave diving cannot be overstated. With the correct equipment, meticulous preparation and an organised approach, it is possible to use Helium based mixtures to extend the range of depth beyond that attainable on air. Even with this approach, procedures cannot be considered failsafe. With anything less, the practice is extremely dangerous. Proper and thorough training, practice and planning are vital for any UK cave diver considering the use of multiple mixed gases.

C) Partial pressure theory

Air provides the diver with a consistent, predicable gas that needs no other description, because the safe limits for depth and duration relating to the percentages of Oxygen and Nitrogen are known. When a breathing gas is blended from several gases the safe operating range for the mixture has to be calculated. Although the amounts of each gas in a mix will be expressed as a percentage, the calculation of the safe working range is best done using partial pressure theory.

To calculate the partial pressure of a gas, multiply the percentage of gas in the mix by the ambient pressure that it is being used at. Thus air on the surface (1 bar) has an Oxygen partial pressure of 0.21 (21% O2 x 1 bar) and at 20m (3 bar) this rises to 0.63, expressed as ppO2 0.63 or PO2 0.63.

To evaluate the correct gas mixture for a dive the highest acceptable partial pressure of the constituent gases at the maximum depth is converted into a percentage. The mixture is then described by these percentages and has a stated maximum safe working depth. For mixtures containing Oxygen, Helium and Nitrogen it is normal practice to calculate the safe percentage of Oxygen first and then calculate the percentage of Helium that will offset narcosis at the maximum planned depth.

D)   Types of breathing gas

i.   Nitrox

Nitrox consists of Oxygen and Nitrogen and is commonly used by the recreational diving community. As a result both the gas and training in its use are readily available. The training agencies offer courses based on the maximum percentage of O2 in the mix that the diver will be qualified to use. The actual percentage varies a little between agencies but most use 40%. Nitrox mixtures that contain more than 40% O2 are used for decompression and are covered by a separate course.

The main advantage of Nitrox is extended bottom time when compared with air. A lower Nitrogen partial pressure (than air) for the same depth results in a reduced tissue loading at depth. Decompression is required when a tissue cannot contain the absorbed gas as a diver ascends, requiring the diver to stop and allow the tissue to unload the stored gas. Because the tissue that would trigger the need for a decompression stop will have less gas loading from a dive using Nitrox, the diver will be able to spend longer at depth. Decompression will only be required after a longer dive.

Nitrox offers no advantages over air for reducing the narcotic effect (see Section 6.e of this chapter).

Manufacturer's of dive computers make a wide range of models that support Nitrox diving. Basic models will support the use of only one gas mix during a dive. More advanced models will support multiple mixtures, calculating the changing decompression requirements caused by gas switching during the dive.

The disadvantages of Nitrox are the shallower maximum depth that must be observed to avoid Oxygen poisoning and increased CO2 retention. Proper breathing becomes more important. The maximum depth for a Nitrox dive is dictated by the highest partial pressure of Oxygen a diver is willing to accept for the planned dive. For a normal dive in UK conditions the diver will typically work with maximum ppO2 of between 1.2 and 1.4 bar. For a dive that will involve a higher work load (such as digging) it may be prudent to reduce the ppO2 to 1.0 bar

The only special equipment considerations that need to be taken into account when using a Nitrox mixture containing 40% Oxygen or less are Oxygen clean cylinders and an Oxygen analyser (see section J.ii of this chapter).

Cylinders containing Nitrox should be labelled "Nitrox" and have the percentage of Oxygen marked; also the maximum safe working depth. The contents of a Nitrox cylinder must be checked when it is first filled and before it is used on a dive.

Rebreather diver in mainland European sump with mixed gas OC bailout.

116

ii.   Pure O2

Although referred to as pure O2 this gas mixture can contain anything from 41% to 100% Oxygen, the balance being made up with Nitrogen (or Helium). It is described by the percentage of Oxygen in the mix. Commonly used mixes are 60%, 80% and 100%. The description of mixtures containing above 41% Oxygen is an arbitrary decision which distinguishes between safety procedures required with different percentages of O2. Oxygen is a very reactive gas and to reduce the risks in handling it at high pressure the diving industry treats 41%O2 mixes as pure.

The main application for pure O2 gases is accelerated decompression. A higher percentage of Oxygen in the mix is used to replace some of the Nitrogen or Helium in the breathing gas used in the deeper part of the dive. The effect by which this works is called the Oxygen window (see Section H.iii of this chapter). Special dive tables or computer programs can be used to generate these tables including accelerated decompression. Dive computer manufacturer's make a wide range of computers that support accelerated decompression, mostly based on air or Nitrox as a bottom gas. Some support bottom gases including Helium. Training to use this type of gas mix is not as widely available as sub 40% Nitrox.

The biggest disadvantage when diving with these mixes is the high level of Oxygen exposure, leading to an increased risk of Oxygen toxicity. There is also the risk of switching to a high percentage O2 mix whilst at depth and exceeding the safe ppO2 limit for that mix.

The greatest reductions in decompression time happen when higher partial pressures of Oxygen are used. Decompression that is carried out at rest can reduce the chance of Oxygen toxicity. For this reason the safe ppO2 for resting decompression in UK sump conditions can be raised but the diver should still not exceed a ppO2 of 1.4 bar.

The biggest disadvantage of rich Oxygen mixes is the extremely reactive nature of Oxygen. To reduce the risk involved, special consideration must be given to all the equipment used with it. The cylinder and all parts of the demand valve (including the pressure gauge) must be Oxygen-clean and the clean status must be maintained. Any decanting or mixing of Oxygen should only be done by qualified people using Oxygen compatible equipment and very low gas flow rates.

Cylinders containing pure Oxygen should be labelled "Oxygen" or "Nitrox" and have the percentage of Oxygen marked on them as well as the maximum safe working depth. The contents of an Oxygen cylinder must be checked when it is filled and before it is used on a dive.

iii.   Trimix

Trimix consists of Oxygen, Helium and Nitrogen, described by the percentage of Oxygen first and then the percentage of Helium, e.g. a 15/35 Trimix contains 15% O2, 35% He; the balance is Nitrogen. Although many mixes are possible, the agencies typically only offer training in mixes suitable for diving down to a maximum depth of around 100 m.

The application for breathing gas containing Helium is deep diving. The Helium is used to replace the Nitrogen to reduce the narcotic effect of the gas at depth; it also reduces the work of breathing owing to its lower density. The percentage of Oxygen in the mix is selected to achieve the highest safe partial pressure at the maximum planned depth for the dive to minimise the decompression burden. This can result in a gas mix that not only has a maximum safe working depth but also a safe minimum working depth. This happens when there isn't enough Oxygen in the mix to support life until the PO2 reaches a safe level as depth increases. When using this type of mix a travel gas (normally Nitrox) is breathed by the diver until the safe working depth of the Trimix is reached.

Trimix is only available from a small number of outlets and is expensive, as is the training which is divided into several levels. Each level requires a separate course; previous qualification and experience with Nitrox, decompression techniques and pure O2 (advanced Nitrox). The different levels of qualification and the range of gas mixes they support vary between agencies. In general they fall into gases that can be breathed at the surface (O2 > 18%) called Normoxic Trimix or Normix and gases not breathable on the surface (O2< 18%) called Hypoxic Trimix. To further complicate matters some agencies also offer courses with O2 percentages of 21% or higher, these gas mixes allow the diver to reach depths in the region of 50m on a single mix with minimum narcosis. Access to training courses is usually restricted to divers with a specified number of dives to a stated depth/duration.

Helium is now used by a sufficiently large number of open water technical divers that equipment, computers, software and general theory now exist to support Trimix diving. It is more common for this type of diving to be done with rebreathers than open circuit equipment; although this adds more complexity, it does reduce the problems related to managing large quantities of gas. The number of cave diving sites in the UK where Trimix diving is needed is very low.

The deep diving advantages of Trimix can be gained only from the proper planning that comes from a thorough understanding based on good training, practice, broad background reading and a full understanding of the cave environment where the planned dive is to take place.

The disadvantages of Trimix are its complexity, cost and increased risk because the theory is less well tested than air or Nitrox. On a more practical level the mixed gas diver using Helium has to be aware that it behaves very differently from Nitrogen, offering new problems.

Greater heat transmission: Owing to smaller molecule size, which results in unavoidable heat loss from breathing; this effect can be reduced by using a rebreather. Any gas containing Helium is unsuitable for suit inflation because of heat transmission. Most Trimix divers will use Nitrox for suit inflation but some will carry a separate dedicated cylinder to supply suit inflation. The gas chosen for this will be air or Argon which gives better thermal protection.

High Pressure Nervous Syndrome (HPNS): This syndrome which manifests as uncontrollable tremors, multiple vision, muscle spasms and nausea occurs at depth of around 160m and beyond. It is thought to be caused by uneven gas absorption between nerve tissue and its casing. The effect can be reduced by including Nitrogen in the gas mix and having a slow rate of compression.

Hyperbaric Arthralgia: This is another direct pressure effect, probably involving differing gas partial pressures between the synovial fluid and cartilage of joints. This effect is not mitigated by the addition of narcotic gases such as Nitrogen. It is only of concern to divers venturing to depths beyond 150 metres.

Although more exact figures will be gained from the training course, typical figures for gas partial pressures are:

PO2: For the deepest part of the dive is between1.2 and 1.4 with an equivalent Nitrogen depth of 30m if possible (this is achieved by reducing the percentage of Nitrogen, adding Helium so that it has a partial pressure of Nitrogen the same as air at 30 m namely around 2.4).

PO2: For decompression and travel mix should be between 1.2 and 1.4 dependent on workload and the gas switch depth is planned so that the partial pressure of Nitrogen never increases at a gas switch (see Section H.ii of this chapter).

iv.   Heliox

Consisting of Oxygen and Helium, this mix is being used by a small number of divers on very deep dives (greater than 100 m) to simplify decompression modelling. It is a very specialist gas mix and there is very limited access to commercial training. Diving practice with this gas at extreme depth represents the limit of knowledge for recreational technical diving and as such should only be pursued by those with considerable experience of all other types of mixed gas diving and strong contacts within the commercial diving industry who are prepared to provide knowledge and support.

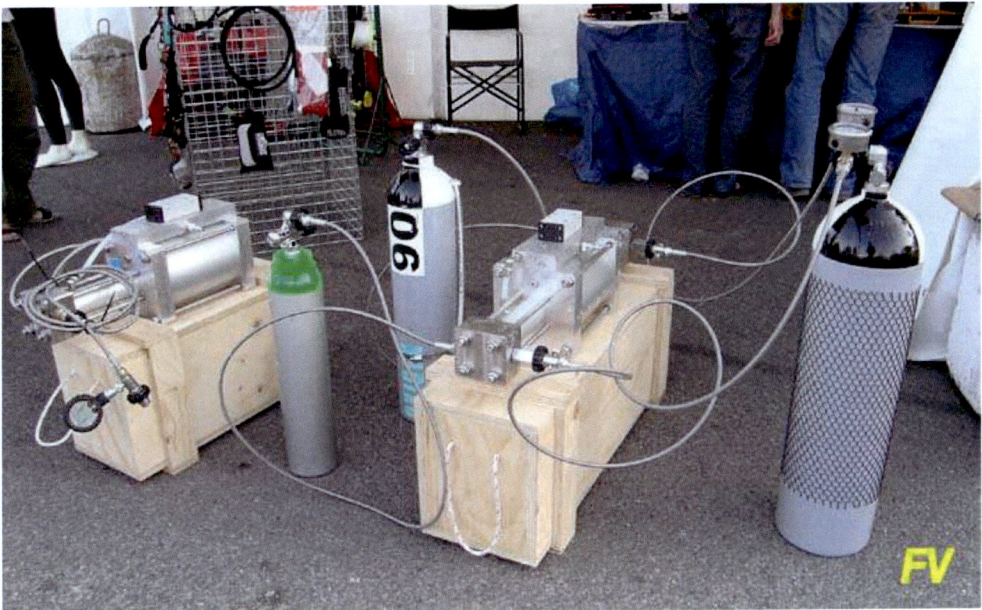

Gas boosters used in mixed gas cylinder filling.

E)   Gas choice

An experienced mixed gas diver will be able to choose the most appropriate gas type for a planned dive. For a diver with only background knowledge and no proper training the starting point for gas choice will be to identify the shortcomings of doing the planned dive on air.

When the correct gas type has been identified the diver can then go about training in the use of the selected gas and building diving experience with it. Training courses are organised in a hierarchical structure and each step has to be completed before the next can be started. The requirement to gain sufficient experience in the use of each gas type before training to use the next can make training a long process. In UK conditions Nitrox is the most commonly used mixed gas. Luckily this is the most basic level of mixed gas training and can be easily obtained.

Nitrox can be used for all UK cave dives that don't exceed the safe working depth of the mixture. Doing so reduces the diver's exposure to Nitrogen during the dive which may have decompression advantages. Divers who don't use Nitrox in place of air should consider doing so when the dive plan brings them close to or into decompression. The longer bottom times offered by Nitrox can provide a safety margin for an overdue diver who may still be able to surface without required stops. Avoiding decompression stops also reduces the amount of gas a diver has to carry to the sump and manage in the water.

When a dive plan cannot avoid decompression even with the use of Nitrox, the use of Oxygen for accelerated decompression should be considered. If the dive plan calls for decompression that is expected to include stops at more than one depth or that will take long enough for the diver to become chilled, accelerated decompression can be used to reduce this risk. The additional equipment and task loading can be justified by the need to do a thorough decompression. With dives that require decompression before surfacing there is an additional risk of a decompression injury. Having pure Oxygen available at the side of a sump and on the journey out of the cave may prove invaluable.

If the planned dive involves the diver having to go beyond the point at which they are comfortable with the level of narcosis on air then Trimix should be considered. This will make the dive plan very complex, involving more than one gas mixture and a carefully planned decompression schedule.

F)   Oxygen toxicity

As stated above, too much Oxygen in a breathing gas can create problems. The exact mechanism for this is not fully understood. The limits set by the diving industry have been identified by practical experience rather than from any solid theory. Knowledge gained from practical experience shows that the limits of Oxygen exposure vary between individuals and from day to day. Because of this the training agencies specify conservative figures for Oxygen exposure. As has already been stated even these figures may be viewed as high for a cave diver coping with the additional stress of UK sump conditions. For the non-saturation diver the type of Oxygen problem that is encountered is central nervous system toxicity (CNS toxicity). This can manifest itself as a reaction to an excessively high ppO2 or as a reaction to prolonged exposure to Oxygen where the ppO2 exceeds 0.5 bar over a period of time.

When a CNS toxicity event occurs the physical reactions are the same for both routes. The diver may suffer from convulsions, unusual vision, ringing in the ears, nausea, irritability and dizziness. The most serious of these is the first which could result in the diver drowning. The other symptoms should be treated as a warning of convulsions and the diver should switch to a low Oxygen mix immediately.

Whilst the reaction to excessive ppO2 can be easily predicted, (a ppO2 above 1.6 bar or a lower ppO2 with a high workload) the reaction resulting from prolonged exposure is less obvious. Thorough planning to predict the level of Oxygen exposure during the dive is needed. Using Oxygen exposure tables or a computer based program it is possible to calculate the percentage of allowed exposure for a 24 hour period. Comparing the duration the diver will spend breathing a ppO2 on a dive and adding all the values together results in an exposure figure. This type of exposure calculation is often referred to as the CNS clock. Results are expressed as a percentage with 100 percent representing the full 24 hour exposure. As exposure increases the chance of Oxygen toxicity increases. The potential for Oxygen toxicity also increases when the CNS clock percentage is rising fast, driven by a high ppO2.

The subject of Oxygen exposure calculations will be included in a mixed gas training courses. This forms one of the most important aspects of mixed gas dive planning, especially for deep dives where the dive time can bring the diver close to the limits during high Oxygen decompression. Correct gas mixture choice is needed to reduce the risk of Oxygen toxicity.

A major contributing factor that can make a diver more prone to Oxygen toxicity is CO_2 retention. If a diver is stressed, has a high workload or is simply breathing badly, CO_2 retention will be increased. It is therefore very important that a diver isn't too ambitious when planning the ppO2 levels.

G)   Relative gas narcosis

Gas narcosis, sometimes referred to as Nitrogen narcosis is the effect breathing a gas at elevated partial pressure has on the brain. A diver's susceptibility to narcosis varies between individuals and on a day to day basis. It is also influenced by other factors such as;

- *Temperature.*
- *Workload.*
- *Diver comfort.*
- *Stress levels.*
- *Work of breathing.*

When a diver suffers a narcotic episode, the effects can be equally varied. Some divers will become euphoric and over confident, some will suffer a panic attack and some may suffer from dizziness or vision problems as well as a variety of other problems. These symptoms will generally develop and increase severity as depth increases, starting with euphoria and dizziness or anxiety and confusion before vision problems start. For a solo cave diver narcosis can be a significant threat that may not always be obvious. When a dive is going as planned an experienced diver will not be under significant stress and will be able to control the dive even with some level of narcosis. If something goes wrong during the dive the stress level will inevitably raise; this may result in an increased rate of breathing and subsequent increase of narcosis.

The narcotic effect of gases increases with higher partial pressure and it starts as soon as the diver descends and increases until it becomes a problem. Since each individual will respond to narcosis at different depths, each diver who is considering deep diving should know the range of their narcotic limit. This will probably already be established over time by each individual whilst diving on air. When this depth is known the partial pressure of Nitrogen at that depth can be calculated.

As has been stated earlier the greatest factor influencing narcosis is the relative narcotic value of the breathing gas. The least narcotic gas is Helium, which is significantly less narcotic than Nitrogen.

Replacing Nitrogen with Helium will reduce the narcotic effect of a mixture. The narcotic limit is used to design a gas mix with a partial pressure of Nitrogen that a diver is confident with. When this is known, the relative percentages of Nitrogen and Helium can be calculated from the partial pressure of Nitrogen at the deepest point of the dive.

Although this considers only the narcotic affect of Nitrogen and Helium, there is also going to be Oxygen in the gas mixture. There has been some theoretical work done that shows that Oxygen is more narcotic than Nitrogen. Because of this, replacing Nitrogen with Oxygen is not considered to reduce the narcotic affect. Nitrox can be viewed as being as narcotic as air. When it comes to adding the percentage of Oxygen with the percentage of Nitrogen for calculating the relative narcotic value of a Trimix the approach is open to debate. Some divers do and some do not, depending on their training and background reading. If the Oxygen percentage is included in the narcotic calculation it should also be included when calculating the initial narcotic limit. Since the percentage of Oxygen in Trimix is likely to be below that of air, this may result in a less cautious gas mix.

H)   Special decompression considerations

i.   Decompression tables and programmes

A number of decompression tables have been produced by the military and commercial concerns, but in some cases these were closely guarded and unavailable to the amateur. Divers in the USA and the UK used the US Navy Surface Supply Tables (or partial pressure decompression tables), which allowed for variable Oxygen partial pressures, and could be used for open circuit Heliox. In France, the tables produced by the Ministere du Travail, for Heliox, were widely used. Also, Trimix tables were obtained from the Comex company and used in the cave diving field.

With the advent of Trimix and Nitrox decompression, an almost infinite number of dive profiles became reality. Processing of the large number of variables involved was perfectly suited to the application of the computer. Since the early nineties, an increasing number of decompression computer programmes have appeared on the market. These are extremely useful tools to the diver, provided their limitations are recognised. The programmes have been written using the formulae developed to represent decompression in the human body, formulae which have only been validated for a certain range of depth and time exposures. Using a computer, it is not necessary to stay within the limits of the ranges and decompression schedules can be computed for massive depth and time exposures. It is possible that this simple extrapolation may not be sufficient to calculate a safe decompression schedule beyond a certain range of values, even though the computer allows us to achieve this on paper. Guidance on which program to use can be gained from active mixed gas divers within the CDG or a mixed gas instructor.

To summarize: personal computer decompression programs will be invaluable for allowing the advance planning of a deep mix dive. Like dive computers, they cannot be considered to be infallible.

ii.   Isobaric counter diffusion

This term refers to the diffusion in opposite directions, through tissue, of gas molecules, at constant pressure. This can occur on re-ascent from a Helium mix dive. At a deep decompression stop, the diver switches to a Nitrox mix that replaces the Helium with Nitrogen with the intention of beginning the one way expulsion of Helium. A parallel effect of this switch is suddenly to increase the partial pressure of Nitrogen in the fluids surrounding the cells at present rapidly unloading Helium. This Nitrogen will tend to enter the cell very rapidly (due to the large difference in partial pressure between blood and tissue) down a concentration gradient. Even though the Helium can diffuse very fast, the Nitrogen is also highly soluble (and can enter cells very quickly) in the lipid cell membrane, so it can possibly enter the cell even faster than the Helium can leave. This results in a total gas pressure within the tissue which is greater than the ambient pressure, and bubble formation. The main consequence of this is that the gas partial pressures are additive with respect to their ability to form bubbles.

Research indicates that the bubbles form and cause damage to the cerebellum, the area of the brain which is responsible for processing the information from the vestibular apparatus (controlling balance). The symptoms are extremely serious for a diver in the water, and planning of the gas switches during ascent should take this into account. The most obvious way to avoid this occurrence is to reduce the partial pressure gradient of Nitrogen across the tissues. Here, Trimix has an obvious advantage over Heliox, as there is already an inherent partial pressure of Nitrogen in the cells during ascent. A balance must be sought between switching from the bottom mix as soon as possible, but not so soon as to expose tissues to a big leap in Nitrogen partial pressure. A switch should not increase the partial pressure of Nitrogen. Reductions in the percentage of Helium should be compensated for by increasing the percentage of Oxygen.

This type of DCS has a significant frequency in practice; it is not a hypothetical scenario and should be taken seriously. Several deaths which have occurred during Helium mix dives have been attributed to severe Nitrogen narcosis resulting from a deep gas switch to a high Nitrogen partial pressure. The possibility of vestibular DCS being a contributory cause of death in these cases cannot be ruled out.

iii.   Oxygen decompression and the oxygen window

During any dive, dissolved gases diffuse from the blood into the tissues and back again. This is a continuous process that results in a balanced level of dissolved gas between blood and tissue after a long enough period of time. When this balance point is reached the dissolved gases are still moving between the two but doing so at an equal rate. When the level of dissolved gas in either blood or tissue is higher than the other, more gas will move from the area of high gas into the area of low gas than will move in the opposite direction. This process appears as a simple migration of gas. The greater the difference in level of dissolved gas between blood and tissue, the faster the migration of dissolved gas appears to be.

An ascending diver will have more dissolved gas held in tissues than will be present in the blood; the gas in the blood escapes through the lungs. While the pressure on the diver is high enough, the gas will remain dissolved within the diver's tissue and slowly diffuse into the blood. If the diver tries to speed up the process by ascending further to reduce the amount of gas in the blood to increase the rate of migration, bubbles will form. The way to reduce the amount of dissolved gas in the blood compared with tissue without inducing bubble formation is for the diver to change breathing gas to one with a lower partial pressure of the gas in the tissue. The difference is usually made up with Oxygen. Doing this will increase the rate of migration of gas from the tissue into the blood.

The maximum amount of gas that can be held by any cell is dependent on the external pressure on it. The amount of gas held within a cell is a result of adding together all the quantities of gases dissolved in it. If the sum of all the dissolved gases exceeds the maximum amount that a cell can hold at the current depth a bubble will form. Increasing the amount of Oxygen to reduce the amount of another gas should therefore result in bubbles forming owing to the higher rate of migration (from the tissues into the blood) that will result. Fortunately not all gases dissolve in the blood in the same way; some take more space than others. Oxygen takes a lot of space when it dissolves in blood, although the majority of it is transported by the red blood cells and therefore isn't included in dissolved gas calculations. Oxygen is absorbed into the tissues as the blood circulates around the body and is replaced by Carbon Dioxide which takes very little space when it dissolves. This results in available space into which the gases from the tissues can dissolve without forming bubbles. The difference between the space taken up by the dissolved Oxygen and the dissolved Carbon Dioxide is referred to as the "Oxygen Window". It allows divers to undertake accelerated decompression.

Higher pressures will increase the size of the Oxygen window and allow faster off gassing. It is for this reason that a higher ppO2 is often used during the decompression phase of the dive and gas mixes are sometimes designed to maximise the ppO2 at each decompression stop.

iv.   Helium during decompression

Helium, which exists in the monatomic state, is very small and diffuses very rapidly compared with Nitrogen, but is considerably less soluble both in water and in lipid. We would therefore expect that Helium will enter the tissues more rapidly than Nitrogen, but that when a state of saturation is reached, the tissues will contain a greater quantity of Nitrogen.

This is more or less what occurs, although gas uptake into the bloodstream is completely limited by diffusion in the alveoli. For this reason, Helium loading of the tissues is far more rapid than for Nitrogen. So during dives of several hours duration, the bloodstream and tissue compartments will contain more Helium than Nitrogen.

Helium uptake into the compartments with shorter half times is very fast, and on re-ascent this Helium is unloaded equally as rapidly. For this reason these compartments will only tolerate a small overpressure ratio before super saturation occurs and bubbles form. As a result, the first stops on re-ascent are at greater depth, and ascent rates are more critical and slower when diving with Helium.

At the deeper, Helium directed stops, Nitrogen uptake will continue for some tissue compartments.

This is then unloaded as shallower depths are reached, and the much longer stops of the "director compartments" controlled by Nitrogen release are commenced.

Decompression during Helium mix diving can be made safer and more efficient by the use of gas switches to one or more Nitrox mixes during ascent, and then to pure Oxygen for the final 6 and 3 metre stops. The result is a one way flushing of Helium from the body and an increased tissue partial pressure of Oxygen. This makes use of the Oxygen window effect.

At this point it may be useful to explain the relative decompression times required for the various gases. It has already been seen that Helium, with its rapid diffusion rate, has faster tissue compartments. It therefore stands to reason that all compartments will become saturated with Helium faster than they will for Nitrogen. During this phase, which represents about 120 minutes of bottom time on a deep dive, the Nitrogen compartments will off-gas faster than those for Helium. For longer bottom times, the Nitrogen compartments will eventually become saturated, and will then exceed the Helium times for off-gassing.

Thus, for normal cave diving exposures, we can use the relationship for decompression times:

Nitrox (air) < Trimix   <   Heliox

From a purely practical point of view, Trimix is cheaper to produce because Helium is decanted as the first gas at lower pressures, and in lower percentage proportions.

I)   Gas planning and usage

Planning of every detail of a mixed gas dive, and adhering to that plan if possible, are the first steps in carrying out a safe dive. The level of planning required will vary with the types of gas or gases to be used.

For a single mix Nitrox dive, the maximum percentage of O2 will be dictated by the sump profile (if known). The ppO2 at the deepest point should be equal to or less than the diver's chosen maximum safe level. If the dive plan could result in the diver going deeper than the current deepest point of a sump, a gas mix with a lower percentage O2 should be selected to allow for this. During the dive the diver can then explore into deeper passage. On no account should the diver exceed the safe working depth of the mix as calculated from pre-dive analysis. The percentage CNS for the profile should also be calculated based on the sump profile. For an un-surveyed sump this will be difficult unless the diver has access to a profile download from a dive computer from a previous dive in the sump. With no access to profile the CNS percentage can be (over) estimated using the maximum depth and the anticipated dive time to provide a square profile. If this results in a high CNS percentage the dive can be re-planned with a lower percentage of O2 until a dive has been completed and improved profile information is available. All other aspects of planning the dive will be the same as an air dive.

For multiple mix Nitrox dives that allow the diver to carry out accelerated decompression or tailor the gas mix to reduce decompression additional planning is required. As with Nitrox (above) the maximum working depth for each mix and the CNS exposure for the whole dive should be calculated. In addition a decompression schedule for the profile and predicted dive time should be calculated. This should include additional schedules for increased run time or the failure of any one of the breathing gas supplies. Next the total amount of gas needed will have to be calculated. Unlike planning a no stop dive the gas margins must take into account the possible additional amount that will be needed if a diver is forced to do a longer decompression by the failure of a high percentage O2 mix. The gas supply plan should also ensure that the diver always has two independent breathable gas supplies at any point on the dive. On Nitrox dives this will mean that two cylinders of the lowest percentage mix are taken. For some profiles it may be easier also to carry two cylinders of high percentage mix rather than rely on breathing the weaker mix for longer in the event of an equipment failure.

Trimix dive planning introduces increased complexity. Firstly, the diver will need to decide on the bottom mix to be used. To do this, the diver will need to balance the degree of impairment by narcosis, length of decompression, Oxygen partial pressure limits, and cold, to arrive at a suitable Trimix for the depth to be dived. As has been discussed already, the diver will already have personal limits for Oxygen exposure and levels of narcosis. The mixes to be used should be based on the sump profile information available. Unlike open water diving, the cave diver may have to travel horizontally for some time before descending to the deepest point on the dive. This can have a significant effect on the decompression requirements for the profile. The bottom mix will normally be calculated first to minimise the accumulation of decompression time whilst staying within the O2 and narcotic limits. From this mix the diver will be able to decide if a travel Nitrox is needed. The percentage of Nitrogen in this must be chosen to avoid a possible isobaric counter diffusion bend as it will be used on the return. A high percentage Nitrox mix can then be chosen for the shallower accelerated decompression phase of the dive. This will include plans for:-

- *At what depth to switch to Nitrox on ascent, considering isobaric counter diffusion.*
- *How many Nitrox mixes will be used during ascent. This will depend on how many cylinders and regulators are available and how complex the diver wishes to make the dive.*
- *Will pure Oxygen be used for the 3 metre and 6 metre stops?*

Then, having completed the dive plan, the Oxygen exposure will need to be tracked to check that it is within CNS limits. If not, the decompression profile may be modified to reduce the exposure to Oxygen, for example, by completing the 3 and 6 metre stops breathing a lower percentage of Oxygen.

The total gas consumption during each stage of the dive will need to be calculated. Two breathable gas mixes must be available at all times. Quantities of decompression gas should allow for extended decompression resulting from longer bottom time or failure of other decompression gas supplies. For dives planned with multiple decompression cylinders, a regulator failure during the decompression phase is not as critical as is the case on the main gas supply. A decompression schedule involving 3 or 4 different Nitrox mixes each in a single cylinder is more difficult to plan and execute during ascent. Planning for a slightly longer decompression phase supported by few different mixes can simplify the dive if the diver can maintain warmth. When planning this sort of deep mixed gas dive, for safety's sake keep it as simple as possible.

J) Special equipment considerations

The equipment requirements for a mixed gas dive are different from those for an air dive. Some of the equipment must be compatible with high percentages of Oxygen for the dive or beforehand during the gas mixing process. Decompression places an extra dependence on some items of equipment, creating a need for additional redundancy compared with an air dive. Additional hazards are also introduced by having a range of different gases to breathe from. To be able to conduct a dive safely, a diver must be able to analyse the breathing gases to be used before the dive and be able to select the correct gas at any depth on the dive.

i.   Oxygen cleaning

The scuba industry has developed a system of "Oxygen cleaning" to reduce the risks of handling high percentages of Oxygen at high pressures. The status of "Oxygen clean" is reserved for equipment that has been prepared and chemically cleaned so that there will be no Hydrocarbons or other material present that will react with high pressure pure Oxygen. Equipment preparation involves replacing some components with a more Oxygen friendly material. This can include;

- *Metal items. Typically in cylinder valves which can release tiny shards when damaged by high pressure gases. With air this doesn't cause any problems but can start an Oxygen fire.*
- *Soft materials. O-rings, diaphragms and hose linings suitable for air diving may degrade faster in a high Oxygen environment creating deposits that can block filters and fuel fires as well as shortening the reliable life of the equipment.*
- *Oxygen grease. Standard silicon grease used for air diving equipment is not considered suitable by the scuba industry for a high percentage Oxygen environment. Special grades of Oxygen compatible grease are available that reduce the risk of Oxygen fire.*

The chemical cleaning process involves stripping equipment down and cleaning it as would be done for a normal service. Then an additional wash with a light acid solution is used to remove any traces of hydrocarbons before drying. For a piece of equipment to be considered as Oxygen clean both stages must be completed initially but for subsequent cleans only a standard service (with Oxygen compatible parts) and a chemical wash is needed.

Once equipment has Oxygen clean status, there are limitations on how it can be used. Breaching these limitations increases the risk of an Oxygen fire. For equipment that will be used at high pressure special marking are used. For cylinders this means an Oxygen clean sticker that records who carried out the clean and how long it is valid for. At the time of writing, in the UK, cylinders have to be re-cleaned every year. Oxygen clean status is needed for any cylinder that will carry either pure Oxygen or be filled using the partial pressure method as pure Oxygen will be used. Other items such as demand valves will have to be cleaned in the same way and maintained as clean by special handling. They are usually marked by replacing some external black plastic components with green components during the initial clean. For maintenance the standard service kit is replaced with an Oxygen compatible kit.

Not all equipment that may come into contact with Oxygen rich gas can be converted to Oxygen compatible status. Oil filled gauges must be replaced with dry gauges. Manufactures of buoyancy compensators and dry suits will specify a maximum percentage of Oxygen tolerance.

ii.   Gas analysers

When a gas is first mixed, the contents of the cylinder will be analysed and marked on the cylinder. The diver will normally confirm the gas mix using a separate set of equipment at this point. In addition the gas will again be analysed just before the dive. For the UK cave diver this may mean testing the gas several hours before the dive if the chosen dive site is located a long way underground.

Analysers used for diving gases measure Oxygen and Helium; the former are the more common and the latter are rare. Oxygen sensors use a galvanic cell to give a voltage reading that can be calibrated to read as percentage of Oxygen. The sensors have a limited life and will need replacing as they become unable to measure high percentages of Oxygen. Calibration is done against air or pure Oxygen. Helium analysers work by comparing the temperature variation between the test gas and a sample gas. Because Helium conducts heat at a high rate, it is possible to calculate the percentage of Helium in a gas mix by measuring the different thermal characteristics of the two gases. Other methods of estimating the percentage of Helium in a gas mix will be covered in a mixed gas course.

iii.   Equipment preparation

To overcome some of the additional hazards of mixed gas diving, a diver will have to develop a new equipment configuration and some new diving procedures. As the number and size of cylinders carrying different gases will vary for dives at different sites, the diver's configuration will vary for different dives. To reduce the risks created by varying configurations, the diver should develop a core configuration which will allow the diver to carry multiple stages. With a basic core configuration the diver will be able to plan for the specific needs of each dive.

For a dive that replaces air with Nitrox to avoid the need for decompression stops, minimal additional equipment preparation will be required. The basic cave diving equipment configuration can be used with two Oxygen clean cylinders. Nitrox tables (hard copy or computer based) or a Nitrox capable dive computer is used to plan the dive. During the dive, a standard dive timer or a Nitrox dive computer can be used if the dive deviates from the plan. If part of the plan is to enter unexplored passage two means of measuring depth should be taken. In the event of one failing, the diver will still be able to stay above the maximum safe working depth of the Nitrox mix.

Dives that include accelerated decompression introduce the risk of gas switching and required decompression stops at multiple depths. Switching from a gas with a low ppO2 to a high ppO2 mix when outside the safe working range of the second mix can result in an Oxygen convulsion. Several methods to prevent the diver using the incorrect breathing supply can be used, these include;

- *Marking the second stage with coloured tape distinct from the colour of the second stages used for bottom gas.*
- *Cutting notches into the second stage mouth piece on the high ppO2 mix so the second stage can be identified with the tongue before a breath is taken. This method is good in low visibility sumps.*
- *Tying a bungee strap to the second stage which is placed over the mouthpiece and removed to allow the gas to be breathed.*

Additional redundancy will also have to be considered. Any item of equipment that by its failure can result in a diver being unable to execute a multiple stop decompression properly should be backed up. Breathing supply failure bailout and redundancy should be dealt with during gas planning. Instrumentation will have to involve redundancy for measuring depth, time and decompression requirement. This can be done by taking two dive computers or a combination of a dive computer plus a digital dive recorder and tables. If specific tables are calculated to cover a range of possible dive plans and bailouts, multiple copies can be produced and one can be clipped to the line at each stop depth.

For a deep dive involving the use of Trimix the methods used for accelerated decompression must be applied to a more complex configuration which will probably have more than two gas mixes. The redundancy requirements for equipment can also be used and further supplemented as follows;

- *A redundant source of buoyancy should be considered, particularly if the profile includes underwater shafts*
- *Thermal protection must be supplemented, as it is essential to remain warm during decompression.*
- *For long, deep dives where hydration plays a critical role in reducing the risk of decompression sickness, a diver should fit a pee valve. Nappies can be used as an alternative.*

Needless to say, all equipment should be well serviced and familiar to the diver using it. Particular attention needs to be paid to breathing resistance of regulators. Demand valves with a high work of breathing can increase the risk of decompression sickness and CO_2 build-up. Some manufacturer's produce special demand valves designed to work at greater depths than are required by the CE marking procedures.

Second stage identification is important when visibility can be lost.

K) DCI events

All diving carries a statistical chance of causing a decompression injury (DCI) to a diver. Some factors increase the chance of this happening. In UK cave diving the main factors will be:

- *Exertion before and after the dive (caving).*
- *Dehydration.*
- *Saw tooth profiles.*

Thankfully owing to the shallow nature of most UK sumps, DCI events are rare. Despite this, when an event occurs it must be considered as much more serious than for an open water dive as the diver may be at a remote location in a cave.

If a dive is contemplated at one of the deeper sites in the UK, the increased risk of a DCI event associated with deeper diving is added to the list of risk factors. Any diver contemplating such a dive should take precautions to prepare for a possible event. The most basic equipment for providing DCI first aid will probably already be used on the dive. There is also an increase in the number of CDG members travelling to remote locations abroad and doing deep dives, sometimes at the limits of decompression theory.

It is useful for all cave divers to be able to understand how to deal with a DCI event.

i.   Types of DCI event

Decompression injuries are either barotraumas (gas expansion in a body cavity) or DCS (decompression sickness). Barotraumas are a rupture in tissue caused by an imbalance in pressure, usually during ascent. Various body cavities can be affected including lungs, ears, stomach, etc. DCS results in a variety of symptoms but all typically include pain for the diver. The effect is caused by gas coming out of solution in the tissues and forming bubbles. Not all bubbles will result in decompression sickness but if it does happen the symptoms can range from skin rash, joint pain and confusion, to collapse. The onset of the symptoms is typically slower than is seen with Barotraumas.

ii.   Treatment

The correct treatment for a diver with a decompression injury is to breathe Oxygen, stay hydrated and rest until the diver can be treated in a recompression chamber.

Commercial training agencies run courses covering Oxygen administration. These cover the use of the typical Oxygen administration equipment. A diver in a cave is unlikely to have a special Oxygen kit and will only have air when doing a normal cave dive. On a mixed gas dive when Nitrox or pure Oxygen is available it should be breathed from a normal (Oxygen clean if needed) breathing set. Staying hydrated may be difficult in a cave if the party has only minimal fluid supplies available. Water purification tablets can allow the injured diver to drink the water in the cave. If this is done then the water should be warmed if possible before the diver drinks it to try and maintain body warmth. Resting will inevitably expose the diver to the risk of hypothermia. Every effort must be made to maintain the diver's body warmth. A drop in body temperature will affect circulation, possibly making the docompression injury worse long before hypothermia sets in.

At a recompression chamber qualified medical staff will chose a treatment regime dependent on the dive profile the diver followed before suffering a DCI. They will supervise both the recompression and medical treatment of the diver. After a treatment has been completed, the diver will be assessed to see what further treatment is needed (if any). The medical staff will give the diver advice about returning to diving.

There is no guarantee that a diver who has suffered a DCI will be free of all the effects on the body caused by the event. Significant long term damage is possible.

Surface situation: Ideal treatment is only possible if the DCI incident occurs after surfacing from a resurgence or some time after the diver has exited the cave and is within easy reach of communications. When a DCI is suspected the diver should phone the emergency services or a hyperbaric chamber, start breathing the highest percentage Oxygen mix available, keep hydrated and stay rested. Any diver who goes to a recompression chamber should take details of the dive profile with them, either in written format or on a dive computer or digital dive recorder.

Underground situation: If a diver has a DCI event underground after a dive, the correct course of action will have to be judged based on the situation. The diver must breathe the highest percentage Oxygen mix available and stay hydrated. The diver must be evacuated to the surface and into a hyperbaric chamber as soon as possible. If the event happens between sumps, the diver will have to choose between staying to be rescued by other divers or exiting despite the injury. The choices taken will be largely decided by the severity of the injury and the speed of onset, as well as the difficulty of the cave passage that has to be passed to exit.

iii.   Portable chambers

For divers planning a trip to a caving area that is very remote from a hyperbaric chamber a portable chamber can be used. They are big enough for one person and are fed from normal dive cylinders. The injured diver is put inside, breathing through a full face mask feed and controlled from outside by a trained individual. A standard recompression programme is followed by the chamber operator, who will be able to contact trained medical personnel via a phone link. This sort of chamber is a second best temporary option for treatment. Once a diver has been treated, a fully equipped hyperbaric facility must be visited, if only to consult with the fully trained medical staff. Under no circumstances should the diver go diving again until cleared to do so by a doctor who is a specialist in hyperbaric medicine.

iv.   In water recompression

It is possible for a diver to have a DCI event in a situation where no treatment will be possible. This will usually be when the diver is the wrong side of a deep sump(s) or in a remote location (expedition cave diving). In water recompression (IWR) is a technique that has not been fully developed or tested and represents the absolute last resort when no other treatment is possible. It is very unlikely that it will ever be needed in any UK sump.

The CDG does not recommend the use of In Water Recompression.

The typical procedure for IWR exceeds the normal equipment taken on most cave dives because it requires that the diver be put onto pure Oxygen from 9 m up, breathing through a full face mask, accompanied by a support diver, kept warm and given the maximum percentage Oxygen mix allowable for the maximum depth planned. The actual recompression profile must be prepared before hand (to suit the dive plan) using a PC based program or be downloaded from the web.

Note: by returning to the water, the injured diver will be exposed to risks of hypothermia and/or Oxygen convulsions.

Chapter 8 Rebreathers

Low profile rebreather with OC bailout.

After falling out of favour for a number of years, rebreathers are just starting to be utilized again in UK sumps for the exploration of longer/deeper systems. On the continent, they have been used for many years in exploration dives and are now being used for tourist cave dives. Rebreathers of a variety of types are now regularly being used by members of the CDG. In the UK, rebreathers are being used for longer/deeper sumps and also for digging projects. The rebreathers being used in the UK are not necessarily commercially available units.

A)   Introduction

i.   Scope

This chapter is aimed at those already fully versed in rebreather use. This can be achieved by taking a course from a recognized training agency (preferably with a well known, respected and proficient instructor). This chapter sets out to provide some detail of current practice and also to identify issues which should be considered by would-be rebreather cave divers, both in the UK and abroad. Many of the configurations discussed in this chapter require modifications to commercial units or complete construction. It should be noted that modifications should only be undertaken when the diver fully understands the implications of the changes being made. This chapter does not consider the specifics of choice of rebreather units or the type of gas to be used for various dives. This chapter does consider the bailout strategies for cave diving; these are significantly different from open water rebreather diving and are underpinned by open circuit cave diving principles.

ii.   Why to use rebreathers

Using a rebreather of any type significantly reduces the volume of gas required on most dives or on a series of dives within a multi sump system. This means that fewer and smaller cylinders are required to complete a specific dive/trip. Often cylinders can be left in place at a sump while a series of dives is carried out, reducing significantly the carrying required. Greater penetration distances and/or depths can be achieved with a given set of cylinders than would be possible on open circuit. The majority of the gas carried is available solely for bailout from the furthest point, whereas with a two cylinder open circuit dive only two thirds of the cylinders' contents remain for this purpose. The consequences of all these are:

- *As a minimum only a third of the gas will be required to be carried when compared with an equivalent open circuit dive, but in practice this margin should be increased.*
- *Where decompression must be completed before surfacing on the far side of a sump, the rebreather can provide suitable gas mixes without the need for carrying open circuit gas for this phase of the dive.*
- *A rebreather can be used for the deco phase of a dive either to save gas usage or when it is more convenient to stage a single rebreather than a number of tanks with different mixes.*
- *A CCR provides a significant decompression advantage. This can give large savings in decompression time, depending on the cave profile. For instance, in a cave with a saw tooth profile, the diver must choose a compromise of open circuit mixes, whereas the rebreather can deliver the optimal ppO2 at all times.*
- *A CCR causes much less disturbance of silt through exhaust bubbles giving better visibility both on the inward journey, but especially on the outward journey.*
- *A rebreather provides a significant time advantage. This results in less pressure to return, is useful for exploration and more conducive for looking at possible ways on. It also gives time for solving other diving problems, such as loss of line, collapse, entanglement, disorientation and loss of visibility.*
- *Warm moist breathing gas helps to preserve body heat and prevent dry throat & dehydration.*

For long/deep sites the best advantage from rebreathers can be gained when used in conjunction with diver propulsion vehicles.

B)   Rebreather suitability for cave diving

i.   When not to use a rebreather

A rebreather is not suitable or desirable for all types of cave diving. Open circuit equipment is still probably easier to carry underground and more suitable for short, shallow, tight sumps.

The rebreather should provide some clear advantage, otherwise its use may cause more problems than it solves. If the dive can be performed using open circuit cylinders that can be transported to the sump easily, this is probably a better option. With a rebreather three cylinders are usually required; one containing Oxygen, one for dilutent and one for bailout. Although the cylinders will be smaller than those required for an open circuit dive, the rebreather itself will also have to be transported. The duration of the dive will have to be long enough to justify the use of a rebreather rather than open circuit.

Other disadvantages:

- *Rebreathers require greater diving discipline.*
- *Rebreathers need longer pre-dive preparation time in assembling and testing.*
- *It is possible for an inexperienced rebreather diver to inadvertently exceed the limits of open circuit bailout.*
- *Additional controls and gauges on rebreathers are more difficult to streamline and can create a higher risk of line entanglement.*

ii.   Types of rebreathers

The different types of rebreathers offer advantages to the cave diver dependent on their design. For certain dives, some types of rebreather may not be suitable, whilst others can be used to great advantage. An understanding of the different designs and their strengths and weaknesses for cave diving must be used when selecting a rebreather.

a.   Oxygen rebreather

In modern cave diving, the Oxygen rebreather is only really useful for decompression. The use of an O2 rebreather can reduce the volume of Oxygen consumed during one or a series of dives. As such, an Oxygen rebreather can be used to replace open circuit Oxygen on an open circuit dive, or provide part of a bailout plan for a rebreather dive.

b.   Semi Closed (SCR): active

This type of rebreather is not considered suitable for cave diving. If the gas injection jets become blocked, the Oxygen content in the loop will drop to a critical level without warning. Unless an O2 meter is used, the diver may never know a problem exists until it is too late. When working properly the advantage over open circuit is limited owing to the need to set the gas flow rate high enough to maintain a safe ppO2 at the shallowest depths. Some units use more than one injection jet to supply multiple gases to reduce this problem. This significantly increases the planning complexity for decompression and turn point calculations when diving saw tooth profiles. Since these units do not operate with a fixed ppO2, but more closely follow a fixed fraction of Oxygen model, there are no significant decompression advantages when compared with open circuit for saw tooth profiles.

c.   Semi Closed (SCR): passive

The passive addition SCR is a reliable, simple gas extension tool. Should the gas injector become blocked, or other supply problems occur the diver receives an intuitive warning—they cannot draw breath. This type of rebreather requires no electronics and has been used to good effect for a number of notable long and deep cave dives. Gas mixing and analysis are however critical.

d.   Closed Circuit rebreather (CCR)

The CCR gives a number of advantages over semi closed rebreathers, providing the most efficient use of dilutent and the optimal gas mix throughout the dive. There are several types of CCR which require varying degrees of user intervention. Manual O2 add requires the user to add Oxygen regularly. Constant Mass Flow adds a volume of Oxygen at a set rate, which is topped up by the diver. Others use electronic control to maintain the loop ppO2. All closed circuit rebreathers require electronic monitoring via commercial O2 sensors. At least one, but preferably more displays of either a passive or active nature are necessary. This is to ensure that the diver knows the ppO2 of the inspired gas. A passive display is one that gives only a measure of O2 partial pressures in the breathing loop, whilst an active setup uses the sensor output to control the O2 injection rate via software and a solenoid.

Non-electronically controlled Manual CCR: is one that requires the diver to maintain a chosen setpoint usually by pressing a button to add Oxygen when required. With no user intervention there is a danger that the Oxygen will deplete to a dangerous level very quickly. The diver has to maintain the setpoint manually even when occupied with other tasks. Direct monitoring of the loop ppO2 results in simple unit operation at all times.

Non-electronically controlled Mechanical CCR (KISS valve): is one that also requires the diver to maintain a chosen setpoint, usually by fine tuning a mechanical O2 addition via a constant mass flow device. When correctly set up, this type of rebreather will generally maintain a setpoint even when the diver is occupied with other tasks except when working hard, especially in shallow depths. Direct monitoring of the loop ppO2 results in simple unit operation at all times.

Electronically controlled:ECCR: an electronic CCR has some form of microprocessor connected to one or more (usually 3) Oxygen cells. The microprocessor attempts to maintain a specific setpoint throughout the dive. When left alone, the microprocessor will use voting logic to select the readouts from the cells it considers "best" and add Oxygen if required to compensate for either a change in depth or usage by the diver. The inherent danger of this type of unit is that it allows the diver to become complacent. The diver has to monitor the operation of the electronic control system which maintains the setpoint. Most ECCR's use a solenoid for O2 injection; this makes a noise that can be tracked by the diver to check for correct unit operation. This noise can be drowned out by some scooters.

What is required in both cases is the discipline to monitor the chosen rebreather carefully throughout the dive, even during stressful situations. This will add to the diver's task loading and ability to handle other problems. Both types of rebreather can be used in "semi" closed mode in the event of Oxygen failure or O2 monitoring / microprocessor failure. This takes practice to achieve safely in a cave and even more practice to be able to assess the decompression obligation.

C)   Rebreather equipment configuration

i.   Rebreather configuration for cave diving

Some units can be configured easily for cave diving, but others need to be adapted. Divers should consider their requirements, which may vary on a cave by cave basis. One cave may require that the rebreather support off board gases and gas switching. Another may require that the diver (and hence the rebreather) are able to pass through restrictions.

Rebreather configurations fall into the following 3 categories:

- *Chest mount.*
- *Side mount.*
- *Back mount.*

Chest mount: this is an ideal configuration for a simple Oxygen decompression unit. Generally chest mounted rebreathers are the smallest and lightest rebreathers it is practical to have in any of the three configurations. When used in constricted underwater passage, a chest mounted rebreather can quickly and easily be detached and repositioned ahead of the diver. They are also reasonably easy to transport underground and can often be disassembled. With the counter lung positioned in front of and below the diver, the work of breathing is often worse than that of back mounted units. Chest mounted units are also less than ideal for scootering as care is required to keep the unit out of the prop wash. This is especially true for tow behind scooters. Chest mount units are generally unsuitable as a backup unit for a back mounted primary rebreather as the overall profile of the diver with both units and other required cylinders attached is very large. Chest mount units have however been used as a secondary unit alongside a side mount rebreather in restricted but deep caves.

Side mount: these units are not readily commercially available. Side mount rebreathers are worn in the same position as a side mount cylinder on an open circuit dive. This results in the same low profile that is good for restricted, low sumps. Side mounting can also be used in conjunction with a twinset in larger sumps, providing an easy way for the diver to carry large amounts of bailout gas.

When the bailout requirements exceed the logistical limit of open circuit systems the side mount rebreather can be used with a back mounted rebreather in a dual rebreather configuration. Size and positioning of the counter lung is critical to the operation of a side mounted rebreather. This positioning includes not just the unit design, but also the mounting of the unit on the diver. If the unit is allowed to hang down significantly, the work of breathing may be unacceptable. To reduce the work of breathing, the side mount unit should be designed and positioned with the counter lung as close to the diver's own lungs as possible. Any difference in height in the water column between the counter lung and the diver's lung will increase the work of breathing.

Back mount: these rebreathers have very limited use in the UK owing to the size and nature of the cave passage. Counter lungs can be mounted either over the shoulder (OTS) or contained within the rear case. OTS counter lungs tend to have a slightly better work of breathing, but can be more susceptible to damage. Rear mounted lungs tend to clear the diver's chest area of clutter, which can be important on dives where many cylinders must be carried. Positioning of the O2 displays & controls is also important; these should be accessible and easy to read whilst not adding to the clutter of equipment.

Back mounted counter lungs keep this divers chest area clear.

ii.   Diving considerations for single rebreathers

When a diver decides to use a rebreather, the mantra "keep it simple" is a good one to bear in mind. If the dive can be accomplished more easily on available open circuit gas, then a rebreather is probably not appropriate.

Rebreathers add a significant task loading to any cave dive. With practice the diver can learn to manage this level of task loading but it should not be underestimated. A rebreather diver must keep track of the ppO2, even whilst performing tasks such as line laying and scootering. Time spent looking at displays is time not spent looking ahead or concentrating on some other task. A head up display (HUD) can help with this problem, but these are generally only commercially available for back mounted units, although kits are becoming available for use with home build units.

For UK, sumps a single rebreather with open circuit bailout is best owing to the poor visibility that can sometimes make monitoring loop ppO2 difficult, requiring a temporary switch to open circuit. A low profile configuration is critical. A diver should ensure that the profile is not significantly larger than that of a two cylinder open circuit configuration. The rebreather controls should also be easy for the diver to operate with thick gloves and cold hands. Considerable thought should be given to hose routeing, in particular for the mouthpiece hoses. For a side mount unit, the hoses may be best routed when a one sided mouthpiece is used. All rebreathers have vulnerable parts that can be damaged by contact with rock. In a sump, suitable protection should be provided for these areas, as the diver will not be able to miss all potential hazards all of the time.

Very small pendulum (i.e. single hosed to mouthpiece) SCRs are starting to be used in very remote or challenging multi-sump situations in UK and abroad. These are mounted on the upper chest/shoulder in a way very similar to those of the WWII 'frogmen' and they contain only around 650 to 800 grams of absorbent. This is taking UK rebreather diving full circle to the early developments of the Cave Diving Group. These units can be used where a sump is known to be short (i.e. under a few hundred meters) where the depth is less than 25 or 30 m and within no stop decompression limits. Whilst being limited in scope compared with conventional larger, better performing units, they still provide many of the normal rebreather advantages and can ease portering logistics over open circuit techniques. It may be possible to wear two such units for redundancy with fewer of the complex configuration issues than with standard CCR units. For dives in known shallow sumps O2 can be used as a diluent thus greatly increasing the duration. Although they are extremely simple in function, extensive rebreather sump diving experience is required for their safe operation and to obtain maximum advantage.

iii.   Diving multiple rebreathers

Using two rebreathers may at first appear to be a convenient solution, providing an apparently simple method for providing bailout requirements. Unfortunately the task loading involved with diving multiple rebreathers is high. Managing multiple counter lungs during ascent and descent is not easy; also ensuring the gas in each rebreather is suitable for breathing takes consideration and fairly complex hose routing and gas pathways. Multiple rebreathers are now being used in both UK and European sumps with success, but in general this technique is best left for long, very deep or more complex penetrations where open circuit back up is less feasible, both for the bottom phase and decompression phase of dive. An example may be passing a sump requiring decompression on the far side or a series of sumps interspersed with difficult carries.

Dual Rebreathers are found in a variety of configurations. Currently there are few commercial systems that support dualling. The diver must select between two identical units or a primary and a simpler/smaller, shorter duration secondary unit, more likely than not in a different configuration: e.g. back and side or chest and side.

Safety is considerably improved if it is possible to cross connect both O2 and diluent into either rebreather. When possible this provides a much greater level of flexibility, the diver being able to suffer multiple failures in both rebreathers, but still be able to survive. For instance, a loop flood on one rebreather, followed by loss of diluent on the other could be fatal without the ability to cross connect gas.

This does however often require considerable thought to achieve fully and becomes quite complex. The diver should carefully consider failure modes of the particular units in use and attempt to mitigate against them. It is wise to ensure that both Rebreathers cannot suffer the same failure at the same time, such as a software bug.

For all but the simplest profile cave dives both units need ADVs (connected and pressurized) and over pressure valves. If the diver does not swap between units during the course of the dive, the secondary unit should be tested periodically for a sanity/reality check especially on/after a descent or every 30 minutes or so. The same diluent that is being used in the active rebreather should ideally be fed into the second unit and any subsequent gas changes should be distributed to both units to ensure a breathable mix is available in the event of a switch of units. To achieve this with least diver intervention, minimal hoses and connections to be made, will require modification or adaptation to a commercial rebreather that may be complex. Before making any such switch, the diver must ensure that there is a suitable breathable mix in the second unit and consult its ppO2 status via the displays.

Buoyancy considerations on ascent and descent are amplified with a second inactive rebreather having full or minimum loop volumes depending on passage through water column. To alleviate this it may be advantageous that the counter lung be restricted in volume by a velco or elastic strap, which is readily removed before use.

If swapping onto a cold rebreather thought should be given to cold CO2 scrubber efficiency being less then optimal. Divers known to have achieved this at depth have done so by operating the rebreather in SCR mode for the first few minutes of operation. This gives the scrubber a chance to warm up by periodically dumping the loop contents (including any un-scrubbed CO2). This is done at the expense of holding the set point during that period.

iv.　　Cylinder configurations

With all types of rebreather, cylinder configuration is important. For many applications onboard diluent is entirely unsuitable, providing insufficient volume or flexibility. Most commercial rebreathers are configured with onboard cylinders. Whilst these can be used for simple square profile dives, longer or more complex profile dives will require one or more off board cylinders of diluent. The cave profile will dictate the number and mixes of diluents required. This is often much greater than may be used in open water in certain circumstances. If a mixture of off board and onboard diluent is used, the diver should ensure that a failure of one cylinder or valve cannot cause loss of gas in the other cylinder(s). This may be achieved through the use of quick disconnects, taps or one way valves. The cylinders should also be configured such that in the event of failure of any manifold used to feed gas to the rebreather loop, it is still possible to add gas by some other means. Some commercial units provide a manual button system which is independent from the rear manifold and can be fed from a separate off board whip.

Even when using a rebreather it will likely be necessary to carry multiple cylinders. The diver should give some thought as to how to best carry cylinders in a streamlined way. It is possible to chest mount cylinders, when using a back mounted ECCR but the chest area can become cluttered. An alternative is to side mount all cylinders, leaving the chest area relatively clear. The important point is flexibility; a diver must be prepared to configure equipment appropriately for each dive – no one configuration works for all situations. Nevertheless, the diver should aim to have access to as much of the gas supply as possible in the event of any emergency. This may be achieved through the use of switching blocks, quick disconnects or similar.

Whilst normally the use of a single source of breathing gas is not appropriate, in some circumstances, the use of a "Y" valve on a single cylinder provides an acceptable level of security. This allows the diver to carry fewer cylinders and therefore become more streamlined. For instance a side mounted rebreather with a single diluent/bailout cylinder is almost as streamlined as two side mounted cylinders, but with greatly increased range. Using this technique the diver must be aware that in the event of a failure such as a burst hose it is possible to lose ALL the available gas. The ability to perform valve shutdown drills quickly is therefore absolutely critical.

D)　Using a rebreather in a cave environment

i.　　Dive duration and turn point

Normal practice is to turn when one third of either Oxygen, diluent or absorbent canister duration has been used, leaving two thirds for the exit. Manufacturer's recommendations as to the duration of the absorbent canister should be observed unless specific first hand evidence to the contrary is available. In reality this practice can be limiting to the available range of many commercial rebreathers, so many exploration divers will turn a dive closer to halves on the three main rebreather consumables. Any final decompression exit stage of the dive is considered separately, so that there are additional breathing means available for this portion of the dive. This would have been considered in the dive planning stage. Once the rebreather is exhausted, two independent gas supplies should be provided for the decompression phase of the dive.

Volumes of diluent and Oxygen and duration of absorbent available should be matched to the anticipated dive and the conditions. For instance colder water will reduce scrubber life and hard exertion will generate more CO_2, also reducing scrubber duration. When diving multi sump systems with rebreathers it is possible to carry additional O2 cylinders and absorbent. Both of these can be swapped in the dry sections of cave, which greatly increase the range of any rebreather. When considering bailout, remember that the rebreather represents your "third in" and "third out" and the bailout provides your "third spare". This guide implies you should be carrying a third of the gas you would expect to require to complete the dive on open circuit plus the diluent you expect to use.

Saw tooth profiles will significantly increase the use of diluent gas. If the dive is just a short bounce to depth followed by a return to the same point then a single diluent cylinder may also become the bailout supply as any return to the surface is unlikely to require the use of further diluent. On longer dives or those with more complex profiles requiring descents and subsequent ascents, there must be two independent sources of diluent available. The diver must be able to plumb either into the rebreather. Both must be suitable for the deepest planned depths to mitigate against a single source failure. Such a failure would effectively trap the diver beyond any elbow with no suitable breathable gas available to feed into the rebreather. The diver would be unable to descend in order to exit the cave.

As with open circuit, decompression requirements should be catered for separately. This may take the form of open circuit bailout gas. For instance, after an uneventful dive, on reaching the entrance area and beginning decompression, the diver may have sufficient reserve of both Oxygen and absorbent to complete decompression on the rebreather. The mixes used for bailout must be taken into account when calculating decompression. Diluent used as open circuit may not offer the same decompression advantage as the rebreather.

Rebreathers can offer a significant time advantage for activities such as digging or surveying. It may be possible to spend significantly longer underwater performing the required activity thus reducing the carrying effort needed to achieve the overall objective. It should be remembered that as dive times increase, other limiting factors may be encountered such as the cold. Very long dive times within cold water may affect the diver's ability to maintain an adequate seal on the mouthpiece thus compromising the rebreather's function. Additional measures such as the wearing of a full neoprene hood covering the cheeks and lips, an additional gag to hold and help seal the mouthpiece to the lips or a full face mask may be employed to counter this.

ii.   Setpoint selection

This should be selected carefully, taking into account the planned duration of the dive including decompression. If the dive is of a saw tooth profile at a shallow depth then attention should be paid to the correct selection of a suitable setpoint when diving with ECCRs. Otherwise a significant amount of O2 can be wasted by the solenoid trying to inject O2 in an attempt to reach relative high partial pressures. It may be necessary to alter the setpoint during these yo-yo sections of a dive. Non-electronically controlled rebreathers may fare better in these circumstances in terms of O2 wastage but it may be better not to attempt to maintain a steady setpoint in these sections but to wait until the cave has either gained sufficient depth or levelled out.

iii.   Bailout gas

Another consideration for turning a dive is the volume of bailout gas carried. The worst case scenario possible with a rebreather is to assume an unrecoverable loop failure at the furthest point into the cave. The diver should plan in advance how to exit the cave safely or how to get to a place of safety. In longer sumps or when multiple divers are operating on the same project, sufficient gas can be pre-staged. Spacing, contents and capacity of these cylinders needs careful thought, but once the cylinders are staged, individual divers can travel lighter. It should be remembered that as with other high stress situations encountered in a cave, the diver's breathing rate is likely to rise during a rebreather problem, which may have an effect on SCR duration. Also, there are some problems which may require either open circuit or significant volumes of diluent (such as vomiting or high CO2) before an exit can be made. These must all be taken into account when deciding on the volume of gas required, but a good guide as stated above is one third of the gas you would expect to use achieving the dive open circuit.

Another critical problem is an O2 supply failure on a CCR; pre-planning can reduce the stress of an incident when it occurs. Having a secondary O2 source as well as sufficient open circuit reserves can allow the diver to continue using the rebreather in closed circuit mode. If the rebreather still has a loop intact with some working CO2 absorbent, a semi closed exit can be made. For this to be effective, selection of diluent & bail out gas is crucial. For instance, where an air diluent may be used for a 35m dive, a Nitrox mix will provide the diver with a much better option should a semi closed exit be required. A much higher utilisation of gas can be achieved along with a significant decompression advantage. This theory is the same as taught in open water courses, but as it is expected that some distance at depth may need to be covered before an exit can be made, this choice is more critical.

iv.   Bailout procedures

Bailout procedures and techniques should be well practised and understood. These include manual semi closed operation, constant volume O2 control with no electronic monitoring or manual (CCR) O2 addition control. These are identical to procedures used in open water; however divers may be required to perform additional tasks, such as scootering or following a line whilst making their exit.

In certain circumstances, as mentioned above, team diving provides a good way to reduce the bailout carried by each member. This may include a team of divers sharing a set of bailout cylinders pre-staged at various points in a sump. This is not however in keeping with the CDG ethos of self-sufficiency. Some agencies suggest that a team should carry enough gas to get one and a half members out from the farthest point and that when used, bailout cylinders should be rotated to ensure that no member has an empty cylinder. This team approach has been shown to work, provided the divers in the team are disciplined and reliable. If secondary rebreathers are being used by a team and these are of a 'modular' type then it would be possible to pass a rebreather from a donor to a recipient; in the same way that an open circuit stage cylinder could be handed over.

Two completely self sufficient and independent divers in a sump are undoubtedly better equipped to solve problems than a team sharing gas. However, when moving independently through a sump, the likelihood of one diver noticing the other has a problem is reduced! This approach probably lends itself more to achieving a specific objective, placing the responsibility of an individual's safety with that diver.

v.   **Notes to help with rebreather diving safety**

Rebreathers are more complex than open circuit equipment. When a problem associated with an open circuit breathing set occurs, the range of causes is very limited, as is the amount of control the diver has over the equipment. By comparison, rebreathers have many more failure modes and the offer divers more methods of control. Because of this greater level of complexity, divers using rebreathers will have to adopt a different mental approach from that they would when using open circuit.

Rebreathers do not save time. In general preparing and maintaining a rebreather requires just as much, if not more, time and care than filling cylinders. The difference is that if the cylinders are not filled this will be obvious, but if a rebreather is not maintained and prepared correctly it may not become obvious until some way into a dive. Most failures can be attributed to errors made in setting up and assembling the unit before entering the water and its subsequent incorrect pre-dive checking. Rebreathers must always be assembled and thoroughly checked every time before diving.

Experienced rebreather divers become aware of the performance of the rebreather at all times during a dive. This comes from reading the displays, listening to the unit and feeling how it breathes. Special attention should be paid during changes of depth or position in the water. Divers should also pay attention to how they feel during a dive. This awareness of both the rebreather and the diver's own body can lead to the diver noticing something odd which could be the early sign of a problem.

Rebreather divers should trust their instincts. If a diver thinks there is something wrong: check and think (the dive can always be resumed after a few seconds if no fault is found). A diver should never become complacent and ignore an instinctive feeling that something is wrong. On a well operated, correctly assembled rebreather a problem may occur only rarely. When a rebreather diver chooses not to check for a problem, it may be the rare occasion when the problem is real.

In the event of a problem a good approach is to think in three stages with the only objective of one stage being to survive until the next.

The next 3 seconds: where is the next breath coming from?—know where the open circuit bailout is. Control the breathing rate.

The next 30 seconds: Get things under control, don't do anything rash—time to think—what is the problem? Can the rebreather still be used in some way?

The next 30 minutes: What is the best bailout plan to use for exiting the cave or getting to an airspace? Choose from the available options open circuit, CCR or Semi closed.

By focusing only on the next step, it is possible to solve the immediate problems and remain in control, reducing the breathing rate and increasing the chance of survival. Breaking the problem into these smaller steps helps to reduce stress and prevent the diver becoming overwhelmed. The transition to open circuit bailout is eased if the second stage regulator is located and maintained in a readily accessed position such as connection to a neck strap. Some rebreathers incorporate a second stage within the mouthpiece design and this can greatly ease the swapping procedure as the stressed diver does not have to remove the mouthpiece & locate an alternative breathing source.

Real life experience shows problems rarely occur singly. Incidents such as a diver wrapping line round the scooter propeller, then puncturing a counter lung as the result of a collision are a lot to deal with in a short space of time. Using the above procedure critical aspects of the problem are quickly addressed, leaving decisions such as whether to abandon or free the scooter until later.

vi.   Decompression

Rebreathers allow longer and deeper dives to be achieved with much simpler logistics. It is much easier to notch up long decompression times. Whilst the rebreather can be used for decompression, facilities should be in place to allow the diver to complete any decompression obligation in case of rebreather failure. This often takes the form of several pre-staged open circuit tanks of suitable mixes, or a single rebreather package including dilutent, O2 & rebreather staged at the deepest stop. An Oxygen rebreather can also be staged at 6m for emergency use to reduce the open circuit gas required.

When a diver plans to travel through a sump the decompression plan should also provide for passing the sump in both directions. In the event of a rebreather failure during decompression at the other end of the sump leading to an open circuit bailout exit, extra decompression will be incurred owing to the doubled profile.

Diver decompressing at the cave entrance.

vii.   Task loading

Rebreathers do require significantly more attention that open circuit diving. This is even more so when things go wrong. The diver must perform all tasks associated with achieving the dive chosen whilst still managing the rebreather(s).

A well built, well maintained rebreather will rarely fail. This can lead to complacency. The diver must be on top of the situation and continuously managing the rebreather at all times—even when other things are going wrong.

The most significant increase in task loading comes from the need to monitor the ppO2 in the breathing loop. A diver with considerable open circuit cave diving experience will find that it is possible to integrate the Oxygen monitoring procedure into the normal line management and route finding procedures. Monitoring the rebreather should not be considered as a separate activity from the normal cave diving procedures; this may cause a diver to fail to monitor the rebreather when other problems occur.

E) Dry caving considerations

i. Caving / transport

When a dive in a sump that is not directly accessible from the surface is undertaken it is important to ensure the rebreather arrives at the dive site in working order.

The rebreather must be capable of surviving all the dry caving on the trip as well as the diving itself. This often means that the unit will need to be disassembled to some degree for transportation. It is important to ensure that the loop of the unit does not become wet during its journey to or through the cave. Any open hole into the breathing loop should be blocked with a waterproof plug. The rebreather can also suffer physical damage that can render it unserviceable. Counter lungs are especially vulnerable and need to be protected with great care. Most rebreathers will have Oxygen monitoring cells which will need special protection.

Some rebreathers are more suitable than others for transport underground. Some designs allow the unit to be broken down into different sections and transported separately in protective containers. Quick connecting couplings are an advantage here, but they must be sturdy enough for caving and be easy to clean in a cave. Some rebreather designs make transport of the breathing loop intact possible, but blanking plugs may still be needed if Oxygen sensors and gas feeds are removed. Rebreathers are best carried by more experienced members of the team and have to be handled with greater care. Settling of absorbent is a possibility, so scrubbers that have some form of springs are ideal. Those without springs need careful packing of the absorbent which is more prone to channelling owing to settlement during the carry through the dry cave passage.

Whenever a rebreather has been transported through a cave, the normal pressure and other pre-dive checks must be carried out. This will mean that the unit will have been checked twice before each dive, as it will be necessary to carry out these checks before disassembling the rebreather prior to packing it for the trip.

ii. Staging equipment

Rebreathers can offer a significant advantage over open circuit diving equipment during a project. Owing to their light weight rebreathers can be easier to carry to and through caves. The lead and cylinders will still be needed for the dive but on a project these can be staged underground. The low levels of gas consumption when diving with rebreathers can mean that only infrequent cylinder carries are needed. It is possible that for a dive that would be best done on open circuit as a one off, rebreathers may be better for the same dive done multiple times if proper use is made of staging.

F) Summary

After cave diving had experimented with home made open circuit and hard hat diving in the 1930s, it was the 1940s when the major gains were made with military rebreathers. This has now come full circle. After decades of neglect whilst open circuit diving was universal, rebreathers can now be found in use in the UK again – providing the ability to push longer, deeper and more remote sumps in a fraction of the time previously required on open circuit.

Rebreathers provide a significant advantage to the cave diver when used carefully and applied correctly. They are however one of many tools in the toolbox and should be seen as such.

Chapter 9 Dry caving and the cave diver

Dry caving skills are used to reach most UK sumps.

The main aim of UK cave diving is to pass sumps and access dry passage beyond. Most sumps are not particularly scenic and are not easily reached without a significant amount of dry caving. As sumps are accessed mainly via dry caves, the correct access arrangements for dry caving must be adhered to, if existing access permissions are to be maintained. This does not mean that resurgences are not covered by the same or similar access arrangements. Quite often permission for resurgences is more delicate than dry caves owing to the easy access to what the landowner may perceive is a hazardous environment.

When moving diving equipment through a cave to a sump, standard caving techniques must be adopted and adapted. Once a diver has passed a sump, dry caving is resumed. This exposes the cave diver to all the normal risks of caving, increased by the remoteness beyond a sump. If something goes wrong beyond a sump the diver may be stranded for a long time before the few people who are be able to assist can be gathered, along with the equipment needed to pass the sump. Careful planning and preparation is therefore important for any project work beyond a sump.

A) Access

Access to caves is controlled by a mixture of organisations, committees, individuals and groups. These may be landowners or somebody who negotiates with them on behalf of the wider caving community. Negotiations are carried out to create access agreements so that the landowner suffers no loss or damage and cavers have a simple, clear system for gaining access. Sometimes these agreements can be sensitive and difficult to maintain, so it is the duty of all cavers (including cave divers) to respect access arrangements for the benefit of other cavers.

Information about access is not published in sump indexes. The majority of sumps are located beyond dry cave passage and do not need any more permission than is needed for accessing the dry cave. There is no special requirement to state that the trip will involve diving for most sites. The exception is when the dive is planned in a show cave open to the public; in this case special insurance considerations may have to be taken into account. The show cave access agreement will have taken this into account and insurance requirements should be queried when permission is sought. The sources of access information are guidebooks, the BCA handbook, BCA regional access bodies, access committees and the local CDG section.

Good relations with landowners are critical to cave access. Cavers should do nothing to damage these relations; just quickly dropping into a site for a look, without securing permission, can cause problems which other people will have to try and sort out. Cavers who take the time to get to know a landowner may be allowed special access arrangements if they wish to undertake regular trips for a specific project. This may include vehicular access, which can be a great help to divers who will inevitably have heavy equipment to carry. Motorised access will also make it easier to recruit assistance to help move dive gear underground as cavers will always welcome a shortened walk to a cave entrance.

For divers wishing to carry out project work in a popular cave where frequent permits are unobtainable, it is possible to join in with other people's trips. If this is contemplated, it is normal to leave the cave rigged in some way so that other parties can have an easy trip without having to carry gear through the cave. In exchange most cavers will not object to divers being down the cave on the same day of their permit.

B) Equipment movement

Many dive sites are far from the surface and owing to the relatively delicate nature of some diving equipment, due care must be given to its packaging and transportation. Some items of equipment stand up to abuse and the rigours of the underground environment better than others. For divers contemplating diving sumps beyond extensive dry passage, the matter of packaging is very important and starts with selecting equipment that can be packed as small and as light as possible.

Normally, cavers will carry equipment to a cave entrance loaded into caving tackle sacks. In certain circumstances other methods have been employed to great effect; these have included rucksacks, Land Rovers (get permission!), wheelbarrows, or a large crowd of willing volunteers. In the case of a very few resurgences, it is possible to don gear directly from the car, and then walk fully kitted to the dive site.

i. Transporting diving equipment on the surface

If the caving party is not large enough to divide diving equipment on a one person one bag basis, strapping bags together provides a simple solution. To use tackle sacks in this way all the dive gear should be packed into bags which can then be clipped together with the hauling cord Karabiner using the various loops and D-rings on the bags. A caver's wide battery belt can then be used to strap the bags tightly together by routeing it through any side handles to hold it in position. The strapped-together bags can then be carried as one unit by using whichever straps are convenient for each shoulder.

Most divers faced with the problem of having to transport equipment on their own will need to rely on a big rucksack. It is essential that this is of high quality construction. Cave divers test rucksacks to their limits (well beyond the demands placed on them by most other outdoor pursuits) as the loads carried are bulky, extremely heavy and often have sharp edges. Most modern products are expensive but many are designed for the requirements of fashion rather than durability. Do not expect a rucksack suitable for a cave diver to be cheap. The features listed below have generally been found to be the most desirable:

- *Large capacity - an absolute minimum of 80 litres, preferably 100 litres or more.*
- *Strong, non-rotting waterproof materials.*
- *Double sewn seams.*
- *Modern high pack design helping avoid major orthopaedic problems.*
- *Well-designed back padding.*
- *Strong, comfortable carrying straps.*
- *Good waist belt system.*
- *Easy adjustment of shoulder and waist straps.*
- *Massive lid flap (with very long securing straps).*
- *Lots of extra attachment points.*
- *Removable outer pockets.*
- *Lid pocket(s).*

On arrival at the cave entrance, if the site is not a resurgence or sink, it is essential to transfer all equipment to more appropriate "cave proof" containers for transport underground. Most currently available rucksacks are not designed for the harsh cave environment and would be quickly damaged.

ii.   Transport of equipment underground

Once diving equipment has been moved to the cave entrance it must then be moved through the cave passages to the sump. For a dive to happen, all the equipment must arrive in working order. This means equipment must be protected against damage, in bags that are easy to handle and compact enough so that a minimum number of bags are required. Some items of equipment are heavy and some represent a considerable hazard if transported incorrectly.

For packaging so that it can be moved through a cave diving equipment can be divided into as follows:

- *Lead.*
- *Cylinders.*
- *Delicates.*
- *Stuff-able equipment.*

Lead: The best way of moving lead is to do so on a separate trip, leaving it in the cave for subsequent diving trips. This is the best option when undertaking a project in or beyond a sump. Carrying the lead in also allows the diver to assess the problems that will be encountered when moving the rest of the diving equipment on later trips. A harness system specially designed for quick lead loading will reduce kitting up time with staged lead. If the dive is going to be a one off then the lead can be distributed amongst the assistants; each can carry a block on their wide battery belts. Alternatively the lead can be placed in an SRT bag with no other equipment.

Note: if the carry to the sump involves swimming, wading or traversing above pools the lead should not be carried on the belt as there is a risk of drowning. In this instance, the lead should be in a bag that is being carried in such a way that it can be dropped easily if the need arises.

Cylinders: Cylinders filled with high-pressure gas are potentially hazardous and must be treated with respect. The weakest point is where the valve joins the neck of the cylinder. Protecting the valve is important. A blanking cap to protect the seating from grit particles is useful, and should be so designed that it does not become a projectile in case of inadvertent operation of the cylinder valve. It should have a pressure release facility. Metal plugs which have a rim that stands proud of the cylinder valve can offer protection against deforming the valve when it is knocked. The cylinder body can be protected by wrapping it in foam or rubber. Cylinders in tackle bags require caution; the bag will wear through quickly if dragged with a heavy cylinder inside. Weaknesses in base stitching and in hauling loops of tackle bags are likely to manifest themselves during hauling operations at pitches. Cylinders should be hauled up pitches by attaching the rope directly to the cylinder as well as to the valve. Cross-flow taps are almost essential for cylinders intended to be hauled up pitches. To reduce the number of cylinders needed for project work it may be possible to choose uneven cylinder sizes and leave the smaller bailout cylinder in the cave. This way only one cylinder will have to be carried for each trip. Cylinders can also be carried uncovered through caves (some cavers prefer this method) using a sling as a carry handle. The sling is attached to the neck of the cylinder below the valve using a secure knot and clipped into the attachment karabiner; the sling then forms a shoulder strap and handling loop.

Delicates: Items such as demand valves, masks, torches, instruments, cutting tool and dive slate with pencil are best transported in a rigid container. This can be a plastic box, tube or ammunition container. Any container chosen should have a wide mouth and be broad enough to prevent sharp kinking of demand valve hoses. Demand valves should be fitted with a blanking cap to prevent water ingress that can damage pressure gauges. Other smaller, easily lost items like the necklace, search reel and belay devices can also be carried in the container. Savings in the bulk and weight of equipment can be made by choosing and building equipment that is lightweight and compact. Each item that goes in the container should be analysed to see if it is possible to reduce weight or bulk. Demand valve pressure gauges should be as small as possible whilst remaining readable (button gauges are too small to be readable in UK sumps) and be mounted on short hoses. LED torches offer a significant improvement in size and weight over the filament bulb variety, owing mainly to the smaller battery sizes used. Some instrument straps can be bulky and may be worth replacing with bungee or snoopy loops. Careful packaging of delicates can greatly reduce the bulk of the equipment that has to be carried. For short caving trips it is possible to wrap the delicate items in spare neoprene and stuff them into a tackle bag.

Stuff-able equipment: This includes fins, hood, harness, gloves and suit. Stuff-able equipment can be used to pad round other items. If tackle bags are used for cylinder transport, fins will sometimes fit in as well. A dry suit or hooded wetsuit jacket can be used to pad round a delicates container in a tackle sack. Although most of these items are of fixed size, special consideration should be given to the harness which can often be very bulky; a lightweight design can make a considerable difference to equipment packaging.

At dive base diving equipment is unpacked and checked before use.

Once equipment has been packed for transportation it needs to be carried to the sump. If regular caving tackle bags have been used and the weight in each is reasonable, normal caving techniques can be used. A word of caution to the assistants about the delicate nature and potential hazards of mishandling some of the equipment is pertinent. Tackle bags can be distinguished from each other to show the type of kit being carried, by using different colour tackle bags or by labelling them. Bare cylinders can be moved using a handling strap if fitted.

For short and easy trips, cylinders can be carried on the dive harness if the American side mount method is used. The British method is usually too uncomfortable except on the easiest carries. In both cases the cylinder valves must be protected as they will be exposed to the cave during the carry.

Trips that involve vertical transport present a significant hazard and require special packaging of cylinders. They have the potential to fail catastrophically if dropped. They can be moved by carrying them slung below a caver on a rope or by hauling them up pitches separately. Whichever method is used the cylinder should be secured by at least two points. If a tackle sack is used the cylinder must be tied to the sack and the haul cord or rope. Then if the tackle sack base gives way the cylinder will not fall. For bare cylinders the karabiner and the neck of the cylinder should be used as tie off points in such a way that the cylinder stays upright during transportation. During hauling cylinders should always be in the upright position to avoid snagging. The cavers doing the hauling should be made aware that they are hauling a cylinder and other cavers should stay clear of the area during hauling. Cylinder valves should be protected during any type of vertical transportation.

On long trips it may be worth carrying a small lightweight tool kit so that minor damage can be repaired. A selection of spare O-rings may also be worth taking to prevent a dive being aborted after a hard carry.

A diver should always give due acknowledgement in dive reports for assistance received.

C)   Caving beyond sumps

Safety within a sump is described in the various and relevant sections of this Manual. It is based on:

- *Good technique.*
- *Good equipment.*
- *Good gas management.*
- *Experience.*

Safety when dry caving beyond a sump will rely heavily on the diver's caving skill and experience linked with good planning and preparation. Any caving trip requires care if accidents are to be avoided. The main difference between a caving trip to a sump and one beyond a sump is that in the latter the difficulty of rescue is greatly increased. Minor obstacles that are negotiated with ease near the cave entrance become much more of a proposition on the wrong side of a sump. It takes only a minor injury to make rescue very difficult and dangerous. Great care must therefore be taken when planning and carrying out caving trips beyond sumps, whether the trip is a one-off visit or a long-term project.

Some of the more notable explorations beyond sumps have been made by divers who, for various reasons, have chosen to dive and cave on their own. Although solo caving and diving is perhaps inevitable during initial explorations when a sump is first passed, it is less inevitable on successive trips. It has been argued that if a diver is competent to operate safely enough alone underwater, solo caving beyond the sump must also be safe. This is simply not true. Although there are many UK sumps in which a solo diver is undoubtedly safer than if accompanied, safety in numbers definitely applies in dry passages on the far side. The lone diver in the caving environment, with its very different hazards, is truly out on a limb. Those contemplating such solo explorations should think seriously about the potential dangers involved, and be more than adequately prepared for all eventualities.

i.   Planning

Cave diving activities have been happening for over half a century in the UK. Historically the people involved have recorded the activities that have taken place at all sites. This has resulted in a large volume of information that can be used to plan trips. The same is true of dry caves. All the available information should be consulted as part of the planning process. First hand knowledge of the cave to be visited is a significant advantage and if the diver does not have this, the cave should be visited prior to doing the dive. On the day of the trip the standard dry caving practices apply and the following should be taken into account:

- *Weather conditions.*
- *Strength of party.*
- *Length of time underground.*
- *Whether the objectives are realistic.*

Be sure to tell someone where you are going, what time you expect to return (allowing some extra time for inefficiency) and what to do if you do not return. Remember to inform that person when you do get out.

ii.   Equipment

The safety and success of any caving trip depends very much on the type and condition of equipment used but beyond a sump it must be even more so. It must be suitable for the planned trip. The information provided below is of a general nature and you may need additional equipment for a particular sort of caving trip.

It is essential to wear the proper equipment for caving trips beyond sumps. This may include:

- *Clothing.*
- *Footwear.*
- *Lights.*
- *Helmet.*
- *Food.*
- *Safety items.*
- *Other items.*
- *Tackle.*

Clothing: Usually, the only suitable clothing for both diving and dry caving is a wetsuit. The best combination is a one piece suit with a separate vest or shorty with an attached hood. Alternatively, there may be situations where the use of a diving dry suit (for sumps), exchanged for a normal caving over suit (for dry passages), is more suitable. The caving suit can be carried through the sump in a bag or, if it is large enough and has cut-outs for valves, it can be worn over the dry suit. (Dry suits with soft boots that allow the diver to wear normal caving boot are an advantage.) There has to be a compromise between over-heating during dry caving and sufficient warmth when diving. Layering of under suits can be useful here. Modern diving undersuits that maintain thermal properties in the event of a flooded suit are available. Carrying a zip cleaning kit can be useful.

Footwear: It is essential that rugged footwear is used in dry passages; it is both unpleasant and unsafe to cave in wet-suit socks or wet booties! The best way of carrying footwear is to wear it, so it is advisable to buy a pair of fins that will fit over boots or Wellingtons.

Lights: Depending on the type of dive light used, a diver may have to take a dedicated light for caving beyond a sump. Both filament bulb and HID dive lights are unsuitable for use in air owing to the lack of cooling when out of water. As a result both types of light may overheat and fail. LED dive lights can be used beyond a sump unless they are particularly high power or the manufacturer's instructions specifically state that the light should be only used underwater. LED lights that are not specially designed to be used as dive lights can also be used beyond a sump; but they will need to be kept dry whilst being transported through the sump because the electronics in LED lights will not tolerate repeated immersion. Whatever type of light is taken, spare batteries (and bulb if applicable) should be taken as a minimum. Best practice is to take multiple lights.

Helmet: The only reliable helmets for dry caving are purpose-designed caving helmets. These have certain disadvantages for diving, so canoeing or skateboarding helmets are used. It is often not feasible to carry a "proper" helmet through a sump for dry caving beyond, so most divers usually forego the security of a conventional caving helmet. When caving in passage that presents a risk of loose rocks, it is advisable to use a conventional caving helmet. This will provide better protection than a light weight diving helmet.

Food: Food and some sort of drink should always be carried. For most trips a number of chocolate bars, cereal bars, energy bars, nuts or trail mix will provide enough food. Drinks are best carried in flexible cartons; several should be taken on a diving trip to maintain levels of hydration both before and after the dive. For longer or more strenuous trips self-heating cans or lightweight stoves to provide warm and substantial meals should be considered.

Safety Items: A caver is not fully equipped without some safety and emergency items. The most important is a survival bag. Once the survival bag has been used it should be replaced. Other items required are spare lights (divers should have these anyway) and a basic first-aid kit suitable for use with the diver's first aid training. Other items could include water purification tablets, notebook plus pencil, spare batteries and thermal clothing such as a balaclava and gloves.

Other Items: A whistle, for signalling on pitches and attracting the attention of a rescue team should rescue be needed, will prove useful, as will an Italian hitch karabiner. This versatile device is excellent for safe life-lining. Consider a small spares kit, including bungee cord, spare O-rings, an Allen key, adjustable spanner and spare mask or fin strap.

Tackle: Any caving tackle required for the exploration of the cave (e.g. electron ladders, ropes and scaling poles) must be in good condition. The use of worn out tackle for leaving beyond sumps is very unwise. When it is anticipated that tackle will remain beyond sumps for more than a few weeks, metal components will need to be protected from corrosion. Permanently fixed metal ladders are increasingly being used beyond sumps; always treat them with suspicion unless they are known to be maintained in good condition.

A diver using a "clothes line" to secure equipment whilst kitting up in a sump.

iii.   De-kitting and stowing gear safely

Once the sump has been passed, the diving equipment must be removed and placed in a safe place. The first priority is to safeguard the air supply by turning it off. The demand valves should remain pressurised to stop the ingress of mud and to reduce the risk of blowing an O-ring when preparing for the return dive (carrying a spare O-ring is advisable). Dry suit zips should be kept clean or the diver may get cold on the return journey in the event of a failure.

After removing the equipment, the diver should find a suitable place to stow it. This should be above flood level so that nothing is washed away and the diver can get back to the equipment if the water should rise. The equipment dump should not be beneath loose rocks that could fall on delicate equipment and the mask in particular must be well shielded. A level floor helps to stop the cylinders rolling around. If there is any chance of the equipment getting washed away, or of it falling, a bolt or similar device should be installed and everything fastened to it. De-kitting should preferably be carried out slowly and methodically with equipment being removed in the reverse order to which it was donned. Once all the equipment has been removed and stowed, the weight belt (if worn separately) should be placed on top of everything else.

If no safe floor area is available for storing equipment a "cloths line" can be constructed from a line between two secure belay points (usually bolts). This is used to hang equipment from either above or below water.

iv.   Moving through the cave and dealing with obstacles

Apart from flooding, fractures sustained by falling or by boulder falls are the most common cause of injury. The way a caver moves through a cave and the care taken will either increase or reduce the level of risk. Other factors that will affect the level of risk, include fatigue and previous caving experience. A constant watch for danger, and slow, methodical progress will reduce the chances of an accident. In a new passage just discovered, it is all too tempting to move along at rapid pace but caution must always be observed.

Special care should be taken when doing the following:

- *Free climbs.*
- *Pitches.*
- *Scaling avens.*
- *Boulder chokes.*

Free Climbs: If there is the slightest possibility of someone falling from a free climb, it should be equipped with at least a good hand line. If an upward free-climb is necessary, be sure to protect it. Most fixed aids in caves are subject to some sort of inspection regime; beyond sumps this is highly unlikely. Fixed aids that have been in place for a long time should not be trusted. Consider taking replacements. Pay particular attention to bolt belays that can corrode.

Pitches: Pitches require great care; beyond sumps they require even greater care. Make sure that the tackle is sound and properly belayed. If ladders are used to descend pitches a lifeline, preferably operated with an Italian hitch or similar device, must always be used. Do not trust fixtures that have been in place a long time. In a new section of cave, remember that ledges and pitch heads may require the gardening of loose rocks and debris.

Scaling Avens: Avens present their own hazards. The risk of falling and the consequences should be considered. Previous experience of scaling avens before attempting it beyond a sump is an advantage.

Boulder Chokes: Boulder chokes can be dangerous caving obstacles. In a new or infrequently visited cave, a boulder choke will not have stood the test of hundreds of cavers, so it may be unstable. Boulder chokes close to sumps may be subject to flooding. Water can wash out sediment from in between rocks and move small boulders. Stable boulder chokes may become unstable after a flood, so a diver caving beyond a sump where this may have happened should always treat any boulder choke as potentially unstable.

v.   Diving another sump

Many caves contain more than one sump. After the first has been passed and any dry passages explored, the time will come when a dive in the second sump will be required. Logistical problems will usually dictate that the first dive in the new sump will be carried out by one diver with the support of others who have passed the first but do not intend to enter any subsequent sumps.

There are two primary considerations for such operations: the total amount of air required and the number of cylinders that contain it. It is important to ensure that all divers have two independent breathing sets available at all times. The volume of gas in each should be sufficient for the diver to reach dive base. (see Section Ch.2.D).

When moving between sumps time can be saved if the diver only removes the minimum amount of equipment. The amount of equipment that a diver repacks for transport will depend on the nature of the passage to be traversed. For harsh passage-all of the delicate items will have to be repacked to protect them. The equipment a diver has beyond a sump is the diver's only route out.

vi.   Digging

Care and forethought are always required when digging, especially, if boulders or unconsolidated deposits are involved. As with all other activities beyond sumps, keep the difficulty of rescue in mind and be prepared to give up if the risk becomes too high.

Thorough planning of the digging methods to be used, spoil storage and equipment requirements will be needed to ensure the correct tools are carried through the sump. Trying to dig with the wrong tools can increase risk and waste time and effort. Do not let the fact that a dig is beyond a sump reduce the amount of shoring that is considered satisfactory. If the shoring can't be moved through the sump, pick another project.

In addition to a digging plan, a rescue plan should also be considered. This may include provision of a rescue dump, communications through the sump to dive base, spare cylinders (and other diving equipment) and in situ cave rescue equipment.

The amount of time available at the dig face must also be considered. Diving trips involve a lot of effort and time, as do digging trips. Combining the two can result in limited digging time. A solution to this is to camp beyond a sump. This will require more setup work than a normal dig beyond a sump but will give the divers considerably more digging time. When planning a camp beyond a sump due care should be given to planning the removal of waste during the dig and the complete camping paraphernalia once the project is over.

D)   Rescue dumps

There can be no definitive list or set rules for the contents of a rescue dump but certain articles will be common to all. Each cave, or section of passage beyond a sump, will determine the contents of a dump. A cave that has a reasonably high proportion of dry cavers free-diving their way through the sump will require different equipment from passage that is visited only by divers. The type of trip planned beyond the sump will also affect the contents of a dump. Projects beyond sumps should involve a much more comprehensive rescue dump. The items discussed below are therefore a suggestion only and must be altered to fit the particular circumstance in which a dump is likely to be used. Common sense, knowledge of dry caving hazards and planning will have to be used to select the contents of a specific rescue dump.

If a Section of the Group, or an individual, installs a dump in a cave then it is vital that someone regularly inspects and maintains that dump. This is especially important in caves where a dump could be raided by persons who do not know better. Particular regard must be paid to the contents of a dump that are perishable, have a relatively short life or that have a certain sell-by date.

A rescue dump will have to contain resources to provide the following:

- *Warmth.*
- *Light.*
- *First aid.*
- *Food.*
- *Water purification.*
- *Rescue equipment.*
- *Communication equipment.*
- *Repair kit.*
- *Spare cylinder.*

Warmth: Survival bag, thermal hood and gloves are suitable for dry caving trips and should be included in a rescue dump, but they may not cope with the extended time involved with beyond sump incidents. For extra thermal protection foam mats to provide an insulated seat can be carried through the sump wrapped around cylinders.

149

Light: Cave divers will already be carrying multiple lights. If these are of an LED type, spare batteries of the correct size can be included for the unlikely event that they will be needed. For divers without LED lights, several can be included in the kit; this should be done anyway to provide light in case a diver suffers a complete loss of all lights. Clockwork driven LED light are available and should be considered for any rescue dump.

First aid: For a rescue dump the basic first aid kit can be extended to include splints (inflatable splints should be avoided owing to buoyancy problems), extra bandages/wound dressings and analgesics (pain killers). Under normal conditions the legal implications of administering analgesic can make their inclusion in a first aid kit problematic. Beyond a sump there is no chance of proper medical help and the resources available will be limited to the contents of the rescue dump. If strong analgesics are chosen, medical advice should be sought to limit the maximum quantity so that a lethal dose is not administered. If the rescue time is longer than the endurance of a single dose, multiple doses can be packed separately and clearly labelled.

Food: Long life high energy food that is normally taken on any caving trip will be needed as a minimum. Also consider including self-heating cans and dehydrated food along with a compact stove to heat them. Stoves should be fuelled by chemical blocks or liquid fuel not gas canisters.

Note: Use of a stove can deplete the available Oxygen and build up Carbon Monoxide in cave passage.

Water purification: Owing to the extended time that any beyond sump rescue will take, provision for clean water should be made. This may involve setting up a water collection system or simply taking water from the sump. Either way the water will have to be purified prior to drinking. This can be done by purification tablets, boiling or iodine straws.

Rescue equipment: If the dry cave beyond a sump includes pitches and/or climbs, it is wise to assess the need for rescue equipment. If extensive equipment is thought to be needed, leaving some in place beyond a sump should be considered. In the event of a casualty needing to be moved through the dry cave to a sump having the equipment available will save considerable time. This may increase the casualty's chances of survival. Any rescue equipment beyond a sump should be stored dry; consider vacuum packing equipment before transporting it through the sump. If a full set of rescue equipment is not thought necessary then the bolts and fixing points that will be used during a rescue should be placed as a minimum.

Communication equipment: In some caves where project work or a large number of diving trips are taking place it may be useful to install communications through the sump. This can take the form of a wire that can carry a telephone signal or be one of the types of cave radio. Whichever method is chosen be sure to inform the local CRO so that they will be able to take the correct equipment in the event of a call out. Good communication through a sump can save time and resources because divers will not have to dive the sump to carry messages. Communication also allows the CRO doctor to talk with and give advice to the people treating a casualty.

Repair kit: Although divers all use different equipment, some items are common: mask straps, fin straps and some O-rings. A small set of tools may also be useful. For project caving the presence of a repair kit beyond a sump can save the divers involved from having to carry their own personal repair kit on every trip.

Spare cylinder: When a project is being worked on beyond a sump, spare cylinders are quite often taken in on separate trips to reduce the amount divers have to carry on diving trips. This reduces the workload and can be very useful if a rescue situation occurs. Storing a cylinder at the far end of a sump may also prove useful in the event of a leak that results in loss of gas from a diver's cylinder whilst it is stowed on a normal trip. Extra gas beyond a sump may also be useful in the event of a rescue.

When putting together a rescue dump for beyond sump use the whole party should be considered as potential casualties owing to the increased risk of hypothermia. For this reason multiple items may have to be packed for some of the equipment listed above.

A rescue dump should include a list of contents so that it can be maintained. When something is removed from the dump, a note is made and the dump is then known to be short. The diver who took something from a dump should ideally replace it, but if this isn't possible whoever maintains the dump should be informed and can then rectify the situation.

E)   Accidents beyond sumps

Ordinary caving accidents happening to divers who are exploring dry passage beyond sumps are rare in cave rescue statistics. This is misleading, however, as there are known to have been several fairly serious injuries in such circumstances, where the parties concerned have managed to effect self-rescue. It is vital to adhere to the standard safe practices recommended for dry caving beyond sumps. In cave rescue terms, any incident beyond a sump is considered as being very remote.

i.   First aid advice

There are a considerable number of first aid training courses available; all will be useful for caving but they can only be considered as a starting point. Caving with its inherent remoteness and difficulty of access presents its own special problems for the first aid provider. Once a "normal" first aid course has been taken a cave diver should then learn cave specific first aid. The best place to receive this training will be the local CRO, who will have medically trained personnel on the rescue team. The information they will give will be cave specific first aid resulting from the collected experience of the various cave rescue teams.

First aid beyond sumps should be aimed at achieving these goals:

- *Treatment of the injury sufficient to allow the diver to leave the cave safely.*
- *Treatment of the injury sufficient to allow the diver to pass the sump prior to receiving further help.*
- *Treatment of any injury to stabilise the victim's condition, hence allowing time for further help to be brought to the victim.*

One of the most important considerations for divers involved in a rescue situation is time. When an incident happens, the rule is to get out of the cave as quickly as possible (if the condition of the casualty allows). The body takes time to react to a trauma and may start deteriorating as time passes. Do not stop and wait to be rescued until the casualty cannot be moved.

ii.   Most likely injuries

Any first aid training must equip the diver to cope with the normal injuries that are experienced in caving.

These are:

- *Lower leg.*
- *Hand.*
- *Head.*
- *Hypothermia.*
- *Drowning.*
- *Spinal.*
- *Crush.*

Lower leg: The most likely lower leg injuries are broken bones, sprains, dislocations, twists etc. First aid training should cover how to splint and immobilise the injured limb with the equipment available on a caving trip.

Hand: Sharp and moving rocks can easily result in damage to a caver's hands. Typically injuries will be crush, cut, dislocations and breakage. First aid training should cover bandaging, strapping and immobilising with the equipment available in a cave.

Head: Injuries to the head will typically result in bleeding and may include unconsciousness, concussion or damage to the diver's teeth. First aid training should include treatment for the bleeding and a basic neural exam. When dealing with damaged teeth, the diver may choose to await rescue as exposed nerve endings can result in a diver passing out in a cold sump.

Hypothermia: Any cave orientated first aid training should include the recognition and management of a hypothermic caver. For divers beyond a sump this is a very serious concern owing to the extra time involved in a rescue and the need to pass a sump to exit.

Drowning: This is the only likely emergency in which cardio pulmonary resuscitation (CPR) would be used with a fair chance of success. CPR means using artificial respiration and heart massage to get the heart and breathing going again. This is not the place to go into the details of mouth-to-mouth respiration or heart massage. In accordance with the CDG training programme any CDG trainee will have been shown how to do this before getting near the water. The only comment that can be made is that efforts should be prolonged before being given up.

Spinal: Usually caused by a fall but can also be the result of being hit by a rock. First aid training will have to cover identification of a spinal injury and how to immobilise the casualty. As any casualty with spinal damage will have to be carried out of the cave in a stretcher; training in the use of the specific stretchers available from the local CRO should be sought.

Crush: The techniques for treating a crush injury will vary, dependent on the body part that is damaged. First aid training should cover strapping, splinting, bleeding, toxic shock and moving onto a stretcher. As for spinal injuries, training to use a CRO stretcher should also be sought.

When a diver is injured the chance of decompression sickness increases. As a precaution Oxygen should be given to the diver if it is available. The advice about keeping the diver warm will automatically be followed to avoid hypothermia. Keeping the diver hydrated will depend on the correct treatment for the injuries the diver has. As the Oxygen is only being given as a precaution, doing so should never compromise the first aid treatment for the injuries that are present.

iii. Dry cave rescue procedures

Accidents that happen underwater will have to be dealt with by the diver's diving skills. For parties beyond a sump and for divers who have exited a sump after an incident, the dry cave rescue procedure is used. No matter what the situation, the greatest enemy of the diver is TIME. The time it takes for the injury to prove fatal, the time to get a message out of the cave and the time it takes for the rescue team to arrive, will largely determine the outcome of the rescue.

As soon as an accident occurs, three responses immediately arise:

- *The immediate response.*
- *The considered response.*
- *The survival response.*

a. Immediate response

STOP and ASSESS the situation. Ascertain the safety of the immediate location and the safety of the rest of the party when they go to offer assistance. Assess the injuries to the casualty. If the location of the incident is hazardous, the risk of moving the casualty must be assessed against the risk of not moving the casualty. If the casualty is in danger of death owing to the location, then the only option will be immediate movement. If the level of risk is lower, the casualty should not be moved immediately. The immediate first aid response in accordance with any training received must be to keep the casualty alive and carry out a medical assessment. Immediate response should only usually take a few minutes.

b. Considered response

This response follows as soon as the immediate response has been completed. The party must plan the next course of action. A more considered assessment of the condition of the casualty must be undertaken. The party must assess whether self rescue is possible. As the quickest form of rescue it is the best option. If the casualty cannot be moved owing to the injury or shortage of equipment, the party must wait for the call out procedure to take effect. This can be triggered by a member of the party exiting the cave and calling cave rescue in the normal way, or by the surface call out being triggered owing to the overdue party.

During this phase of the incident the party should focus on keeping the condition of the casualty stable and preventing hypothermia in the casualty and the rest of the party. The equipment the party has to do this will depend on what has been brought on the trip by the party and the contents of any rescue dump in the cave that the party can get to.

c.   Survival response

If the plan involves waiting for the rescue team, the casualty and the rest of the party will be exposed to hazards by the length of time they have to wait. At this point the survival response must be considered. This includes practical details such as:

- *Lighting.*
- *Thermal protection.*
- *Food.*
- *Water.*
- *Location.*

Lighting: Clearly fundamental. Obviously conserve light by using lights on their lowest power setting. Turn off lights when not required. It may be necessary to have one light on at all times to monitor continually the condition of the casualty.

Thermal protection: Hypothermia will soon become a problem. Move to a drier and less windy area if possible, wear hoods and gloves, use tackle bags to insulate the body from wet ground, use survival bags and candles for heat.

Food: Beware giving the casualty food. There are some instances where food must not be given. These include - any significant head injury or a state of altered consciousness (risk of vomiting, choking or inhaling vomit); abdominal pain (risk of vomiting and exacerbating symptoms); anyone likely to be operated on in 6-8 hours (feeding may delay safe anaesthesia); and any serious injury such as fractured limbs (may cause diversion of blood to the stomach and worsen shock).

Water: Take small sips of water regularly, rather than drinking large quantities that will reduce body core temperature. As with food, beware giving the victim water if certain injuries are known or suspected. As with food, there are some circumstances where drink should not be given, such as a bad head injury or serious abdominal injury

Location: Move to a better location if possible/necessary; if in a remote side passage leave a message on a slate (or some other sign) at a main junction to warn arriving rescuers. There is a problem that if the party moves too far away from where the incident took place, the rescuers may be confused when they arrive.

In a normal wet British cave, an enforced stay for any length of time with minimal survival or comfort aids and with a significant injury will be a very serious proposition. This will almost certainly result in serious hypothermia, increased physical trauma and very possibly death. Prevention is the answer.

iv.   Self-rescue

As is stated above the greatest enemy of an injured caver is time. This exposes the party to increased hazards such as hypothermia and will allow the condition of the casualty to deteriorate. The best option for any party is self rescue. How practical this will be will depend on the injuries the casualty has sustained, the level of first aid knowledge, the amount of rescue equipment available and the level of training the team has in using it. Current knowledge and recent practice in these areas will increase the chances of a self rescue being possible. So will a well supplied party and well maintained rescue dumps.

The best answer is prevention but it must be backed up by preparation for what will take place when prevention fails.

The problems of rescue through some cave passages should not be underestimated.

F) Conservation

Caves take a long time to form and have many delicate features. These features not only include the obvious formations; the mud deposits in many caves have not been disturbed for thousands of years. There is also the matter of cave life particularly in sumps in the UK. Every effort should be taken to protect the delicate cave environment. Viewing caves is a privilege taken up by a few. Those few have a duty to those who follow to avoid damaging the cave environment. Once a cave formation is damaged it is unlikely to be repairable. Mud banks that are unaffected by water can never be put back once disturbed. Each individual's caving career may only last a few years or decades, but the cave will remain for future generations who will also want to see the cave environment at its very best.

Several methods have been used to protect cave passage from damage by visiting parties of cavers. The more successful methods involve taping off delicate areas to mark a limit that nobody should enter. This method can be applied beyond sumps if a particularly decorative section of passage is found that will attract a lot of visitors. It is also useful to record details of the appearance of cave passage so the level of impact that cavers are having on the passage can be monitored. If the condition of the passage is found to be deteriorating, better underground controls should be considered or access permissions could be altered. This is particularly important when a cave is located in a SSSI as damage to any part of the cave can result in court action.

For cavers involved in project work beyond sumps the conservation aspects of the project should not be ignored. There should be a plan at the beginning of the project for the removal of all the equipment from the cave passage once the project is over.

154

Chapter 10 Cave diving outside the UK

Cave diving outside the UK can offer the diver the chance to use different equipment and techniques.

CDG members dive outside the UK for both tourist trips and original exploration. A wide range of sump conditions have been created in the different types of limestone around the world by various geological processes. Conditions similar to UK sumps can be found as well as very large clear passages. Although some of the techniques of cave diving are common to all sump environments, there are considerable variations between regions. All divers should be aware of these variations in practices. When diving sump conditions that are significantly different from those found in the UK, CDG members may have to use a different equipment configuration. Cave diving outside the UK also offers the opportunity to dive sumps that are longer and deeper than typical UK sumps. In some cases this will be easier if the diver is using equipment that would not normally be used in a typical UK sump such as a scooter or a habitat.

Cave diving is a sport that is practised the world over and divers have benefited from the easy communication that has been made possible by the Internet. Information about caves and access to them is typically provided by divers active in the region.

A)   The UIS

Internationally cave diving has an organisation based on the recognised governing body in each country. These groups are represented on the cave diving commission of the UIS.

UIS stands for the Union Internationale de Spéléologie, in the original French.

The UIS is a:

- *Non-profit.*
- *Non-governmental organization.*

It aims to promote the development of interaction between academic and technical speleologists from a wide number of nationalities. This is to develop and coordinate international speleology in all of its aims which are divided into four areas:

- *Scientific.*
- *Technical.*
- *Cultural.*
- *Economic aspects.*

Within the structure of the UIS is the Department of Exploration. This covers the commissions of:

- *Cave Rescue.*
- *Materials and Techniques.*
- *Cave Diving.*

Cave diving has a Cave Diving Commission. "Commission de la plongée souterraine". The UIS also publishes a code of ethics to cover exploration. The aim of the Cave Diving Commission is to bring together the various national bodies of cave diving and discuss cave diving exploration and their common interests on a global scale. The Commission will attempt to protect the interests of committed cave divers to practise their activities as appropriate. The Commission will try to establish a true representation of committed cave divers around the world. The UIS Cave Diving Commission will establish a framework of principles and guidelines regarding:

- *Safety.*
- *Cave protection.*
- *Landowner relations.*

This framework is to be implemented according to the local technical, legal and cultural situation. The Commission will not seek to impose, but will try to convince, and because of the diversity of cave diving techniques used worldwide, the Commission will not set up rules. It will invite, encourage and support local cave divers, or, preferably, their organizations, in the implementation of principles and recommendations. Whatever the framework or guidelines the Commission might devise, local practice will be respected.

B)   Respecting local practices

Cave divers in any part of the world will have developed a standard mode of operation in their local area. This may be for safety reasons or political reasons. It is important that when diving outside of the UK, divers apply the same level of respect to these factors as they would apply inside the UK. Different procedures are a response to different risks or an altered balance of risks to those present in a UK sump. Divers should fully understand these different procedures and the rationale behind them. Access permission can be as sensitive outside of the UK as it is in the UK and maintaining it will take considerable effort from the local divers. Although it is not possible to list all the regional differences that may occur in this manual some of the more common variations are:

- *Line laying and following.*
- *Access agreements.*
- *Rescue procedures.*
- *Hiring equipment.*
- *Equipment transportation.*

Line laying and following: Different line laying techniques are used in many parts of the world. There will also be variation in the type of line used which will sometimes be thinner than typical UK line. The principle of a fixed line running from air into the flooded passage is not always used. In some areas the line will start inside the sump and the diver will start the dive by laying a temporary line between the surface and the main line. This line is removed when the diver exits. This system is used to discourage divers who are not suitably trained from entering the sump. At line junctions the main sump line may not be attached to branch lines. Again the diver will have to lay a temporary "jump line" to link the main line to the branch line in a side passage. The temporary line is removed when the diver exits. This method is used to avoid confusion at junctions as there will be only a continuous line on the route the diver used on the way into the cave. To simplify line laying for junctions and short breaks in the main line divers take short lengths of line into the sump on spools. Each spool will have a clip for line attachment at the start of the line, once part or all of the line has been used and tied off the spool is left in place for later retrieval. Divers will take multiple spools into a sump. In addition a main reel can be carried to replace longer sections of damaged line.

Well tagged thin mainland European line.

In some parts of the world and in sumps that are not frequently visited divers will lay new line rather than make multiple repairs to older flood damaged line. As a result multiple lines are common in some areas and there is the risk of following the wrong line on the way out. When multiple lines are encountered divers should maintain a high level of vigilance and make careful note of compass bearings on the inward journey. For specific details of line laying practice in any area the best information will be from the local cave divers. To avoid confusion divers should comply with local practice.

Access agreements: UK caving has a well developed and organised political structure that deals with access agreements in a variety of ways. Outside of the UK careful investigation may be needed to gain access to a site. The local cave divers are an essential first contact. In some countries access agreements will be organised through local government agencies. In all cases local cavers and cave divers are the best source of information. Many guide books will contain no information about access to sites; this does not mean that access is not sensitive. Access should be checked before diving or a local agreement could be breached and access to the site lost.

Rescue procedures: UK rescue procedures rely on the local caving community and are provided free of charge. Cave rescue outside the UK is not always free. The local emergency services will be involved. These rescue services may need recompense in the event of a call out. To cover this cost cave divers should have rescue insurance. This will normally take the form of both caving insurance and recompression treatment insurance. When organising insurance for cave diving trips it is very important to study the small print, as many policies do not cover both caving and cave diving and may have a (shallow) maximum depth limit. In some parts of the world there may be no rescue services capable of undertaking a rescue to the limits of the planned trip. In this case the party should be prepared to provide its own cover in the event of a rescue. This will mean divers staggering dives so that there is always a team available for a rescue should it be required.

Hiring equipment: In some parts of the world it is possible to hire equipment for cave diving, which can reduce inconvenience and cost if flights are involved. Any equipment will probably be unfamiliar and a diver should become completely conversant with it before diving in a sump. Hiring equipment also offers the diver the chance to dive with types of equipment that the diver has not previously used. Although most places that hire equipment will expect the diver to have some proof of qualification in the use of equipment, some will not. It is the responsibility of each diver to ensure that they are diving within their own limits of knowledge and capability.

Equipment transportation: The legislation relating to the transportation of diving cylinders will vary between countries and modes of transport. For some types of transport cylinders will have to be empty. Prior to moving equipment by air a diver should always check that the aircraft's hold will be pressurised and heated. This will vary between airlines and flights; most holds will be pressurised, not all will be heated. Some items that may suffer from cold temperatures and low pressures and will have to be packed in hand luggage on flights that do not offer the right hold conditions. If cylinders have to be empty for transportation the local regulations relating to cylinder filling should be checked prior to the trip. Information about transportation of diving equipment should be obtained from the company providing the transportation. Check with the consulate for general legal information about the laws relating to cylinder transport in the country to be visited.

C)   Back mount equipment configurations

Diving outside the UK will often be easier using back mounted cylinders. Many commercial training organisations use manifolded twin cylinders as the basis of their cave diver training. CDG training will not cover the use of a manifolded twin set and all the team procedures that go with it. Because of this CDG members should dive independent cylinders unless they have trained in the use of a manifolded twin set.

When renting equipment it may not always be possible to obtain independent cylinders. Divers who have experience only of independent cylinder configurations should ensure that they are fully conversant with the techniques used with the manifold configuration, in particular the shutdown procedure for the manifold. Team procedures are an important part of manifolded twin set diving; these will include communication, gas sharing and division of tasks.

With a manifold it is possible for a diver to suffer a complete loss of breathing gas. This can happen if a diver is unable to isolate a free flowing valve or the manifold has been damaged. When this happens the diver will need to get gas from another team member. CDG members should be aware of this weakness in the manifold based dive configuration. If they are diving with a diver using a manifolded twin set, a safety procedure must be agreed before the dive to deal with this situation should it occur. CDG divers should also be aware that the diver using a manifolded twin set is not diving as an independent individual in a group, but as one member of a team. Mixing the two types of dive configuration and procedures will increase the risk to the divers involved.

Setting up for a back mount configuration will require some additional equipment. This may include:

- *Backplate and harness.*
- *Wing.*
- *Cylinder mounting.*
- *Stages.*
- *Umbilical light.*

Backplate and harness: Although most open water diving is done with a buoyancy compensating jacket and some of these jackets can be used to mount twin cylinders, a stainless steel backplate and harness is the best option. The backplate is a single plate that holds the cylinders and buoyancy compensator in place and allows the diver to attach many other items of equipment. The backplate is carried on the diver's back, normally using a continuous harness. This consists of two pieces of webbing; one goes over the diver's shoulders and around the waist and the second goes between the backplate and the waist band to form a crotch strap. Correct fitting of this type of harness is important to ensure that the backplate is held firmly and comfortably on the diver's back and also allows the diver to get in and out of the shoulder straps easily. Careful thought must be given to the placement of these D-rings as poorly distributed equipment can alter a diver's trim and increase drag.

Wing: For cave diving using a back mounted configuration the best type of buoyancy compensator is the wing. It offers low drag and keeps the diver's chest and sides clear for other equipment. For most cave diving a single wing designed for use with a twin set and having a lift of about 27 kg will be ideal. For long penetrations with multiple stage cylinders that mean the diver cannot rely on a dry suit for backup buoyancy a second wing may be considered. This may take the form of a separate wing or a dual bladder wing. A two bladder system (either dual bladder or two wings) will add to the complexity and will introduce a potential hazard of the second (unused) bladder becoming inflated owing to a faulty inflator. When using a two bladder configuration a diver should check the second bladder for inflation in the event of unexpected buoyancy changes. Wings should be transported separately from the cylinders and backplate as they can be easily damaged by these heavy items.

Cylinder mounting: For a backmount configuration using a stainless steel backplate and wing the best method of securing cylinders are stainless steel twinning bands. These allow the diver to separate the backplate and wing from the cylinders for transportation and filling whilst making re-assembly easy. The bands are tightened around the cylinders with a threaded bar or long bolt leaving enough thread proud towards the diver's back to secure the backplate. The wing is sandwiched between the cylinders and backplate. Only enough thread to hold the backplate should protrude; too much thread can damage the back of the diver's suit. Cylinder positioning is important for both diver trim and control of gas supplies. A diver should be able to reach both cylinder taps (and the isolation valve if a manifold configuration is being used) and turn them on and off whilst in the water. Having the taps close to the shoulders helps with this and divers should avoid positioning the cylinders too high which moves the taps away from the body. Once the cylinders have been correctly positioned, the holes in the backplate should be marked so that the same ones are always used.

Stages: When additional cylinders are needed for a dive using a back mounted configuration, the normal practice is to side sling them. Unlike side mounted cylinders, side slung cylinders hang down from the diver's body, allowing several cylinders to be easily clipped onto the same side. Seven litre Aluminium cylinders are popular for side slinging owing to the more neutral buoyancy characteristics that can simplify staging. The cylinders are mounted by two clips onto D rings on the harness. One clip is located at the balance point of the cylinder about half way down and links into a waist D ring.

The second clip is located at the cylinder shoulder secured by a cord or tape between the lower clip and the cylinder neck. The second clip links into one of the shoulder D rings on the harness with enough slack to allow the cylinder to hang in line with the diver's body, thus reducing drag. Demand valves second stages should be secured to the side of the stage cylinder with a length of bungee when not being breathed to avoid confusion and reduce entanglement hazards.

Umbilical light: If the sump passage is large then a more powerful light than a diver would normally use in the UK should be used. A typical back mount configuration will use one main light with two smaller low power backup lights. Divers working in teams can share light for the outward journey when a light failure occurs and the diver who has suffered the failure can use the backup light for instrument reading. A more powerful light requires a larger battery pack to drive it for the duration of the dive. For this reason most high power lights use a waist mounted battery canister and a hand held/mounted light head. The battery canister will usually have a switch built in and the light head will often be fitted with a Goodman handle. The light head can be used in either hand and is clipped to a D ring on the harness when not in use. A variety of light types are available but HID and multi-array LED designs are widely used by cave divers.

Once a diver has put a backmounted configuration together it should be tested in an open water site before taking it into a sump. Only when the diver is confident that all the normal drills (including cylinder shutdown) can be executed along with buoyancy control should the diver go underground. Diving with a backmount configuration can only be done in larger passages; in these passages it is possible to render assistance to another diver in the team. Divers contemplating diving together in the normal independent CDG way should develop communication and joint bailout procedures. These will add to the safety of the normally total autonomy of CDG divers.

Team diving is used when the site is large enough.

160

D) Habitats

A habitat is a contained bubble of gas which the diver can enter to make decompression, or other long stays underwater more comfortable. Habitats can provide a significant advantage on a long dive both psychologically and physically, offering a "haven" where the diver can to some degree remove equipment, read, eat, drink and be warmer than the surrounding water. Habitats can also provide a good "base" for securing both equipment that is no longer required during a dive and also equipment (such as gas or heating batteries) that will be required for decompression.

Structurally habitats generally fall into two categories:

- *Rigid.*
- *Flexible.*

Rigid habitats: Are fixed structures such as a large plastic container/bin or more commonly a standard one metre cubed liquid bulk container with the bottom cut out. If one of these is used, it should be ensured that the previous contents were non toxic. Rigid habitats are best suited to being secured to the roof of a cave (held in place by the upthrust of gas contained in the enclosure) or to the floor/wall of the cave by ropes to anchors.

Flexible habitats: Are normally comprised of an envelope of waterproof material and in some cases a frame which either takes the strain of the up-thrust, or simply holds the opening of the habitat in a required shape

Size can vary from a large two person habitat or similar where the diver can lie completely out of the water to a small 80cm diameter light weight one person unit which is easily deployable during the decompression phase of the dive for immediate use.

Another type of habitat that has been employed consists of lining roof scallops with waterproof material. In every case, the habitat will have an opening at the bottom of the bubble to allow the diver to enter and exit. The depth of this hole is the depth at which the habitat can be considered to be anchored for decompression purposes.

i.   Installation and setup

The habitat must be anchored securely either to the floor or to the ceiling. For a habitat to provide a psychological advantage to the diver it should be as secure as possible. A large 2 person habitat can provide over 2 tonnes of up-thrust. Anchors must be suitably strong to withstand this. To combat this some habitat designs have the addition of large weights to minimise the load on the anchoring systems. Most habitats have some valve at the top to let the gas out, but this is not a necessity as a siphon hose can be used. Generally, the heavier and more rigid the habitat the harder it is to manoeuvre and install.

A rigid habitat placed upside down on the roof is often the easiest solution if there is a suitable level ceiling close to the entrance. Minor irregularities should be levelled out with the use of packing. Once the habitat is more or less level, then filled with gas, no further anchorage is required.

Anchors for mid water habitats can include natural features in the cave walls or floors to belay the securing ropes, and climbing protection devices and bolted anchors drilled into the rock at convenient places. Another method is to use expanding building props to span across narrow passages. Webbing slings can be used around large boulders on the passage floor so long as it is certain that they will not be moved by the up-thrust of the habitat. A counterweight belay can be created by placing sufficient smaller stones/boulders/gravel in a suitable receptacle.

In awkward shaped passages or to set the habitat at a certain depth where the floor is not suitable (i.e. composed of mud or silt) a system of wire strops could be spanned between the passage walls. The habitat is then attached to an intermediate point along these. It must be remembered that immense forces will be placed on the belays if using this arrangement.

If dynamic ropes are used to anchor the habitat consideration must be given to the stretch of the ropes during the rigging process, positioning a virtually empty habitat at exactly 6m using long lengths of dynamic rope could result in the habitat breaking surface before it is full!

Similarly, consideration must be given to the equipment being suspended from the habitat. A small habitat of around 200kg up-thrust may sink when loaded with a couple of J cylinders and a fully equipped diver.

The habitat should be filled and continually flushed with some breathable gas which is not too high in Oxygen content. High Oxygen content open circuit gas should ideally be exhausted outside the habitat to minimise the fire risk, especially if an electrically heated jacket is used. In practice, most divers exhale Oxygen into the habitat without problems, but it is important to be aware of the fire risk.

Diver approaching a habitat.

ii.   Use

If the diver intends to remove equipment to enter the habitat, this manoeuvre should be well practised. The diver must also be able to reverse the manoeuvre and re-kit in case of an emergency. Correct weighting is essential and a diver is likely to need additional weight to maintain neutral buoyancy once equipment has been removed. Clip lines on the habitat can be used to store equipment as it is removed. One or more cylinders with long hoses clipped to the habitat provide a gas supply for the diver during the de-kitting manoeuvre. Once complete, the diver will have removed all equipment and ideally be neutral in the water next to the habitat before entry. It is advisable to keep as a minimum a mask round the diver's neck, lights if required and possibly fins. In the event of habitat failure, the diver will have some chance of survival without surfacing and facing a possible bend.

Consider breathing from an oral/nasal mask; this is often better than biting on a regulator mouthpiece for long periods above water.

Where the cave permits, habitats can be configured to move in the water column, ascending through various levels as decompression requires. The use of a variable height habitat can allow the diver to enter the habitat at a much earlier stage in the decompression, but also maintain good off gassing by decreasing the depth of the habitat as required. The methods used to do this are chains or wires with a Tirfor winch, where the habitat is winched up by the support divers. The CDG has generally drawn methods from cave rigging and used pulleys, caving rope and abseil devices to achieve this. When configured correctly, the diver in the habitat can raise the habitat, in some cases, without even getting wet! This must be done slowly and carefully.

If the habitat allows the diver to sit, consideration must be given to allowing blood flow to all extremities; for instance, any seat should be wide and comfortable, allowing uninterrupted blood flow to the legs, ensuring off gassing is efficient.

A rigid platform or at least a trapeze type bar suspended a metre beneath the air surface so that a diver standing on it is at waist height in the habitat is useful in assisting entry and exit as well as the removal and replacing of equipment. It is also useful in assisting visiting support divers in their task.

iii.   Gas considerations

Oxygen exposure is an important consideration for any dive, whilst PPO2 limits and CNS exposure are significant considerations. Exposure in a dry environment may be considered less risky, especially if the habitat atmosphere is breathable and the diver cannot fall into the water. In these circumstances Oxygen convulsions are less likely to prove fatal

Most divers use a mixture of high Oxygen content gas, low Oxygen content gas and possibly closed circuit for decompression. This normally provides for an adequate flushing of gas in the habitat to allow for comfortable eating and drinking during the stay in the habitat. It is normal to keep periods of breathing habitat gas to a minimum to adhere as closely as possible to the decompression schedule; this means that CO_2 build-up is not usually a problem.

Whilst the subject of in-water re-compression is controversial, many cave dives take place a long way from help and from the nearest recompression chamber. A habitat anchored at 6 metres and prepared with fluids and either a rebreather or open circuit Oxygen can provide a massive safety advantage to any decompression dive.

iv.   Diver preparation

Divers considering the use of a habitat should seek advice from active divers who use habitats. They must be prepared to put considerable time and thought into developing procedures for the use of the habitat. These procedures will then need to be practised on no-stop dives before the diver commits to using the habitat for a decompression dive. If a habitat is to be a sanctuary and provide psychological advantage, divers must be absolutely confident they can remove their equipment and make use of the habitat in a comfortable and relaxed manner. A diver laying line may be distracted by additional stress if the entry to the habitat is complex and poorly practised.

E)   Diver propulsion vehicles

Until the late 1990s the use of diver propulsion vehicles (DPV) or scooters in Europe was limited to exploratory cave divers. Recently however their use has been more widespread. Here in the UK the nature of the cave environment has restricted their use.

The two main advantages over swimming are greater distance penetration especially when heavily laden with equipment and the subsequent reduction in time spent at depth.

i.   Types

There are two basic types of scooter. Each type has its own advantages and disadvantages, and each will require a different technique.

The two types are:

- *Tow behind.*
- *Ride on.*

Tow Behind: When using this type of scooter in a cave it is usual to be pulled along by a secure tow strap, which takes the strain away from the arms. This strap is normally attached to the rear end of the main body or to the propeller shroud at the handles and is then fastened onto the tow ring on the front of the diving harness. This ring applies the towing force to the diver via the crotch strap. For very long scooter penetrations some divers additionally wear a climbing style harness and attach the scooter lanyard to this thus spreading the tow force to the diver's buttocks rather than crotch.

The operating control is of the dead man's handle variety, situated so it can be operated with the thumb or forefinger from the pistol or twist grip situated on the side or top of the main body or propeller cowl. With a properly adjusted tow strap and a correctly trimmed machine, one-handed operation is possible with the handle used to operate it held (usually with the right hand) at the top. This usually involves twisting the unit through 90 degrees. During the dive a scooter is simply controlled by pulling or rotating with one or both arms, so pointing the unit in the intended direction of travel and then twisting the body to follow on behind. These tow behind scooters are more suited to small passages, as they are more easily manoeuvred and also produce a smaller end-on profile. As the propeller is forward of the diver and within vision, it is less likely to foul on equipment or entrap any loose line. The speed on many of these scooters is controlled by altering the pitch of the propeller blades, whilst others have electronic means of altering speed by changing the voltage or operating a phase shift on the motor.

The scooter should exhibit correct buoyancy and trim. This can be finely tuned by shifting the battery and placing small weights to achieve neutral buoyancy. It should also lie in its proper orientation with the handle in the appropriate position. When operating a tow behind, especially with one arm, divers find the torque reaction from the motor will rotate the unit by varying amounts depending on the model. This can be compensated for by trimming the scooter when stationary so that it adopts a position that is rotated by a corresponding amount in the opposite direction to this torque rotation. This is done by rotating the battery and trimming weights within the hull, thus shifting the centre of gravity. When in use under power it will then naturally adopt a neutral handling position.

It is this type of scooter that is becoming more popular with cave divers as they are simpler to operate, lighter to handle and more versatile in the range of caves where they can be used.

Ride On: The ride-on type is in fact laid upon by the diver. They are fitted with a T- bar type saddle that allows the diver to slide the legs beneath the top of the bar and astride the vertical section, thus providing a pushing force via the crotch. The T section of the bar can be positioned to help with the thrust by pushing against the base of the back-plate. The handles and switching mechanism are usually identical to the tow behind models. The position of the T-bar toward the rear end of the torpedo-style body allows the diver's legs and fins to hang over and behind the propeller of all but the very largest of ride on scooters. The diver's fins can then be used to steer by using them to direct the propeller wash. Used in conjunction with judicious leaning allows for great control even at speed. If the propeller on exceptionally long scooters is set further back than the fins then the turning reaction becomes slower and the scooter is less manoeuvrable. There is also a greater danger of the propeller cowl being damaged or picking up unseen stray line because of this 'rear overhang'.

This style of scooter is generally capable of greater speeds over the tow behinds. One problem with too fast a speed is the tendency to plane up towards the cave roof. Some models have a canard at the front to control pitch and help overcome this tendency. Sometimes in the past two such DPVs have been coupled together side-by-side for greater range, speed, and redundancy (better if they can be uncoupled quickly for redundancy).

ii.   Scooter adaptations for cave use

The first thing that needs to be fitted is a tow strap; 3 or 4mm cord is ideal. The length of this should place the tow tug in the optimum position - that is with the propeller well ahead of and below the diver, but so that the control arm is not over-stretched. It can be fixed in length or adjustable by, for example, wrapping the cord around a handle or with a prussik knot on a loop.

Even ride on scooters can benefit from a permanent connection to the diver. This assists in pulling the diver along and to act as a secure tether so as to prevent separation. The tether also allows the scooter to hang beneath a stationary diver so that it does not have to be placed down and is always ready for use.

Many scooters come with a headlight at the front; these are not often useful for cave diving because of the back-scatter they create, as well as taking power away from the propulsion battery. Lights are mainly hand-held but many divers with ride on models also place lights underneath the front of the scooter tube, angled down towards the floor, not only for better lighting but to keep the hands free. This can be accomplished with snoopy loops. A number of such loops along the length of any scooter can be useful for carrying many smaller items and they can also be used to protect the more vulnerable plastic bodies from knocks and scratches. On the larger ride on scooters, some instruments such as a secondary depth gauge and timer may be placed on the top of the tube in such a way that they are in permanent view. It is also possible to carry larger items such as line reels and stage cylinders on ride on scooters as they perfect trim and buoyancy is not so critical and minor adjustments can be made by the diver's buoyancy compensator.

iii.　　Depth

All scooters have a maximum depth rating, provided by the manufacturer. This should be adhered to. Pressure at depth will distort the housing especially if made of plastic resulting in ingress of water across the seals. As scooters get older and more worn the depth at which they will flood may decrease. Distortion will be greater wherever there is play because of worn fittings. The margin of error on depth limits is not great. Many models are rated at 40m, others at 90 or even 180m. It is possible on some models to increase the depth limits with the addition of internal bracing or bulkheads. Any failure is likely to be sudden and catastrophic.

iv.　　Transport

Some of the largest scooters weigh around 70kg and the smaller ones range down to 20kg. This presents a transport problem before entering the water. The grab handles on some models are prone to breakage; some divers therefore build a light tubular frame to protect them and to assist in handling. In a car or van they are best transported on a custom-made stand to stop them rolling around. This also acts as a stable platform for supporting it whilst fitting batteries or completing maintenance.

It is fairly rare to take a scooter for any great distance into a dry cave, but if this is done it must be well protected from shocks (some of the PVC body tubes are quite brittle). Internal shocks can be avoided by carrying the battery pack separately. The larger models may be too heavy and awkward to carry for even a short distance, so are best moved without the heavy batteries.

v.　　Advantages of using a scooter in a cave

There are many advantages offered by the use of scooters. The obvious ones are that the diver can travel further and with less gas consumption, and spend shorter times negotiating deep sections of underwater passage (thus giving significant decompression advantages). Secondly with less exertion by not swimming combined with being relaxed comes a lesser gas absorption rate by the bodies tissues; this provides an additional decompression advantage compared with a swimming dive of equal duration.

vi.　　Primary considerations

Whilst one of the main advantages is increased penetration, more intricate dive planning needs to be carried out to maintain safety. This is especially so with regard to gas management. The diver must always work on the premise that the scooter may break down at the furthest point of penetration and the diver will have to swim out from that point. Thus it can be seen that the basic rule of thirds has to be revised. A diver new to scooters must use it in territory that is already known, providing previous knowledge of the amount of gas needed to swim out from any point. It should never be used to penetrate further than the diver has experience of swimming, nor used at depths or in conditions not previously encountered. With increased experience divers can then evaluate their own gas reserves for any given situation.

As there are many variables, there can be no rigid rules for the gas safety margin required. Such factors as depth, current strength and direction, stress, and individual differing gas consumption rates between swimming and scootering all play a role in determining the turn around point. A basic rule of thumb however can be diving to a fifth rule when using two cylinders, so retaining four times as much air to swim out as was used to scooter in.

Another dive planning factor that needs to be considered is the range and operating duration of the scooter that is being used. The manufacturer's exaggerated claims will bear little resemblance to what is really possible when wearing full cave diving equipment. The only way of finding out is by extensive testing, preferably in open water or in progressive stages underground, or by talking to others with experience of that model of scooter. Scooters should not be run until the batteries are deeply discharged, as this will cause permanent damage and a reduction in capacity. A scooter should ideally not be run beyond the point when a marked loss of speed or change in operating noise is noticed. Experience of the individual unit is required to best determine this. The range should be evaluated using the same equipment configuration as would normally be used. Any additional equipment and therefore increased drag will reduce the range, as would the ageing of the battery pack through its service life. Once a range profile with various kit configurations has been established, the diver can use these distances. Run time in minutes is often considered a better indicator because factors such as drag play no part in this; the diver can then turn a dive before half its operating time has elapsed. With the stop/start nature of many dives however it is often hard to account for how long the scooter has actually been in operation.

Batteries should be chosen for cyclical use, these are normally higher in quality than those used in float or brief discharge situations. Batteries will deteriorate with time and it is useful to get a measure of this before starting out on a major dive. One way would be to run the scooter to full duration in water but a more precise way is to burn test. A base level should be set for the batteries when new, drawing current up to a timed point beyond which the voltage drops a significant amount. This is then used as a comparison for subsequent tests and will give an idea of the total capacity available with age and therefore the expected range that could be achieved.

As mentioned above, overall range can vary depending on equipment drag factors. For maximum effectiveness the diver should attempt to become as streamlined in the water as possible. This means no extraneous or dangling equipment, but more importantly good buoyancy and trim play a key role. The propulsive power of a scooter can be used to overcome deficiencies in buoyancy but with the trade-off of reduced range. A scooter diver should maintain neutral buoyancy throughout the whole dive and not rely on the thrust to compensate for being either positively or negatively buoyant. Many small corrections should be used, just as on a normal dive. When beginning, take time to stop at changes of depth and at regular intervals to ensure that buoyancy is correct and that reliance is not being placed on the scooter for this.

Good trim is also essential for good technique. Maintain a position in order to present the least amount of frontal surface; raising the chest is a common fault that creates drag. On a fast machine the aileron effect causes a rise up to the ceiling. Steering and all other movements should be done gently so as not to affect trim and create a smooth flow of water past the diver.

On a tow scooter, the propeller is in front of the diver who is positioned at arms-length behind and slightly above the machine. The prop wash should have an unimpeded exit path for maximum efficiency and comfort. If the diver is operating the unit with one hand, the wash tends to be to one side of the diver and it is better to keep this side free from equipment, which could interrupt the water flow. With a ride on style, the prop is somewhere between the diver's legs and it is more important to watch that equipment does not restrict the flow of water into the prop cowling as this will have much the same affect.

vii.   Safety and other considerations

Whilst some consider a helmet and its attached lighting creates too much drag, the nature of the cave environment should determine whether a helmet is used for personal protection. In many European caves with poorer visibility helmets are an essential item; an impact with rock can momentarily stun at the very least.

The cylinder valves on back-mounted cylinders may be prone to damage by gross pilot error. Cages are available to protect them but these devices can also become line traps, so attention should be paid to their design to minimise this potential problem.

Be aware that even in gently rising passage it is possible to exceed a safe ascent rate. Depth gauges should be monitored more regularly than when swimming to avoid this.

Warmth is another factor of concern on a scooter dive. Heat generation is reduced as little work is being done and the increased rate of water flow conducts heat away quicker leading to chilling. The scooter diver has to compensate for this with additional clothing and possibly other measures. This can then present a problem if the diver is forced into a long swim for any reason and overheating may occur.

Silting can be a major problem with misdirected scooter wash. Avoid pointing the propeller at silt deposits as poor visibility will quickly result. When starting off from rest on a cave floor, always adjust buoyancy and rise off the floor using buoyancy. Clear any debris that may be within the prop shroud which could damage the prop. In low or awkward sections it is best to stop and swim through, not only to prevent silting but any other mishaps. When operating in low visibility the speed may have to be reduced and an extra vigilant watch kept on the line.

With increased speeds comes the risk of losing sight of the line, especially thin lines. Speed needs to be modified to suit the cave environment. In poorer visibility a lower speed needs to be selected.

One of the main problems on a scooter dive is the fouling of the propeller by equipment or stray line; both of these are readily sucked into the propeller. Anything dangling in reach of the prop must be avoided.

Tow behinds have the advantage here as the diver and gear are behind and so any possible problems can be observed and in advance. Large items, especially stones may snap the blades and line rapidly wraps round the boss bringing the scooter to a halt. It is all too easy to drive straight over loose dive lines. Care must be taken while crossing loose lines, preferably with the motor off. Most scooters have a clutch device to prevent damage to the internal drive train – make sure this is set to slip at the correct torque. The best way to deal with any line entanglement is not to cut it into small segments but to unwind it in one length by turning the boss whilst maintaining tension on the line. Ensure that all traces are removed before continuing.

Pay heed to the normal operating noise produced. Any change in this signals a problem which should be rectified immediately. Internal motor problems can also be diagnosed before they become too serious.

Changes in buoyancy may be noted indicating that flooding has occurred. To avoid damage to motors and electronics, partially flooded scooters should not be powered up until they have been dried out and inspected. A flooding is not so serious in fresh water but the internal parts must be dried and then inspected as soon as possible.

Recovery of partially or totally flooded scooters or retrieving abandoned ones can be best accomplished by using another scooter to assist in the tow of the dead one. Migrating trapped bubbles of air may cause a problem with trim, especially with long scooters and they will be also be very heavy to move. Strapping on some form of additional buoyancy, i.e. a BCD at either end will be of assistance.

Inability to turn off the motor is another common failure, often caused by a sticking reed switch or jammed relay, or just silt in the trigger mechanism. It would be wise to plan before the dive a strategy for what to do should this happen. It can often be rectified by a sudden jolt to the specific area to release the affected components. If not, the consequences could be serious, options are to either ride it out with no control or leave it tied to the line or wall to discharge itself and collect later. Pointing a run away scooter at a wall will bring it to a halt, and allow the chance of fixing the problem quickly in many instances. Where the scooter has an adjustable propeller pitch it may be set to the lowest torque setting whilst it is rotating by placing the palm of the hand on the end knob; thereafter the scooter will have little speed and may be handled easily.

viii.   Speed

Running a scooter at maximum speed continuously may result in the motors becoming burned out; it will also drain the batteries faster. Some scooters have adjustable settings, either controlling the voltage applied to the motor or varying the pitch of the propeller blades. The lower speed settings will result in increased duration. Lower speeds result in less overall drag, and greater distances can be achieved at low speeds. In certain situations if it is noticed that the scooter is running low on power whilst running at a higher speed, changing to a lower setting may give the diver sufficient duration to exit the cave without completely draining the batteries.

An advantage of using two or more scooters is that it allows the rider to swap between them thus allowing each a recovery period. When using this approach it is often normal practice to rest each scooter intermittently.

ix.   Laying line

It is common practice to drive the scooter to the end of the existing line and then lay line by hand. It is possible however to lay line from a moving scooter. Great care must be taken to maintain a steady pace and avoid a stop/start motion. Keep a constant gentle tension on the reel to avoid slack line that can be sucked into a ride on scooter's propeller.

x.   Expeditions

For major expeditions staged safety cylinders can be placed in the cave for all personnel to use, rather than having to carry them on every dive. On really long penetrations multiple scooters may be staged beforehand as well. Scooters can be used to move supplies of cylinders on specially designed sleds that are towed along behind. If neutrally buoyant cylinders are available they can be linked end to end and towed in a chain. With ride-on scooters cylinders can be strapped underneath; the rider then adjusts buoyancy with the scooter's additional load and moves off. Tow behind scooters cannot be used in this manner unless fitted with their own independent buoyancy compensator. This is impractical and in this case it is easier to carry the additional cylinders attached to the diver.

To extend the available range and for increased redundancy additional scooters may be towed behind. This is best done via a short lanyard from the nose cone clipped into a ring either at the rear of the crotch strap or off to the side of the back mounted equipment. In this way it will be concealed immediately behind the back so creating little drag of its own. It is possible to tow three or more scooters using this method attaching one either side with another centrally. Larger ride on scooters are not well suited to this as they protrude too far behind; thus tow scooters are ideal for secondary use.

xi.   Team work

Divers operating in teams can extend their safe penetration distances, and increase their overall safety in many situations. To work as a team however it is necessary to stay in touch with each other and this requires discipline. When using light signals the lead rider needs to control the scootering speed to remain within light communication of the diver behind. The rear diver needs a light strong enough to be visible to the lead diver. Matching speeds is easier if similar scooters and equipment packages are used. If this is not possible, the slower scooter can take the lead position. Matching speeds with dissimilar scooters and general team skills requires practice.

In the case of a total scooter malfunction it is possible to hitch a lift from a team member. The towed diver tucks in tight behind the backpack of the towing diver and holds or clips onto the crotch strap or other suitable handle. Any dead scooter is then towed behind in the usual manner. This needs to be practised between team members so as to attain the best and most streamlined position. A tow strap is sometimes carried by each diver to assist with this type of exit.

If a significant speed differential between scooters has occurred because of some problem, this tow strap could be employed to keep the team together and balance out the scooters' performance. The faster scooter can be used in the lead position, thus pulling the slower scooter and rider on a tow line. Alternatively it can be used to push the slower diver from behind. This is another skill that requires time and practice.

Abandoning a dead scooter and other used equipment may be necessary in certain situations.

It is wise to remember however that dead batteries will recover enough to supply some power after a period of rest. So a 'dead' scooter that has been towed for a distance may have enough power to get out of trouble later. Once the gas has been used from a cylinder however it will only act as a drag. In emergency do not hesitate to jettison depleted cylinders.

xii.   Maintenance

Become familiar with your scooter, its mechanical components and the maintenance requirements from the makers hand book so it can be looked after correctly.

In general:

- *Open the scooter as soon as possible after diving to release any gas from the batteries and to verify that no flooding has occurred.*
- *Always charge the batteries immediately after use.*
- *Connect the charger to the battery before switching on the mains power.*
- *Ensure batteries are properly charged before use.*
- *If it is not being used for a period of time, maintain charge in the batteries.*
- *Maintain O–rings carefully by keeping them clean and greased. Sealing surfaces should be checked for damage prior to assembly.*
- *Store batteries in a well-ventilated, cool but not cold place.*
- *In the field maintain a supply of suitable spares.*

Scooter used to decrease effort in passing a sump.

F) Submarine cave diving

i. Considerations for sea diving

When considering the topic of cave diving under the sea, it is worth going back to first principles and considering the differences between fresh water and seawater sites.
The main ones are:

- *Salinity.*
- *Tides.*
- *Weather.*
- *Marine life.*
- *Boat handling.*
- *Harbours and controlled areas.*

Salinity: The salinity of the sea means that all electrical equipment and non-stainless steel equipment is liable to corrode quickly. Lights need to be thoroughly sealed to prevent damage if they leak. After diving in saltwater, rinse all equipment well to prevent corrosion and the accumulation of salt deposits. If electrical equipment is flooded, abort the dive immediately and flush it with freshwater. The density differences between salt, brackish and/or fresh water result in a halocline, a boundary layer that may appear as a sharp transition or as a fuzzy mixing zone. Passing through a halocline produces an alteration in visibility, which can be seen as a haze or a shimmering effect as the changing densities refract light differently. Haloclines occur where freshwater overlies salt water, or freshwater resurges in saltwater. Such density changes can have an effect on buoyancy. Similar alterations in visibility can occur at thermoclines, where layers of seawater at different temperatures meet.

Tides: Find out the tidal range of your proposed diving site and to what degree it is affected by local currents at each stage of the tide. Extreme examples are the ocean Blue Holes of the Bahamas, where entry is governed by tidally-related ebb and flow currents at the entrance. Such currents are often out of phase with surface tidal changes, and may change two to three hours later. At other locations, there may be a negligible tide, as in the Mediterranean. Apart from the presence of tidal currents in the caves, entry and exit into the water may be affected. Check that the point of entry is not affected by the tidal range. Tides also produce currents. Check tidal streams and the time of slack water, near high or low tide, before tackling a site that can be swept by strong currents. Boat cover may be worthwhile. If currents are not a problem, check that your site is not out of the water on a low spring tide. Diving at low tide may give you a shorter dive (less air consumption, fewer decompression problems) and fewer problems with swell. Diving at high water may give better visibility, but swell surges into sea caves (particularly those which funnel in) may force a diver into passage from which it is difficult to escape. Diving in shallow caves with airspace may become unpleasant with pronounced surges, when a considerable shock wave may occur as air is compressed suddenly. This shock wave can be felt by the diver.

Weather: The effects of wind on the sea can be sudden and dramatic. Sometimes storms many kilometres from the diving site (particularly ocean-facing sites) can generate a huge swell which converts into pounding surf when it reaches the shoreline. Study the weather forecast each day and inspect the site before diving. Entry and exit into the water may become difficult if surf is breaking. Getting into the water is always easier than getting out, and a fully-kitted diver can encounter difficulties in a strong undertow. Underwater, the surge from a big swell can reach depths of many metres and affect not only the swim into the cave and the subsequent dive but also seriously affect any decompression stops. The best weather for diving an exposed coastline is probably when the wind is coming from onshore and the weather is settled. Unsettled weather can have a bad effect on underwater visibility, which may take several days to clear fully. Additionally, where submarine caves are active resurgences, strong currents may be encountered running out of the caves and visibility may be impaired by organic run-off from the inland end of the cave systems in bad weather. The calmer weather immediately after a heavy storm may, however, be a good time to go looking for active marine resurgences from the shoreline.

Marine Life: Obviously, the sea contains many living creatures, most of which are not only harmless but make diving a positive pleasure. Visibility may be affected by the smallest - plankton - to the extent that the diver can only peer through a soup-like haze of life. Jellyfish of some species can sting, and it is worth noting that they can be swept by wind and tides into sea caves in large numbers. In tropical waters, corals can cause nasty scrapes, and some small attached creatures can give nasty stings (e.g. fire coral, hydroids). It is always worth wearing some form of complete body cover, even a set of light overalls, when diving in close proximity to hard surfaces in the sea. Fish of any kind are unlikely to present a hazard if left alone, whatever their size. Crustaceans such as the spider crab or crawfish are often found in caves, and the former has a habit of dropping from the roof when disturbed by exhaust bubbles. None of these will cause harm if not handled, and do remember that in most parts of the world it is illegal to take shellfish, lobsters, crabs and many fish from the water when using SCUBA gear. Check local regulations, and do not break them.

Boats: If a boat is used to reach the diving site it must be controlled by a competent boat handler. Divers should be familiar with the use of boats for diving, and also make sure that the boat is up to the task. It is not advisable to dive and leave a boat unmanned, for obvious reasons. Check the weather before setting off in a boat and use the international "diver-down" flag when in the water if other boats are likely to be present. Seasickness afflicts some divers, even when finning in a choppy sea. If prone to seasickness when travelling in a boat a diver should try and keep their eyes on a static object, like the shore or the horizon. Seasickness from finning on the surface usually disappears when the diver submerges. Divers should descend below the surge zone quickly and settle for a while before moving off.

Harbours and Controlled Locations: Some diving sites may be in controlled locations such as harbours or shipping lanes. The presence of divers can be a hazard to both parties. Check to see if there are any local regulations affecting diving at a particular site. Using the international diving symbol on the support vessel will hopefully warn other vessels to keep away. If you are underwater and hear a boat engine, remain submerged at a safe depth until it has gone.

ii.   Equipment considerations

The equipment required for sea diving will differ from UK cave diving. It is rare for any submarine cave dive to start directly from the shore, and a buoyancy compensator will be needed during the surface swim to and from the site. Salt water is denser and therefore more buoyant than fresh water, so weights will need to be increased accordingly. It may be that weight belts will need to be jettisoned on the surface, either in an emergency or for getting back into the boat, and it may be worth altering normal cave diving practice and wearing the weight belt on top of the cylinder harness. A surface marker buoy may be useful at some sites. Remove these when diving is completed Such buoys can also aid in identifying locations from onshore, and enable precise bearings to be taken. For initial exploration, it may be sufficient to attach a small buoy to the end of the line reel and run the line from the surface, belaying at the entrance before penetrating the cave.

iii.   Line laying

Techniques in line laying will be similar to those used in freshwater cave diving. Some discussion has revolved around the permanence of any line laid in areas that may later be visited by sport divers. In general, leaving line at an entrance is an open invitation for non-cave divers to go beyond the safe limits of their training. It is best to belay the line beyond the limits of daylight and make sure any line laid has direction tags that clearly indicate which way the nearest entrance lies. Belaying line well inside the entrance has the further benefit of reducing storm damage. Any permanent lines should be thick and capable of coping with storm surges and strong tides. It should be well laid and well belayed. Do not lay several lines down the same passage on successive explorations. If the original line is sound, use that. If it is damaged, then it must be removed and replaced. Broken lines can pose an entanglement threat not only to cave divers, but to marine life. Remember that a line reel may not last long in seawater if left in the cave.

Appendix 1: CDG Documentation

All documents in this section are current at the time of publication. These documents will be updated as the body of knowledge relating to cave diving in the UK changes and adapts to new techniques, equipment and the legal environment. For the most recent up to date copy of CDG documentation please visit the CDG website on:

www.cavedivinggroup.org.uk

i. CAVE DIVING GROUP SAFETY CODE

1. A trainee should be accompanied by a qualified diver unless he has had considerable cave diving experience before joining the Group.

2. A trainee diver on his first cave dives should either be accompanied by an experienced diver, or should have a fully kitted, experienced diver at base.

3. A diver should always take steps to ensure that there is an effective alert and rescue in the case of an emergency.

4. A diver should always be connected to base by a line.

5. A diver should ideally have a 100% safety margin of breathing gas for the planned dive. This means consider the thirds rule of gas consumption. The limitations of the thirds rule must be considered.

ii. The Cave Diving Group Constitution

Including amendments of the 2007 AGM

Objects

1) The name shall be the Cave Diving Group. The objects of the Group shall be;

a) To explore submerged caves and cave passages.
b) To lay down codes of practice for that purpose.
c) To review and publicise new diving techniques.

Central Committee

2) The cave diving group shall consist of any number of regional sections and a central committee. The central committee shall consist of a President(s), a Chairperson, a Secretary, a Treasurer, a Foreign Officer, a Technical Officer, an Editor, and a Distribution Manager each elected at the Annual General Meeting; and in addition to these officers there shall be appointed by the Annual General Meeting the posts of a Librarian, a Nitrox Instructor Trainer and a Web Site Manager. The posts of any two of these Officers or Appointees may be combined. In addition to these Officers and Appointees there shall be two Committee members for each regional section, who will have one vote between them at committee meetings.

3) The committee shall meet at least once a year between one A.G.M. and the next, the meeting places being in each region by rotation, unless agreed by a simple majority of those entitled to attend. The committee shall deal with the following matters:

a) General administration and policy.

b) To supervise and finance the publication of sump indexes, technical reviews, newsletters, updates to the group's manual and the five year index of dives.

c) To maintain public relations with other bodies on a national and international level.

d) To initiate new regional sections as and when they become necessary.

e) Finance; in respect of powers delegated by regional sections under paragraph 23.

f) To consider appeals against expulsion from membership.

Regional Sections

4) The function of regional sections shall be as follows:

a) Finance, except where delegated to central committee under paragraph 23.

b) To encourage all members to use the safety code for divers and follow the group's rules.

c) To supervise the cave diving and training of its members.

d) To elect or expel members.

e) To establish and maintain a regional equipment store.

f) To consider all new forms of diving equipment and to make recommendations regarding their use.

g) To furnish the editor with material for his publications. To prepare a regional sump index.

h) To award or remove diving status or any category thereof.

j) To present a report of their activities to the A.G.M.

5) The regional committee members shall be responsible to the central committee for ensuring the functions of the regional sections are implemented. They may delegate responsibility for any section.

6) The regional sections shall be named by reference to their geographical location, or by such other name as the members shall determine, providing the words Cave Diving Group appear in the title.

7) Each regional section shall elect at its annual meeting a secretary and a treasurer. The treasurer shall receive all subscriptions from the region, present properly audited accounts to the section once a year for approval, and send a copy to the secretary of the central committee. He or she shall be responsible for forwarding the annual subscription to the central committee. Where the regional section has no treasurer, the regional secretary must observe the rules relating to annual accounts.

8) Subject to the provisions of this constitution and the rules, the business of the regional sections may be carried out in whatever manner the members of that regional section shall determine.

Membership

9) There shall be four classes of membership, namely Honorary, Diving, Non-diving and Temporary Membership.

10) Honorary members are to be proposed by regional sections for consideration by the central committee. The central committee will put its recommendations to the A.G.M. where election shall be by simple majority vote. These positions shall be awarded to persons who have made a valuable contribution to cave diving or the Group. Honorary members are entitled to receive all the Group's publications and attend and vote at all general meetings and attend but not vote at Regional Section meetings. They are covered by the Group's insurance as non-divers and pay no subscription. Honorary members who wish to be covered by the Group's diving insurance must apply to the treasurer on an annual basis.

11) There shall be two classes of diving membership, namely trainee diver and qualified diver. The election of diving members and the award of qualifications is the function of Regional Sections in accordance with the rules. All diving members are entitled to receive the Group's publications and attend and vote at all general meetings and Regional Section meetings of which they are a member, except Trainee divers who cannot vote on the election of new diving members or matters of qualification. All diving members shall use the Group's safety code for divers and follow the Group's rules. Any diver wishing to rejoin the group after a period of non-membership is subject to a review of

their qualification status by a section meeting.

12) Non-diving members are elected by the regional sections. They must be proposed and seconded by existing members of the group and shall be entitled to receive the group's publications. They are also entitled to attend and vote at all general meetings and regional section meetings of which they are a member, except that they cannot vote on the election of new diving members or matters of qualification. They are not covered by the group's insurance and cannot borrow group equipment or take part in group dives. Members ordinarily resident abroad will normally fall into this category.

12a) Temporary Membership is limited to a maximum of 15 days in a Year, and is open to overseas cave divers, who should be judged suitable by the Section Committee, in advance of their attendance.

13) Permanent Diving and Non-Diving members will pay an initial joining fee when first joining the Group or when re-joining after a period of lapsed membership.

14) Subscriptions are due on 1st January and shall be paid to the Regional Section except as provided in paragraph 15. Annual fees for the following services shall be determined by a majority of members attending and voting at the annual general meeting:

i. Charge for the Group's publications for domestic and overseas subscribers.
ii. Non-diving membership fee.
iii. Diving membership fee.
iv. Temporary membership fee.
v. Regional section levy.
vi. Joining / re-joining fee.

Non-diving members shall pay the sum of i, ii and v and diving members shall pay the sum of i, iii and v with the Regional Section levy being retained by the Regional Section and the balance being forwarded to the Group's Treasurer. Membership of additional Sections is charged according to v. and is retained by the appropriate Regional Section. Temporary membership fees should be forwarded to the Group's Treasurer as well as any joining / re-joining fee from new or lapsed members. In the event of a failure to determine the charges for the following year, the existing rates shall continue to apply.

In addition to the membership fee, members will pay an annual levy to cover the cost of the Group's insurance policy. The amount of the insurance levy will be set by the central committee before 1st November each calendar year.

15) Payment for subscription to the Newsletter by non-members will be made to the Distribution Manager. The Distribution Manager will inform the Central Treasurer and Central Secretary of the details of all non-member Newsletter subscribers.

16) Members expelled by their regional section shall have a right of appeal to the central committee whose decision shall be final. The appeal must be made in writing to the secretary within three months of the member being notified of the expulsion by the regional section.

Meetings

17) There shall be an Annual General Meeting, to be held in the months of April or May. The secretary shall give six weeks notice of the meeting and twenty one days notice of all proposals to be put to the meeting. Notice shall be circulated to all members

18) The central committee or a regional section may call an Extraordinary General Meeting by giving twenty one days notice to all members and a similar notice of their proposals.

19) Proceedings at general meetings of the group shall be decided by a simple majority of those attending and voting. The decisions of a general meeting are binding on the central committee.

20) There shall be a quorum of 5% of the membership at any general meeting before the meeting is

deemed validly constituted.

21) Amendments to the constitution take effect as soon as they are passed by a general meeting.

Officials

22) The secretary of the central committee shall call a committee meeting when necessary, at his or her discretion, in accordance with paragraph 3, giving notice of not less than one month to all committee members. After every committee meeting he or she shall circulate minutes to each committee member. He or she shall keep the minutes of all meetings called (ref. Paras. 1 7&1 8.); keep the membership list, maintain contacts on a National level, and be responsible for general correspondence.

23) The function of the Central Treasurer is to receive the annual subscription from the regional sections, to keep up to date the Group's insurance policy, to pay the expenses of the Group, to pay for Group publications and deal with all other matters relevant to the group's finances. The Central Treasurer shall present properly audited accounts to the Annual General Meeting.

24) The function of the Foreign officer is to establish and maintain contacts with overseas groups including the exchange of newsletters. He or she shall also ensure group representation at relevant overseas meetings where possible and maintain a library of overseas publications.

25) The Technical officer is responsible for the up-date of the group's manual. He or she is also responsible for the review and publication of all items of technical interest and correspondence on all technical matters.

26) The Editor will keep a record (supplied by regional sections) of all dives carried out by the group and will be responsible for the publication of a five year index of dives. He or she will also publish a newsletter quarterly, the deadline dates for which will be March 1st, June 1st, September 1st. and December 1st.

27) The Distribution manager, operating with the Editor is responsible for distribution and production of the group's publications.

28) The President shall preside over all general and central committee meetings, but these meetings shall be chaired by the Chairperson.

General

29) Every person whether a member or not, taking part in any activity or expedition organised by the group, or in which any member or officer of the group takes part, shall do so at his or her own risk, and he or she or his or her legal and personal representatives or assigns or dependents shall have no claim or right of action against the group or any member thereof in respect of damages or injuries to person or property and whether fatal or otherwise notwithstanding any negligence of any member or officer of the group or of the body of members of the group.

30) Recommendations for changes of the group's Rules or Safety Code shall be put forward to the central committee for consideration. All such changes must be adopted at a general meeting.

31) Any member standing for office in the CDG shall provide the central committee with details of any business interest that could affect their judgement or ability to carry out the duties associated with that office. If the office is subject to election at the AGM those details should be made available to all members attending the AGM.

iii. The Cave Diving Group Rules

a.   Administration of Membership - 8th May 2005

1 - CDG Membership is as stated in the Constitution.

2 - Regional Sections are responsible for the administration of membership including the acceptance of new members and matters of expulsion.

3 - Regional Sections will maintain accurate memberships records. The details will be made available to officers of the Central Section for purposes of administration of the Group.

4 - There are four classes of membership:

Diving
Non-diving
Honorary
Temporary

5 - There are two classes of Diving Member:

Qualified Diver
Trainee Diver

6 - All Diving Members must have attained 18 years of age.

7 - All Diving members must be physically fit and not suffering from epilepsy.

8 - All new permanent and temporary members must apply to join a Regional Section of the Cave Diving Group as either Trainee Divers or Non-Divers.

9 - Two Qualified Divers must sponsor all new permanent members and their acceptance is subject to approval by a simple majority vote at a Regional Section meeting.

10 - Temporary membership is granted by a Regional Section committee.

11 - All members must sign the RELEASE AND WAIVER OF LIABILITY AGREEMENT.

12 - All members must pay the appropriate membership fee at the start of each calendar year. If the membership fee is not paid by the 1st of January, then the membership will be deemed to have lapsed.

13 - Lapsed members may rejoin the Group by paying the appropriate annual membership fee and any additional re-joining fee.

b .   Cave Diver Education - 8th May 2005

1 - It is the responsibility of the Regional Section to ensure that Trainee Divers have reasonable access to suitable training.

2 - Each member is responsible for establishing mentoring relationships both as mentors and mentees with other members of the Group.

3 - The mentor and mentee should discuss the mentee's requirements for cave diver education in a manner that is suitable for both parties.

4 - The mentor should provide advice on obtaining suitable; training, practical experience, an understanding of risk, theory, knowledge and maturity in order to educate the mentee to the point where they are able to pass the assessment for Qualified Diver status.

5 - The mentor must acknowledge the limitations of their own mentoring ability and communicate those limitations to the mentee.

6 - The mentee should obtain advice from more than one source.

c.   Assessment Schedule -13th May 2004

1.   Roles and Responsibilities

1.1 A Trainee Diver may be elected to Qualified Diver subject to satisfactory performance in the CDG Qualified Diver Assessment.

1.2 Trainee Divers are responsible for providing evidence of their competence of Part A of the Qualified Diver Assessment to the Regional Section. This evidence can be of any form but must be made available for review by the Section prior to election to Qualified Diver.

1.3 Trainee Divers are responsible for presenting themselves to a Section Examiner (who must not be the Trainee Diver's sponsor) for Qualified Diver Assessment Parts B and C.

1.4 Regional Sections are responsible for appointing Section Examiners who administer Parts B and C of the Qualified Diver Assessment. Examiners must be active, Qualified Divers, with suitable experience, nominated and appointed at a Section Annual General Meeting. A Regional Section may appoint up to five examiners whose status should be reviewed on an annual basis.

1.5 Section Examiners are responsible for proposing a Trainee Diver for Qualified Diver status at a Regional Section meeting and for providing evidence of the Trainee Diver's competence within Parts B and C of the Qualified Diver Assessment to that meeting.

1.6 The Central Committee is responsible for appointing an Exam Committee to provide Section Examiners with written questions and specimen answers for Part C of the Qualified Diver Assessment.

1.7 Regional Sections are responsible for reviewing the performance of Trainee Divers under 1.2 and 1.5 and to elect them to Qualified Diver by a simple majority vote at a Regional Section meeting.

2.   Qualified Diver Assessment Standard.

The CDG Qualified Diver Assessment consists of three parts:

Part A - Submission of a record of caving and cave diving experience
Part B - Practical Test
Part C - Theory Test

2.1 Qualified Diver Assessment Standard Part A - Submission of a record of caving and cave diving experience.

2.1.1 The Trainee Diver will keep a Documented Record of their caving and cave diving experience.

2.1.2 The Documented Record will be made available to all Qualified Divers attending the Regional Section meeting at which the Trainee Diver wishes to be considered for Qualified Diver status.

2.1.3 The Documented Record must demonstrate the Trainee Diver's experience of caving and cave diving using a range of techniques under a variety of conditions. It is recommended that the Trainee Diver has completed a minimum of twenty cave dives at a variety of sites to include: caving to a sump, caving beyond/between sumps, vertical access (requiring a rope or ladder) and the use (or simulation) of decompression techniques).

2.1.4 The Trainee Diver must demonstrate awareness of the caving environment both in a physical sense (e.g. cave formation and development) but also in terms of cave conservation and access.

2.2 Qualified Diver Assessment Standard: Part B - Practical Test

2.2.1 The Practical Test must be carried out at a diving site with poor visibility and a muddy bottom, with a minimum depth of three metres.

2.2.2 Full kit as chosen by the candidate for cave diving, must be worn.

2.2.3 Full kit shall include two independent breathing sets suitable for a dive of at least 30 minutes duration.

2.2.4 Assemble and check breathing apparatus and weight for neutral buoyancy.

Demonstrate the use of a buoyancy compensator and/or dry suit for controlling buoyancy (if a dry suit is worn).

Demonstrate the ability to change between breathing sets.

2.2.7 Demonstrate the ability to control a failed regulator due to:

A damaged or clogged exhaust port by purging the regulator for each breath.

A free-flowing regulation by turning the cylinder tap on and off for each breath and also to give a controlled slow free flow so as to free both hands.

2.2.8 Demonstrate how to clear a flooded mask and reinstate an interrupted breathing supply.

2.2.9 Lay a tagged line for fifty metres using a variety of belaying techniques, belay the end and survey "home".

2.2.10 Lay a branch line to the surface, and fit a buoyant aid, having previously marked the main line with a home tag. Remove the buoyant aid, branch line and home tag.

2.2.11 Having "lost" the main line in bad visibility, demonstrate the use of a search reel to regain the main line.

2.2.12 Survey the line back to the reel. Release the belay and reel in back to "home".

2.2.13 Demonstrate to the examiner's satisfaction the ability to clear tangled line.

2.2.14 Demonstrate the ability to recognise a cardiac arrest, how to perform cardio-pulmonary resuscitation, maintain an airway and control bleeding.

2.3 Qualified Diver Assessment Standard: Part C - Theory Test

2.3.1 The Trainee Diver will answer a written paper relating to cave diving problems including; navigation, open-water diving problems, physiological problems, elementary first aid, standard and specialised equipment, equipment maintenance, porterage, cave rescue procedures, in-water decompression techniques, use of decompression tables and specific decompression problems relating to cave diving.

2.3.2 The Exam Committee will provide the questions and answers for the written paper to Section Examiners. Section Examiners will ensure that the written paper accurately assesses the Trainee Diver's understanding of cave diving.

iv. The Cave Diving Group Training Standard - 13th March 2004

This Training Standard is a code of practice for UK cave diver training published by the Cave Diving Group of Great Britain. It does not represent a Rule of the Group.

Part 1 – Diver training to Qualified Diver level.

1 Scope
This Training Standard is intended to guide the tuition of amateur cave divers who wish to engage in cave diving for leisure purposes under the conditions commonly found in UK sumps.

This Standard addresses the tuition of the diving skills required for cave diving. Matters pertaining to caving, physical access to diving sites and dive-project planning are specifically outside the scope of this Standard.

This Standard is intended to teach cave diving skills using open circuit air diving equipment with a dry-suit or with a wetsuit and a buoyancy control device to divers who are already experienced in open-water diving techniques.

2 References
The Cave Diving Group Constitution (http://www.cavedivinggroup.org.uk/Articles/Constitution.html)
The Cave Diving Group Safety Code (http://www.cavedivinggroup.org.uk/Articles/safetycode.html)
The Cave Diving Group training manual (Mendip Publishing 1990 ISBN 0-905903-14-5).

3 Responsibilities
Trainer
At all times the Trainer must maintain the safety of the Trainee above the needs of the training.
The Trainer must fully explain the risks associated with cave diving.
The Trainer must provide direct tuition in person for a total of at least 10 hours on at least two different occasions.
The Trainer must provide in-water tuition to no more than three Trainees at any given time.

Trainee
The Trainee must inform the Trainer of all previous caving and diving experience.
The Trainee must inform the Trainer of all medical or physical conditions that might affect the trainee's ability to participate in diver training.
The Trainee must explain their motivation for wishing to be trained in cave diving techniques.
The Trainee must understand the risks associated with cave diving and must give informed consent to enter into the training on a voluntary basis.

4 Pre-Training Requirements
Trainer
The Trainer must belong to a national organization with recognized expertise in training cave diving in UK conditions. The Trainer must be fully recognized by that organization and be qualified and insured to conduct the training of inexperienced cave divers.
The Trainer must ensure that there is suitable access to out-of-water, open-water and sump sites that will enable controlled and relevant demonstration and practice of cave diving techniques.

Trainee
The Trainee must have had some experience of the cave environment before commencing cave diver training.
The Trainee must be able to demonstrate to the Trainer's satisfaction that they have basic cave, open-water diving and first aid skills that include the following:
- Carry a 20Kg load for 200m through simple, walking, wild-cave conditions.
- Conduct a 30 minute dive to a maximum depth of 30m in open-water conditions using commonly

recognized diving practices with adequate planning and preparation for emergency situations.

- Demonstrate the ability to recognise a cardiac arrest, how to perform cardio-pulmonary resuscitation, maintain an airway and control bleeding.

5 Training

5.1 Delivery of Training
The Trainer will ensure that the Trainee is introduced to the skills of cave diving in a progressive fashion starting out of the water, then practicing the skills in open-water and finally using the skills in a cave diving situation. The open-water sites should, where possible, simulate the cave diving environment. The cave diving site should be suitable for tuition and practice of cave diving skills but still have a muddy floor and no clear air surface. Either natural cave sumps or flooded mines can be used at the Trainer's discretion. The Cave Diving Group Safety Code must be observed at all times.

5.2 Out-of-water Training
The following topics should be explained, demonstrated and practiced out of the water:
UK Caves
The formation of caves
- The physical environment
- Classic sites
- Access
- Sources of information
- Cave conservation
- Legal aspects to cave diving

Equipment configuration
- Suits
- Buoyancy compensation devices and techniques
- Harnesses
- Cylinders
- Regulators
- Lighting
- Ancillary Equipment

Underwater Skills
- Buoyancy control and recovery from failure
- Air contamination identification and responses
- Mask clearing
- Total mask failure
- Sinus and ear clearing failure
- Regulator swapping
- Breathing supply failure procedures
- Multiple cylinder diving
- Underwater transportation of equipment
- Fin strokes
- Removing and replacing equipment
- Emergency rescue procedures
- Zero visibility techniques

Above water skills and theory
- Pre-dive planning
- Gear assembly and pre-dive checks
- Kitting-up underground
- Air margin calculations
- Porterage to dive base
- Equipment maintenance
- Oxygen cleaning

- Compressors and compressing
- Cylinder markings and testing
- Risk assessment and mitigation
- Emergency rescue procedures

Physiology and Medicine
- Diving on medications (e.g. decongestants)
- Arterial gas embolism
- Pulmonary barotrauma
- Dysbarism

Psychology
- Motivation for cave diving
- Setting personal limits
- Pre-dive mental preparation
- Solo diving
- Multiple divers – single sump
- Coping with adversity

Line Management:
- A brief overview of the history of line laying and following in the UK
- The risks and benefits of using a dive line in a sump
- Line construction and properties
- Line tagging and junctions
- Line reels
- Common codes of conduct for line usage and maintenance
- Describing and navigating using lines
- Line laying and belaying techniques
- Branch lines and out tags
- Lost line procedures
- Line cutting procedures
- Clearing tangled line
- The affect of your actions on other divers

First Aid
- Cardiac arrest
- Cardio-pulmonary resuscitation
- Maintaining an airway
- Controlling bleeding

Surveying
- Surveying to true north
- Recording data underwater
- Drawing up surveys

Decompression Diving Techniques
- Gas laws
- Decompression diving physiology
- Decompression sickness
- Oxygen toxicity
- Nitrogen narcosis
- Development of the multiple compartment decompression algorithms
- Use of tables in square profile diving
- Use of dive computers in calculating decompression schedules
- Dangers associated with non-square profile diving
- Micro-bubble theory
- Flying after diving and diving at altitude

- In-water use of Oxygen during decompression
- Decompression incident emergency procedures

Awareness of advanced diving techniques
- Nitrox
- Mixed gases
- Scooters
- Rebreathers
- Habitats

5.3 Open water practice
The Trainee should conduct at least two open-water dives totalling at least 60 minutes underwater practicing the following skills:
- Equipment assembly, check and weight for neutral buoyancy
- The use of a buoyancy control devices and techniques
- Changing between breathing sets
- Controlling a failed regulator due to:
- A damaged or clogged exhaust port by purging the regulator for each breath.
- A free-flowing regulation by turning the cylinder tap on and off for each breath and also to give a controlled slow free flow so as to free both hands.
- Mask clearance and total failure
- Reinstating an interrupted breathing supply
- Line laying and following
- Zero visibility techniques
- Line surveying
- Simulated emergency procedures

5.4 Cave diving under supervision
The Trainee should conduct at least two cave dives totalling at least 60 minutes underwater practicing the following skills:
- Line laying and following
- Simulated emergency procedures
- Surveying

6 Appraisal of Training
The Trainer should provide regular appraisals of the Trainee's progress with their development of cave diving skills to help the Trainee to plan further training and diving within safe personal limits.

v. Risk Assessment

Cave diving is a hazardous activity that carries significant inherent risks of personal harm or injury, including death.

The Cave Diving Group is a volunteering body whose main goals are the promotion of safe cave diving practices and the exploration of flooded caves. Its members consist of explorers who carry out sport and exploratory cave diving both in Britain and abroad. These members also assist newer members on a volunteer basis to safely use well established safe cave diving techniques, so that they may further their experience.

By participating in voluntary, recreational cave diving under the auspices of the Cave Diving Group you are considered to have read and understood this Risk Assessment, to have acknowledge that accidents can occur without negligence and to have accepted your personal responsibility for the safe conduct of cave diving.

This Risk Assessment is provided by the Cave Diving Group of Great Britain as a generic illustration of some of the risks that are associated with recreational cave diving in a voluntary setting under the Constitution and Rules of the Group. Individuals are obliged to consider other further risks relevant to their own personal situation.

In addition to the risks associated cave diving a caver diver will also be exposed to the risks associated with caving. This Risk Assessment does not assess the risks associated with general caving either on approach to a sump or beyond a sump.

This Risk Assessment was compiled by voluntary cave divers and does not represent a professional Risk Assessment of the risks associated with cave diving.

This Risk Assessment is not exhaustive and there will be additional risks, both foreseeable and unforeseeable, that will affect the safety of any cave diver.

This Risk Assessment is relevant to cave diving by cave divers of Trainee or Qualified status, operating either independently, in a team or in a concurrent group of solo divers, for recreational or exploratory purposes in accordance with the Constitution and Rules of the Group. The Risk Assessment does not include open water hazards, nor is it relevant to the buddy system. It is provided as a training aid and is no substitute for instruction in cave diving.

Risk	Preventative actions	Mitigation actions
Any obstacles, elements, actions or inactions that might affect the safe completion of the activity	*Any actions or inactions that may reduce the risk*	*Any actions or inactions that may reduce any damage resulting from the occurrence of the risk*
Equipment failure		
Total mask failure	Check the mask carefully before entering the water.	Practice diving with no mask. Consider the risk and benefits of carrying a second mask on a dive.
Single lighting failure	Check all lights before diving. Purchase primary cells from a trusted source. Regularly run lights flat to check expected duration of rechargeable batteries and efficiency of chargers. Recharge cells in a known environment to prevent charging errors.	Carry multiple sources of light. Always carry enough emergency lighting capable of lasting long enough to reach safety.
Failure of all lighting sources	Check all lights before diving. Regularly run lights flat to check expected duration of rechargeable batteries and efficiency of chargers. Purchase pre-charged cells from a trusted source.	Practice diving in blackout conditions. Ensure lines are suitable for following in blackout conditions.
Equipment servicing failure	Be aware that servicing failure can cause failure of critical equipment required to support your life. Always check all equipment immediately prior to entering the water. Ensure that equipment is serviced in accordance with the manufacturer's specification by appropriately qualified individuals. Consider the use of different equipment for each breathing system, to guard against common mode failures.	Carry at least two fully independent breathing supplies that are capable of sustaining life long enough to reach safety.

Risk	Preventative actions	Mitigation actions
Gas contents gauge failure	Regularly calibrate contents gauges against other gauges. Service contents gauges regularly and replace worn parts.	Look for signs of malfunction such as twitching, sticking or illegible displays. Be prepared to abort the dive early. Carry at least two fully independent breathing supplies that are capable of sustaining life long enough to reach safety, in the event of a single failure.
Depth gauge failure	Regularly calibrate gauges against other gauges. Consider the use of duplicate depth gauges in situations where depth is a safety issue, e.g. decompression.	Look for signs of malfunction such as twitching, sticking or illegible displays. Be prepared to abort the dive early.
Decompression computer failure	Regularly calibrate computer against other computers. Service computer regularly and replace worn parts. Consider the use of duplicate sources of decompression information in situations where decompression is required, e.g. additional computers, or tables and depth gauge.	Look for signs of malfunction such as twitching, sticking or illegible displays.
Dry suit failure	Ensure that dry suit is well maintained. Ensure that the dry suit is constructed from materials that are suitable for the environment in which it is used. Protect vulnerable parts of the suit from abrasion and damage where possible. Avoid using the drysuit as the sole means of buoyancy control.	Abort the dive.
Damage of equipment during transportation	Protect or otherwise take care of equipment when carrying. Check all equipment for correct function prior to entering the water.	Recovery will depend on the circumstances.
Failure to check equipment adequately prior to entering the water	Monitor the function of all equipment during the course of a dive.	Carry at least two fully independent breathing supplies that are capable of sustaining life long enough to reach safety, in the event of a single failure. Change to your alternate breathing supply if you detect any malfunction and retreat to safety.
Failure of any artificial aid, e.g. ladder, bolt, belay, bridge, step, rope, roof ... etc	Test all artificial aids before use. Expect artificial aids to have been placed to assist the original user during original exploration and not to be suitable for subsequent usage.	Recovery will depend on the circumstances.

Risk	Preventative actions	Mitigation actions
Loss of only buoyancy control device	Consider the use of a second buoyancy control device prior to entering the water. Plan the dive to account for the suitability of the physical environment of the cave or the artificial structures (e.g. ropes or diving lines) in place to be used to counteract the effects of too much or too little buoyancy.	Consider underwater climbing. Pull on fixed lines as a final resort only.
Loss of all buoyancy control devices	Plan the dive to account for the suitability of the physical environment of the cave or the artificial structures in place to be used to counteract the effects of too much or too little buoyancy. Be aware of the potential for increased air consumption.	Consider underwater climbing. Pull on fixed lines as a final resort only.
Physical loss of equipment during kitting up	Plan your dive, including the above water aspects of gear transportation and preparation, to ensure that your safety is not compromised by the malfunction or loss of a piece of equipment.	Recovery will depend on the circumstances.
Diver propulsion vehicle (DPV) drive failure	Ensure that the DPV is serviced in accordance with the manufacturer's specification by appropriately qualified individuals. Complete a thorough pre-dive check of the vehicle. Regularly run batteries flat to check expected duration of batteries and efficiency of chargers. Charge cells in a known environment to prevent charging errors. Purchase pre-charged sells from a trusted source. Expect failure of a DPV's propulsion. Plan your dive to allow for a retreat to safety by free swimming, including adjustment of the thirds rule.	Start swimming, or use alternative DPV
DPV buoyancy failure	Ensure that the DPV is serviced in accordance with the manufacturer's specification by appropriately qualified individuals. Complete a thorough pre-dive check of the vehicle. Expect failure of a DPV's buoyancy. Know the buoyancy characteristics of your DPV when flooded. Plan your dive to allow for a retreat to safety.	Start swimming, or use alternative DPV.

Risk	Preventative actions	Mitigation actions
Decompression habitat failure	Ensure that the habitat is serviced, checked and deployed as intended by the manufacturer. Ensure that emergency procedures are in place to ensure continuation of breathing supplies and maintenance of the correct ambient pressure in the event of a sudden catastrophic failure of the habitat.	Recovery will depend on the circumstances.
Lack of emergency, rescue or medical personnel or equipment at the site of an accident	Make contingency plans in the event of a cave diving emergency based on the resources that you know will be available on site. Do not expect any additional emergency, rescue or medical personnel to be able to reach you in time to offer substantial assistance.	Recovery will depend on the circumstances.
Unsuitable equipment	Test equipment suitability in an environment where escape is available. Consider the use to which untried equipment will be put.	Recovery will depend on the circumstances, but will be aided if it has been fully considered beforehand.
Loss of usable breathing gas		
Breathing gas contamination of single source	Use breathing gas sources that are known to deliver a good quality of gas. Test all breathing gases on the surface prior to diving to look for obvious failure such as a bad taste or fainting. Be aware of the possible modes of failure when filling breathing gas supplies and take steps to reduce possible errors.	Carry at least two fully independent breathing supplies that are capable of sustaining life long enough to reach safety.
Breathing gas contamination of all sources available to the diver	Use breathing gas sources that are known to deliver a good quality of gas. Test all breathing gases on the surface prior to diving to look for obvious failure such as a bad taste or fainting. Be aware of the possible modes of failure when filling breathing gas supplies and take steps to reduce possible errors.	Abort the dive.
Incorrect measurement of Oxygen concentration in breathing gas	Always calibrate and service any gas analysis equipment in accordance with the manufacturer's instructions. Ensure your competence to use any gas analysis equipment properly. Be aware of the consequences of Oxygen toxicity. Be aware of the special needs of rebreathers.	Carry at least two fully independent breathing supplies that are capable of sustaining life long enough to reach safety. Be aware of the signs and symptoms of both Oxygen toxicity and Oxygen starvation during a dive. Change to your alternate breathing supply if the signs or symptoms of either Oxygen toxicity or Oxygen starvation occur during a dive and retreat to safety.

Risk	Preventative actions	Mitigation actions
Incorrect measurement of gas fractions in breathing gas	Always calibrate and service any gas analysis equipment in accordance with the manufacturer's instructions. Ensure your competence to use any gas analysis equipment properly. Be aware of the potential for common mode failure when filling and checking gas mixtures.	Carry at least two fully independent breathing supplies that are capable of sustaining life long enough to reach safety. Be aware of the signs and symptoms of both the surfeit and the lack of any of the constituent gases that form your breathing supply. Change to your alternate breathing supply if the signs or symptoms of either surfeit and the lack of gas occur during a dive and retreat to safety.
Running out of breathing gas	Use a gas contents gauge to regularly monitor the contents of breathing supplies during the course of a dive. Always maintain a reserve of breathing gas that is sufficient to reach a place of safety including an additional safety margin for any delays and decompression schedules. Monitor your personal gas consumption over a number of dives and ensure that your diving plan is supported by sufficient supplies of breathing gas. Allow for the effects of external factors such as: current, fatigue, equipment porterage, task loading, poor visibility, navigational difficulties and any technical issues of the ability of the delivery system to use all available breathing gas supplies.	No mitigating action identified.
Loose material breaking diaphragm on exhaust of regulator second stage	Be aware of any design features of your breathing apparatus that may allow ingress of foreign material to the exhaust of regulator second stage. Consider options for eliminating these features. Consider options to aid removal of foreign material from the exhaust of a regulator second stage whilst underwater. Practice changing mouthpieces whilst under stressful conditions. Practice clearing foreign materials from a mouthpiece and reinstating the breathing apparatus to a functioning condition.	Carry at least two fully independent breathing supplies that are capable of sustaining life long enough to reach safety.
Single regulator failure	Test regulators on surface immediately prior to entering the water. Service regulators regularly. Replace worn parts (particularly hoses) prior to failure. Practice the rule of thirds.	Carry at least two fully independent breathing supplies that are capable of sustaining life long enough to reach safety.

Risk	Preventative actions	Mitigation actions
Failure of all regulators	Test regulators on surface immediately prior to entering the water. Service regulators regularly. Replace worn parts prior to failure.	No mitigating action identified.
Cylinder tap failure – no gas	Test taps on surface immediately prior to entering the water. Regularly service taps.	Check that taps do not become turned off during a dive. Carry at least two fully independent breathing supplies that are capable of sustaining life long enough to reach safety.
Cylinder tap failure – leaking gas	Test taps on surface immediately prior to entering the water. Regularly service any blow-off devices such as bursting disks. Regularly service the pillar valves.	Carry at least two fully independent breathing supplies that are capable of sustaining life long enough to reach safety.
Loss of breathing gas	Regularly service and test sources of breathing gas. Carry at least two fully independent breathing supplies that are capable of sustaining life long enough to reach safety.	No mitigating action identified.
Use of inappropriate breathing gas	Be aware that all mixtures of breathing gases have limitations on their minimum safe depth, maximum safe depth, decompression schedules, ascent rates, descent rates, storage, transfer, analysis and narcosis factors. Always know the exact composition of the breathing gas that you are using. Be thoroughly familiar with the practices and theories associated with any breathing gas that you use and the implications of switching between supplies of differing compositions at differing depths. Mark all supplies of breathing gas with their composition and consider marking with the safe usable depth to remove ambiguity. Never make assumptions about the composition of gases in unmarked supplies.	Recovery will depend on the circumstances.
Common hazards		
Mask flooding	Ensure the mask fits well and is in good repair. Be aware that mask flooding is a potential problem if the mask is knocked against rock, and in particular for dives in constricted cave passages.	Practice mask clearing drills. Practice diving with no mask. Consider the risk and benefits of carrying a second mask on a dive.

Risk	Preventative actions	Mitigation actions
Becoming physical stuck – underwater	Be aware that some sections of sump have been explored by extraordinarily thin divers using specialized techniques for "pushing" confined spaces. Some cave features change shape between dives or during a dive (e.g. gravel banks) and may become impassable very quickly. Do not expect always to be able to follow any line or cave passage in existence and plan dives accordingly. Critically examine your equipment configuration and your ability with respect to passing confined sections of sump before entering the water. Research the dimensions of the passage for your planned dive before entering the water. If in doubt, abort the dive and come back another day.	Stop. Presence of mind will be of primary assistance in recovery from this hazard. Recovery actions will depend on the nature of the obstacle, but the opportunities for external assistance will probably be limited.
Collision with physical objects	Expect to collide with objects. Wear protective clothing such as a helmet appropriate to the nature of the site, the speed of progression through the water and any hazards either natural or unnatural. Ensure that equipment and its location can survive the impact.	No mitigating action identified.
Line problems		
Line entanglement	Lay lines that are suitable for the cave environment. Use thicker lines in areas of lower visibility. Use intermediate belays to improve the course of the line. Remove any slack in lines where possible. When following pre-existing lines, continually assess the risk of entanglement and take appropriate preventative action such as tidying or relaying line. If necessary, delay the completion of a dive objective in order to safeguard the route. Practice line disentanglement drills. Assess personal equipment for features that may cause entanglement such as hanging objects and open clips. Be aware of difficulties in line handling due to gloves.	Carry a sharp knife or other cutting tools, and practice using them underwater. Be aware of difficult-to-cut lines such as wire, cable and chain, etc. Consider personal equipment features when attempting disentanglement. Cut the line as a last resort only. If this is necessary, ensure that the end you hold on to is the one leading to the way out.

Risk	Preventative actions	Mitigation actions
Cut line	Be aware that lines regularly become cut or broken by natural acts such as flood. Always allow for the possibility of lines becoming cut or broken before, during or after you enter the water. Assess the state of lines on entry and take appropriate actions to mend any lines that appear in danger of breaking. Assess the artificial hazards in the water, including yourself, that might cut a line that you are following or intend to follow. Assess the possibilities that other divers in the water, either known or unknown may cut a line. Consider diving solo. Prepare contingency plans for any cut line situations. Practice cut line drills.	Be aware of the cave's general route. Carry a search reel and compass, and know how to use them.
Losing the line	At all times be aware of the location of any dive line in the water. Consider following the line by hand when visibility is poor. Prepare contingency plans for a lost line situation. Be prepared to abort the dive if deteriorating visibility would cause the line to be lost. Lay line so that it is suitable for following in poor visibility.	Carry a suitable search line to enable you to execute a lost line procedure effectively.
Unexpected line junction	Reduce the incidence of unexpected line junctions by planning dives. Obtain descriptions and surveys of known passages, lines and junctions where possible. Be aware of the risks associated with navigational errors and the ability to reach safety within current resources of breathing gases or other resources. Be prepared to undertake several dives to familiarise yourself with the line route.	When encountering an unexpected line junction underwater then stop to assess the situation. Use navigational aids such as line marking conventions, compass bearings and out tags to mark selected lines.
Line belay failure	Be aware of the possibilities and consequences of both terminal and intermediate line belay failure. Create belays that are likely to be fit for purpose. Assess line belays when following existing lines and correct any obvious deficiencies. Be aware that line following difficulties can be caused by line belay failure.	When encountering an unexpected line route underwater then stop to assess the situation. Use navigational aids such as line marking conventions, compass bearings and out tags to mark selected lines.

Risk	Preventative actions	Mitigation actions
Line routing failure, e.g. line pulls in to a bedding or rift that is too small for the diver to follow	Use intermediate belays to route line on an acceptable course. Be aware that both poor lining techniques and natural changes in the environment can cause line routing failure.	In the event of line routing failure the diver will need to take exceptional action to reach safety. This may involve line rerouting, line cutting or diving without a line. The diver should plan for and practice these procedures prior to entering the water. A good understanding of the cave environment and speleogenesis will assist in understanding the topography of the situation. Be aware that a line that is visible but not reachable on the way in, may not be visible on the return.
Multiple lines	The diver should always maintain a continuous line to safety. Be aware that multiple lines increase the risk of unexpected line junctions, unrecognised destinations, inadvertent jumps between unconnected lines and cut or broken lines.	Observe heightened line disciple when diving in a multiple line environment. Clearly mark all jumps between unconnected lines. Consider removal of redundant lines.
Lack of a line junction, e.g. failure to notice an existing junction or removal of a jump line that created a junction	Be aware that line junctions can change before, during or after you enter the water. Assess the artificial hazards in the water, including yourself, that alter line junctions that you intend to use. Assess the possibilities that other divers in the water, either known or unknown may alter line junctions. Prepare contingency plans for line junction confusion. Be aware of local conventions regarding line junctions and line management.	Assess the state of junctions on encounter and take appropriate actions to mend or mark any junctions that appear in danger of changing or would be difficult to recognise later in the dive, possibly in poor visibility.
Failure in line following	Be aware that a diving line may unexpectedly fail to lead to safety. Practice line management skills prior to entering the water.	Stop. Slowly retrace your route to where the line was last seen. Be prepared to use the search reel to look for the line continuation.
Unexpected removal of a line	Be aware that long sections of line can be removed before, during or after you enter the water by both natural and human actions. Assess the natural and artificial hazards in the water, including yourself, that may remove line that you intend to use. Assess the possibilities that other divers in the water, either known or unknown, may remove line. Be aware of local conventions regarding line management.	Prepare contingency plans in the event of line removal.

Risk	Preventative actions	Mitigation actions
Route finding failure	Follow and stay with an existing safe guide line where possible. Obvious exceptions to this include exploration of previously unlined cave or in the event of an emergency. A good understanding of the cave environment and speleogenesis will assist in understanding the topography of the situation.	If progress cannot be made then the diver should attempt to return to safety.
Unrecognised destinations	Be aware that it is sometimes impossible to recognise a destination either above water or below water due to the confusing nature of caves. Plan your dive with an option to retrace your route from an unknown destination to a place of known safety.	Return along the incoming route.
Visibility failure		
Poor visibility	Be aware that poor visibility through the water in the cave diving environment can affect your ability to execute a dive safely. Poor visibility increases all risks associated with any activity that uses sight including: line management, line following, navigation, communication, and decompression. Before entering the water you must practice in a zero visibility environment all of the activities that are required for you to reach safety. Be prepared to follow the line by touch alone.	Practice and experience in poor visibility will assist in escaping safely.
Deterioration in visibility	Low visibility increases all risks associated with any activity that uses sight including: line management, line following, navigation, communication and decompression. Before entering the water you must practice in a zero visibility environment all of the activities that are required for you to reach safety.	Be aware that visibility through the water in the cave diving environment can deteriorate to the point where you are unable to see your lights. Be prepared to follow the line by touch alone.
Medical problems		
Hypothermia	Check temperature of water prior to entry. Wear sufficient thermal clothing to guard against both hypothermia and hyperthermia.	Abort the dive.

Risk	Preventative actions	Mitigation actions
Blocked sinus	Be aware that a blocked sinus can cause difficulties in changing depth due to build up of pressure within sinus cavities. Assess sinus health before entering the water. Do not commit to diving where changing depth is a requirement to reach safety.	Abort the dive.
Unable to clear ears	Be aware that blockages in the inner and middle ears can cause difficulties in changing depth due to build up of pressure within the inner and middle ear cavities. Assess the health of your inner and middle ears before entering the water. Do not commit to diving where changing depth is a requirement to reach safety.	Abort the dive. Be aware of the consequences of changing depth without clearing your ears and take steps to minimise the impact of further hazards that may result.
Respiratory illness	Be aware that respiratory illness can cause sudden and disorientating physical symptoms when underwater. Assess respiratory health before entering the water and do not dive if respiratory problems are suspected.	Abort the dive.
Physical or mental impairment due to alcohol or other substance	Avoid diving when under the influence of alcohol or other substances.	Abort the dive.
Mental impairment due to pre-existing psychological condition	Obtain advice on your ability to cope mentally with cave diving from a suitably qualified medical professional prior to entering the water if you have ever suffered from a psychological condition.	Abort the dive.
Impairment due to pre-existing physical condition	Obtain advice on your ability to cope with cave diving from a suitably qualified medical professional prior to entering the water.	Abort the dive.

Risk	Preventative actions	Mitigation actions
Mental impairment due to psychological condition emergent during diving, e.g. stress or panic	Expect to suffer from mental impairment whilst diving and plan your dive accordingly. Research the nature of the "incident pit" before entering the water. Plan the dive thoroughly before entering the water to minimise the number of unexpected situations faced and decisions taken underwater. Build experience of cave diving gradually and incrementally. Do not over extend yourself mentally or allow others to encourage you into a situation that you are not comfortable with. Think through the compounding of problems that can occur when decisions are made in an impaired state.	Be prepared to abort the dive.
Mental impairment due to narcosis caused by breathing gas	Expect to suffer from depth-related mental impairment whilst diving and plan your dive accordingly. Research the nature of narcosis caused by breathing gas at depth before entering the water. Build experience of cave diving, under increased partial pressures of narcotic gases, gradually and incrementally.	Be prepared to abort the dive.
Lack of diver fitness	Plan the dive appropriate to your personal level of fitness.	Be prepared to abort the dive early.
Sudden medical emergency, e.g. anaphylactic shock, asthma attach, heart attack, hypoglycaemic attack	Obtain a regular medical check up from a suitably qualified person. Plan your diving in accordance with any medical advice you receive regarding pre-existing medical conditions.	No mitigating action identified.
Pulmonary barotrauma	Observe correct ascent procedures.	Stop ascent if possible and regain control of the ascent.
Fatigue	Avoid diving when overly fatigued. Plan diving around your expected level of fatigue when entering the water.	Be prepared to abort the dive.
Lack of sleep	Avoid diving when lacking sleep. Plan diving around your expected level of lack of sleep when entering the water.	Be prepared to abort the dive.
Insect bites	Be aware of the effect that allergic reactions to insect bites can have on your diving. Prevent insect bites prior to entry to the water. Check equipment for the ingress of insects prior to entering the water.	Be prepared to abort the dive.

Risk	Preventative actions	Mitigation actions
Animal attack (eg sharks, snakes or crocodiles)	Take local advice on the risks posed by the local wildlife.	Be prepared to abort the dive.
Overheating	Check temperature of water prior to entry. Wear sufficient thermal clothing to guard against both hypothermia and hyperthermia.	Stop. Move more slowly.
Lack of food	Ensure that you have adequate but not excess food in order to complete the dive.	Be prepared to abort the dive.
Dehydration	Ensure that you have adequate but not excess water in order to complete the dive. Be aware of the dehydrating effect of diving and of options for handling micturation during a dive.	Be prepared to abort the dive.
Medication	Obtain medical advice from a suitably qualified person before diving whilst taking any prescription or over-the-counter medication. Plan your diving in accordance with any medical advice you receive. Be aware that medication that does not affect one diver at depth, may still affect another.	Be prepared to abort the dive.
Vomiting underwater	Avoid diving when feeling nauseous. Be aware of the capacity of your breathing apparatus to pass vomit into the surrounding water without malfunction. Be aware of the difficulties associated with vomiting underwater without a mouthpiece. Practice changing mouthpieces whilst under stressful conditions. Practice clearing foreign materials from a mouthpiece and re-instating the breathing apparatus to a functioning condition.	Carry at least two fully independent breathing supplies that are each capable of sustaining life long enough to reach safety.
Psychological disturbance as a result of being present when a diving accident occurs	Expect an underwater incident to a fellow cave diver to be a harrowing experience. Before you enter the water when diving in a concurrent group of solo divers, discuss the psychological issues of being physically close to a fellow diver in trouble but being unable to help them without compromising your own safety. Clearly communicate that your own safety is your primary concern whilst underwater and any efforts to assist a diver in trouble will be secondary to that primary concern.	Consider professional counselling after being present at any accident involving a fellow diver. Seek medical advice if necessary.

Risk	Preventative actions	Mitigation actions
Dental emergency	Ensure good dental health before entering the water.	Abort the dive.
Traumatic injury or acute medical condition.	Be aware that cave diving can aggravate the effects of a traumatic injury or an acute medical condition. Avoid diving when suffering from these conditions. Avoid activities that have an increased risk of inflicting a traumatic injury or an acute medical condition if it is necessary to execute a cave dive in order to reach safety.	Be aware that there is a risk of aggravating an existing condition if attempting an emergency evacuation of a casualty through a sump.
Serious harm including death	Do not dive if you are uncertain of the risks associated with cave diving.	No mitigating action identified.
Weather problems		
Underground flood pulse	Check the weather forecast before going underground. Assess the likely impact of a flood pulse on any of the factors that may affect cave diving such as length of sumps, kitting up areas or support from "dry cavers.	Take remedial action where appropriate.
Underground and underwater flood pulse	Check the weather forecast before going underground. Assess the likely impact of a flood pulse on any of the factors that may affect cave diving such as current flow or visibility.	Take remedial action where appropriate.
Cave problems		
Falling natural and unnatural objects – above water	Plan diving operations such as transportation and kitting up with the possibility of falling natural and unnatural objects in mind. Wear protective clothing, e.g. helmet, as appropriate.	No mitigating action identified.
Falling natural and unnatural objects – below water	Be aware that objects can fall underwater and cause both direct harm and entrapment. Assess the dive site for the possibility of falling objects and plan the diving accordingly. Consider the use of reinforcement or support at potential collapse sites.	No mitigating action identified.
Physical changes in the cave whilst diving	Some cave features change shape before, during or after a dive (eg boulder slopes, excavated shafts, gravel banks...etc) and may become impassable during the course of a dive. Assess the dive site for the possibility of physical changes to the cave and plan the diving accordingly.	No mitigating action identified.

Risk	Preventative actions	Mitigation actions
Strong currents	Assess currents when diving with particular attention to changes that may occur to the strength or direction of a current during the course of a diver. Plan the dive to account for currents with particular attention to progress and breathing gas consumption. Avoid unexpected currents.	Be prepared to abort the dive.
Falling whilst entering or leaving the water	Observe good caving practices whilst entering or leaving the water.	No mitigating action identified.
Falling underground whilst beyond a sump	Observe good caving practices whilst moving underground.	No mitigating action identified.
Air contamination in confined air spaces above water, e.g. low partial pressure of Oxygen in air bells or presence of poisonous gases	Be aware of the danger of the depletion of Oxygen in air confined in a small space such as an airbell. Be aware of the signs and symptoms of common non-air situations such as lack of Oxygen, increase in carbon dioxide and the presence of carbon monoxide.	If the risk of contamination is high or if abnormal signs or symptoms are suspected, then reinstate your breathing supply and retreat to safety.
Unusual problems		
Nearby use of explosives	Check the local vicinity for the use of explosives.	No mitigating action identified.
Procedural problems		
Inadequate or incorrect pre-dive planning materials, e.g. descriptions and surveys	Use planning information to provide guidance about the likely situation underwater, but always include the possibility that the information was gathered under less than optimum conditions or by inexperienced divers and consequently may be inaccurate or incorrect. Get to know the dive site over several dives. Include a retreat to known safety in your diving plan.	Abort the dive early.
Failure to observe gas margins	Work to pre-planned gas margins based on the gas available at the start of the dive. Use margins appropriate to the dive conditions, the size of the cylinders used and techniques adopted. Note that a strict interpretation of the rule of thirds may not be appropriate.	Carry at least two fully independent breathing supplies that are capable of sustaining life long enough to reach safety. Switch to alternative supply on failure of initial supply.
Failure to interpret decompression tables correctly	Regularly practice the application of decompression theories. Build in a margin for safety. Plan for the onset of decompression sickness, both during and following the dive.	No mitigating action identified.

Risk	Preventative actions	Mitigation actions
Inadequate understanding of decompression techniques	Regularly review your understanding of decompression theories. Obtain feedback of understanding from a suitably qualified individual. If in doubt – ask.	No mitigating action identified.
Failure to observe correct decompression profile	Regularly practice the application of decompression theories. Use pressure gauges and physical landmarks to assist in maintaining the correct profile. Plan for the onset of decompression sickness, both during and following the dive.	No mitigating action identified.
Failure to observe correct ascent rates	Correct use of buoyancy control devices. Correct weighting. Use of appropriate physical structures within the cave environment.	Stop ascent if possible, regain control of the ascent.
Failure to observe correct descent rates	Correct use of buoyancy control devices. Correct weighting. Use of appropriate physical structures within the cave environment.	Stop descent if possible, regain control of the descent.
Lack of judgment of personal capabilities to execute a planned dive safely	Research and practice the practical and theoretical aspects of cave diving before entering the water. Build experience of cave diving gradually and incrementally. Do not over extend yourself. Obtain feedback on your current abilities from a suitably qualified cave diver.	Abort the dive as necessary.
Communication failure between divers underwater	Expect communication failure underwater. Plan all diving so that it can be completed safely without intervention thorough either action or inaction from a fellow diver. Never allow your safety to depend on communication with another diver. Plan and communicate the expected actions of all concurrent divers before the first diver enters the water. Include likely optional reactions to differing but possible scenarios. Allow for the fact that the actual reactions may be substantially different. Dive solo.	Abort the dive as necessary.

Risk	Preventative actions	Mitigation actions
Confusion over the expected actions of other divers whilst underwater	Expect the actions of other divers to be confusing and confused. Plan all diving so that it can be completed safely without intervention thorough either action or inaction from a fellow diver. Never allow your safety to depend on communication with another diver. Plan and communicate the expected actions of all concurrent divers before the first diver enters the water. Include likely optional reactions to differing but possible scenarios. Allow for the fact that the actual reactions may be substantially different. Dive solo.	No mitigating action identified.
Over-familiarity with a situation	Asses the risks before diving. Always plan a dive to allow for possible risks as well as expected risks.	Recovery will depend on the circumstances.
Public interference by a non-diver	Assess the ability of a member of the public to compromise the safety of your dive, e.g. through blocking of exits or removal of breathing supplies or guide lines. Take action to prevent any compromise.	Recovery will depend on the circumstances.
Increased or decreased buoyancy due to loss of breathing gas or other discharged materials or materials gained	Assess the likely change in your buoyancy that will occur during your dive. Carry sufficient buoyancy control measures to allow you to maintain your buoyancy within tolerable limits. Be aware of the potential for empty cylinders to be come buoyant near the end of a dive.	Large stones can be used as an improvised weight.
Failure to locate alternative breathing supply during swapping of breathing supply.	Ensure your gear configuration places breathing supplies in a reproducible and accessible position at all times. Practice changing between breathing supplies.	Revert back to your previous breathing supply.
Obstruction of alternative breathing supply during swapping of breathing supply.	Ensure that your gear configuration or the physical nature of the cave does not compromise your access to your alternate breathing supply.	Revert back to your previous breathing supply.
Loss of above ground communications (e.g. failure of telephones or radios)	Be aware of the limitations of ground communications when making diving plans such as surface coordination of support or contingency plans in the event of an emergency. Plan your diving on the assumption that above ground communications are outside of your ability to control.	No mitigating action identified.

Risk	Preventative actions	Mitigation actions
Lack of or unexpected loss of underground to surface communications	Expect failure of underground to surface communications. Do not plan your dive to rely on underground to surface communication for safety.	No mitigating action identified.

Appendix 2: Accident analysis

The Learning Curve: A Quantitative Analysis of Fatal British Cave Diving Incidents from 1980 to 2005

David Brock, 24th January 2006

Abstract

A description is given of nine fatal cave diving incidents in the 26 years between 1980 and 2005. The overall fatality rate for all dives is estimated at 1 in 3,286 dives. Experience is identified as the main variable and an experienced diver is estimated to be 25 times more likely to survive a dive than an inexperienced diver. The most significant hazard to experienced divers is inadequate line management and the most frequent major hazard to inexperienced divers is lack of training. Cave diving safety has advanced considerably over the last 26 years for experienced divers. An experienced cave diver is 39 times more likely to survive a dive than his counterpart from 26 years ago. Unfortunately this improvement in diver safety has not been matched for inexperienced divers. There remains a lot of work to be done in understanding the safety issues for new cave divers and in developing suitable training programmes and education opportunities to get them up the learning curve safely and quickly.

Method

Data was collected in a standardized form to allow analysis of fatal incidents by divers who have deliberately entered into the overhead environment of the natural caves of Britain (excluding Ireland) using breathing apparatus. Fatalities from open-water training, breath-hold diving, diving in mines or diving in countries other than mainland Britain were not analysed. Information was obtained from published sources and by direct accounts from the people involved with the incidents.

The following information was collected for each incident:

- *Name:*
- *Age:*
- *Date of incident:*
- *Location of incident:*
- *CDG Qualified Diver: Yes/No*
- *CDG member: Yes/No*
- *Estimated to have previously completed more than 45 dives: Yes/No*
- *Line management was a significant contributory factor: Yes/No*
- *Equipment failure was a significant contributory factor: Yes/No*
- *Training was a significant contributory factor: Yes/No*
- *Something else was a significant contributory factor: Yes/No*
- *Narrative: About 100 words summarizing the event and probable causes*

Statistical Considerations

Although quantitative information is presented, a fair degree of caution must be exercised in interpreting their meaning. A major confounding factor is the timescale from the first to the last incident. Cave Diving technologies and practices have improved considerably from 1980 to 2005 and the probability of a fatal incident has fallen considerably. The number of incidents is also very small. This can produce gross sampling errors so although incidents rates are presented, there is an unknown degree of accuracy. There is still value in producing these rates as they allow the Group to observe changes over time and to compare incident rates between sub-groups of divers. A word about incident rates; if the fatal incident rate is 1 in 3,286 dives then this does not mean that the 3,287th dive a person does will be fatal because the odds of survival improve with experience. It means that if 3,286 people dive once in identical circumstances, then the likely number of fatalities is one.

This analysis will also contain data sampling errors. Given the close nature of the cave diving community, it is highly unlikely that there have been any unreported deaths in natural caves. Deaths in artificial cave-like structures such as mines have not been included to maintain the completeness of the incident dataset. The information about the incidents is less complete and some of the contributory factors for some of the incidents remain unknown. Lastly, values for the quantity of diving have been drawn from estimates that contain an unknown margin of error. The restriction of scope to incidents from mainland Britain goes some way to reducing the scale of this estimation error.

Incident Data

Location	Date of incident	Variables			Major Contributory Factors			
		CDG Qualified Diver	CDG Member	More than 45 dives	Line Management	Equipment failure	Training	Other
Bull Pot of the Witches, Cumbria	16/3/1980	Yes	Yes	Yes	Yes	No	No	No
Keld Head, North Yorkshire	23/11/1980	No	No	No	Yes	No	Yes	Yes
Wookey Hole, Somerset	14/11/1981	No	Yes	No	No	No	Yes	UNK
Hurtle Pot, North Yorkshire	6/1/1985	No	No	Yes	No	No	No	Yes
Unnamed Hole, Barbondale	23/4/1988	No	No	No	Yes	No	Yes	Yes
Joint Hole, North Yorkshire	June, 1992	No	No	No	No	No	Yes	UNK
Birkwith Cave, North Yorkshire	9/7/1994	No	No	No	No	No	Yes	Yes
Ogof Pont Y Meirw, Merthyr Tydfil	30/12/1998	No	No	No	Yes	Yes	Yes	UNK
Low Birkwith Cave, North Yorkshire	13/3/2005	Yes	Yes	Yes	Yes	No	No	No

UNK = Unknown

Narratives

1980 - Bull Pot of the Witches

A diver lost the line in sump 2 of Bull Pot of the Witches and ran out of air before finding his way out of a complicated area in poor visibility [CDG NL 56].

1980 - Keld Head

Four divers embarked on a training dive. One of their number, a relatively inexperienced diver became entangled in the line just before a kicking water airbell 100m from the entrance. On freeing himself he surfaced in the 100m airbell in a state of panic. A second diver was nearby but had to adjust his own buoyancy before offering help. By the time his buoyancy was sorted, the first diver had descended back in to the sump and was presumed to be making an exit. A few minutes later the second diver found the first diver laid on his back without his mouth-piece in place. The second diver recovered the first diver some 50m towards the entrance but was unable to save him. The body was recovered later that day [CDG NL 58].

1981 - Wookey Hole

A trainee diver, died during a training dive in Wookey Hole. He appears to have lost his mouthpiece a short distance from the surface in chamber 20 [CDG NL 62].

1985 - Hurtle Pot

An experienced diver drowned 14m from the surface during a routine dive. Subsequent tests of the equipment found no defects and the cause of the accident is uncertain [CDG NL 75].

1988 - Barbondale

An inexperienced 18 year old diver became physically wedged whilst trying to push a tight, unexplored sump with a base fed line. The sump was pumped out and the body recovered with much effort [CDG NL 80].

1992 - Joint Hole

A diver failed to return from a routine dive to the first airbell. He was later found dead near the entrance on the line with air available. There was nothing obviously wrong with the equipment on later inspection [CDG NL 105 & 118].

1994 - Birkwith Cave

An inexperienced diver, disappeared in the final 20m sump whilst on the through trip from Old Ing to Birkwith with a less experienced diver. The diver was found dead the next day some 3m from the line and about halfway through the sump near a "letter box" constriction. The diver's equipment was old but was working correctly when checked after the incident. The contents gauge was connected directly to the first stage and not via a hose so it would not have been possible to read the cylinder pressure whilst in the sump [CDG NL113].

1998 - Ogof Pont Y Meirw

A diver drowned whilst returning from exploring beyond the first sump with another diver. The line had become fouled in undercuts and the diver was found drowned a short distance from surface with no air left in his cylinders. Later examination of his equipment showed one of the demand valves to have a fault [CDG NL 134].

2005 - Low Birkwith Cave

An experienced diver, was engaged in a project to revisit a low, silty cave last extended in the 70's. The diver became entangled in old, loose line and ran out of air before he could free himself [CDG NL 155].

Amount of Diving

The amount of diving was investigated previously and the details are reported in CDG Newsletter 159:1 [Brock & Cordingley, 2006]. The following estimates are taken from that work.

The estimated total amount of diving performed between 1980 and 2004 is 29,149 man-dives of which 1,140 were conducted in 1980. Information for all dives in 2005 was taken from CDG Newsletters 154 to 157 which reported a total of 335 man-dives for the year. Using the reporting rate estimate of 78%, the estimate for the total amount of diving in 2005 is 429 man-dives. The total amount of diving for 1980 to 2005 is 29,578 man-dives. The total amount of diving for 1981 to 2005 is 28,438 man-dives.

It has been estimated that new cave divers performed 6,750 man-dives between 1980 and 2004. The full estimate from 1980 to 2005 would therefore be 7,020 man-dives. The estimate from 1981 to 2005 would therefore be 6,750 man-dives.

Analysis of Incident Rates

Incident rates have been calculated and are presented below.

The time between the first and the last incident has been identified as a confounding factor. Line management was identified as a major problem in 1980 and a Technical Review was published to address this issue [Yeadon, 1981]. Since then the quality of line management has improved and a sub-group of dives from 1981 to 2005 has been analysed to give an incident rate that may be more appropriate to modern circumstances.

Experience has been identified as a variable. Three interpretations of experience were collected during the data collection phase. Membership of the CDG is not used as a definition of experienced for the purposes of this analysis. Both being a Qualified Diver and having completed an estimated 45 dives are analysed as being an experienced diver.

Previous work [Brock, 2005] has identified that line management, equipment failure and training are the three most important hazards faced by British cave divers. Incident rates are reported for these three factors.

Rates of Fatal Incidents			Time Period	
			1980 - 2005	1981 - 2005
Divers	Variable	Factors		
All Divers		All Factors	1 in 3,286	1 in 4,063
Experienced Divers	Qualified Divers	All Factors	1 in 14,789	1 in 28,438
		Line management	1 in 14,789	1 in 28,438
		Equipment Failure	0	0
		Training	0	0
	Over 45 Dives	All Factors	1 in 9,859	1 in 14,219
		Line management	1 in 9,859	1 in 28,438
		Equipment Failure	0	0
		Training	0	0
Inexperienced Divers	Not Qualified Divers	All Factors	1 in 1,003	1 in 1,125
		Line management	1 in 2,340	1 in 3,375
		Equipment Failure	1 in 7,020	1 in 6,750
		Training	1 in 1,170	1 in 1,350
	Less than 45 Dives	All Factors	1 in 1,170	1 in 1,350
		Line management	1 in 2,340	1 in 3,375
		Equipment Failure	1 in 7,020	1 in 6,750
		Training	1 in 1,170	1 in 1,350

Discussion

The overall fatal incident rate is 1 in 3,286 dives but the rates for the sub-groups show a more complex picture.

Clearly there is a major confounding effect with time and removing 1980 from the analysis reduces the overall incident rate to 1 in 4,063 dives. The accuracy and applicability of the rates to modern cave diving activities is questionable. Robust incident statistics are available for current open water diving [BSAC, 2005] however the confounding of the cave diving data renders it inappropriate to compare the two sets of incident rates. It is however possible to make observations about the relative rates within the cave diving incident rates. The differences are perhaps best observed by looking at the data from 1981 to 2005.

The greatest difference is seen between experienced and inexperienced divers. The difference in defining experience as either a Qualified Diver or having completed more than 45 dives is not extreme. Taking Qualified Diver status as the most precise and documented determinant of experience then the picture is clear.

CDG Qualified Divers have an overall incident rate of 1 in 28,438 dives whereas unqualified divers have an incident rate of 1 in 1,125 dives. It appears that Qualified Divers are 25 times more likely to survive a cave dive than an inexperienced cave diver. A similar effect was found by the HSE [Paras, 1997] when examining open water diving. They found that "There are a small number of repeated causes associated with the majority of fatalities. If these causes are eliminated then the number of fatalities would have fallen from 286 to 8". This equates to a 36-fold difference in the incident rates between true accidents and fatal incidents involving repeat causes.

The last quantitative analysis of fatalities conducted by the CDG covered the period 1957 to 1978 and indicated an overall fatal incident rate of 1 in 620 dives [Churcher & Lloyd,1980]. Excluding the non-cave and non-British dives there were 6 fatalities from 4338 dives, of which 3 were experienced divers and 3 were inexperienced divers. The overall fatality rate was therefore 1 in 723 dives. There was no obvious difference between the number of fatal incidents for experienced and in-experienced divers. The analysis did not report the proportion of the 4338 dives that were conducted by inexperienced and experienced divers so the assumption is made that an equal number of dives were performed by both subgroups.

In the 26 years between the two analyses of cave diving figures there has been a great step forward in the safety of experienced divers. The fatal incident rate of 1957 to 1978 was 39 times higher for experienced divers than for their counterparts 26 years later. Unfortunately the same improvements for safety have not been made for inexperienced divers for whom the fatal incident rate improved by only a factor of 1.6. Although there are sampling and assumption errors, there is no evidence of a significant improvement in the safety of inexperienced cave divers over the last 26 years.

Three main causal factors were analysed; line management, equipment failure and training. Equipment failure and training were not major factors in either of the recorded incidents for experienced divers whereas line management figured in both. Experienced divers clearly need to take account of all hazards affecting cave diving but should pay particular attention to line management.

All factors contributed to the incidents for inexperienced divers and it comes as no surprise that training was the predominant factor. The take home message for inexperienced divers is to get trained and become qualified. As this group of divers is at a significantly higher risk of a fatal incident, the training should be controlled by very stringent safety standards. There was also a high incidence of uncategorized contributory factors recorded as "other" affecting inexperienced divers. A number of factors fell into this category such as panic or irrational decisions. Brandt claims that anxiety or other psychological problems affect 12% of non-fatal incidents [Brandt, 1980]. It is probable that inexperienced divers are far more susceptible to these issues than experienced divers and more work should be done in this area.

Conclusions

Fortunately there have been too few fatal cave diving incidents for robust fatality rates to be calculated. It is not possible to make meaningful comparisons between the risks faced by cave divers and the risks faced by other kinds of divers. It is clear that cave diving safety has advanced considerably over the last 26 years for experienced divers. It is also probable that this improvement in diver safety has not been matched for inexperienced divers. There remains a lot of work to be done in understanding the safety issues for new cave divers and in developing suitable training programmes and education opportunities to get them up the learning curve safely and quickly.

No activity is without risk but it is important to balance the risks of any activity against the benefits of that activity. There are multiple health and happiness benefits derived from participating in an intellectually, socially and physically challenging pastime like cave diving.

Appendix 3: Further reading

Caving information

Caving Practice and Equipment edited by D. N. Judson.............................ISBN 1-871890-75-6

SRT by D. Elliot .... ISBN 0 904405 68 0

The Complete Caving Manual by Andy Sparrow ....ISBN 1-86126-022-9

An Introduction to Cave Surveying by Bryan Ellis ....ISBN 0-900265-07-8

Life on a line by Dr Dave Merchant...ISBN 978-1-84753-281-7

CDG History

A Glimmering in Darkness by Graham Balcombe ....ISBN 978-0-901031-03-7

The Darkness Beckons by Martyn Farr...ISBN 0-906371-87-2

Basic use of scuba equipment

The Diving Manual – BSAC ....ISBN 0953891925

Open Water Diver Manual – PADI (course material)

Decompression theory

The Decompression Matrix by Bob Cole...ISBN 0-9520934-2-1

Basic Decompression Theory and Application by B R Wienke ....ISBN 0941332179

A Simple Guide to Decompression Illness 2nd Ed by Lee Griffiths ....ISBN 1-905492-05-7

Reduced Gradient Bubble Model in Depth by B R Wienke ....ISBN 1930536119

Deeper into Diving 2nd Edition by J Lippman..ISBN 0959030638

Mixed gas diving

Recreational Nitrox Diving by R N Rossier...ISBN 0941332837

Technical Diving From the Bottom Up by Kevin Gurr...................................ISBN 1904381200

TDI course books on Nitrox, Trimix and Decompression procedures

IANTD course books on Nitrox, Trimix and Decompression procedures

Getting Clear on the Basics: The Fundamentals of Technical Diving by Jarrod Jablonski

Rebreathers

Mastering Rebreathers by Jeffery E Bozanic ....ISBN 0941332969

First aid

Oxygen First Aid for divers by John Lippman and Trevor Davis ....ISBN 0959030654

First Aid Manual St Johns Ambulance Brigade and British Red Cross ....ISBN 1405315733